THE STORY OF THE PHILIPPINES

THE STORY
OF THE
PHILIPPINES

GOD'S RAMPART IN ASIA

by
Phillip Campbell

Arx Publishing, LLC
Merchantville NJ
2022

Arx Publishing, LLC
Merchantville, New Jersey

The Story of the Philippines: God's Rampart in Asia
©2022 Arx Publishing, LLC

All rights reserved. No part of this book may be reproduced, transmitted, or stored in any form without the express written permission of the publisher.

Printed in the United States of America

First Edition

ISBN 978-1-935228-24-0

DEDICATION

*To all the lovely Filipino Catholics I have had
the privilege of meeting over the years.*

ACKNOWLEDGMENTS

A work like this is never a one-man task. With sincere gratitude, I would like to acknowledge the assistance of the following individuals: Louis Gerard del Rosario, for his friendship and the resources on Filipino culture and history that he generously made available to me; Rev. Allain Caparas, for thoroughly going over the draft of the manuscript and making abundant comments and suggestions which helped improve it significantly; Lori Kauffmann who provided the cover art and excellent illustrations that complement the text so nicely; and a heartfelt thanks to the Tolentino family from Mr. Campbell.

TABLE OF CONTENTS

Introduction v
Map 2

Chapter 1: The Land of Ma'i 3
Chapter 2: Coming to the Philippines 11
Chapter 3: The Jade Culture 19
Chapter 4: The Rajahs of Butuan 23
Chapter 5: The Kingdom of Cebu 33
Chapter 6: The Kingdom of Tondo 41
Chapter 7: The Coming of Islam 49
Chapter 8: The Sultans of Brunei 55
Chapter 9: Magellan and the Spaniards 61
Chapter 10: The Spanish Conquest of the Philippines 71
Chapter 11: The Spanish East Indies 79
Chapter 12: The Castilian War 89
Chapter 13: The Moro Fight Back 95
Chapter 14: The Philippines in Crisis 103
Chapter 15: Christianizing the Philippines 111
Chapter 16: Life in the Spanish Philippines 119
Chapter 17: The Great Manila Galleons 131

(Continued...)

Chapter 18: The British Interruption..139
Chapter 19: The World Meets the Philippines 149
Chapter 20: The Philippine Revolution....................................157
Chapter 21: America Versus Spain 165
Chapter 22: The Philippine-American War 173
Chapter 23: Moros and Modernization.....................................183
Chapter 24: Between the Wars 193
Chapter 25: The Japanese Invade.. 203
Chapter 26: Island Hopping to Freedom...................................211
Chapter 27: The Third Republic 221
Chapter 28: The Dictatorship of Marcos 229
Chapter 29: Return to the Republic 241
Chapter 30: Into the 21st Century 249
Chapter 31: Facing the Future...257
Chapter 32: Catholicism in the Philippines............................. 265
Chapter 33: The Filipino Diaspora 275

Index... 279

INTRODUCTION

Writing a book about the history of any country is a big job. To do so about a country as complex as the Philippines is an undertaking monumental in scope. Any decent history author tries to take in all the information he can about a place or time and distill it down into a single, understandable narrative for his audience. The Philippines makes this task extremely challenging. With 134 ethnic groups speaking 120 dialects, spread out over 7,640 islands, drawing out any single narrative is impossible. When we study Philippine history, we are not following a single storyline—rather, we are weaving together the complex histories of multiple regions and ethnic groups.

In weaving this rich tapestry, it was regrettable that I had to leave out many things. For every historical person mentioned, I had to omit twenty others. For every battle described, ten went unmentioned. Entire regional sagas occasionally had to be left out in the interest of space. And when I got into the modern era of post-independence Philippine politics, the interplay among the various political parties was so dizzying that I could only present the most basic sketch. Therefore, to those who may already be familiar with Philippine history, I apologize if one of your favorite persons or episodes was left out.

But enough about what is not in the book, because what *is* included is an amazing tale of one of the most interesting places in the world. The adventures of the Conquistadors in the Philippines are every bit as exciting as the Spanish conquest of Mexico or Peru. The escapades of Miguel López de Legazpi were epic enough to rival those of Cortez and Pizarro. The 1646 Battle of La Naval de Manila against the Dutch was a more improbable and miraculous victory than the better-known Battle of Lepanto. The Philippine Revolution, the sudden intervention of the United States, and the struggles of World War II, are all fascinating tales of heroism, betrayal, and struggle. The laborious efforts of the Filipino people to overcome obstacles of geography, culture, and history to forge a single nation deserves the highest admiration. It is my hope that all who read this book will be inspired by these stories to learn more about the Pearl of the Orient.

Catholics, especially, should take a lively interest in the Philippines. The Philippines remains the only predominantly Catholic country in Asia—the center of the Catholic religion in the Far East. Marinated in the Christian culture of Spain for centuries, Filipino Catholicism is a particularly rich blend of Christianity, an exemplar of a society that has truly "inculturated" the Gospel, to use the term coined by the Second Vatican Council. And with four million Filipinos living and working in the United States, Filipinos are the second largest minority group within the American church after Hispanics. In his World Youth Day address to the Filipino Church in Manila in 1995, St. John Paul II expressed his desire that the Philippines would be the jumping off point for the Catholic faith to take root in Asia. As you can see, it is a place that should be of interest to every Catholic!

Though this book is about the Philippines, it is primarily intended

Introduction

for an American audience. As such, it is colored by an American lens, so to speak. Many Americans are completely ignorant of U.S. involvement in the Philippines. There are certainly millions who are unaware that the Philippines was an American colony from 1898 to 1946. The American legacy in the Philippines is not always spotless. The seizure of the archipelago from Spain when it was on the cusp of liberty is hard to justify. Events like the 1906 slaughter of almost 1,000 Moros at the Massacre of Bud Dajo were atrocities committed by U.S. soldiers accustomed to thinking of the Filipino peoples as savages. The U.S. saying of the day was "Civilize 'em with a Krag"—referring to the Krag–Jørgensen rifle used by American servicemen. While the Americans helped modernize the Philippines, and were certainly preferable to the brutal Japanese who occupied the nation from 1942 to 1945, the fact remains that the American presence in the Philippines was an exercise in raw imperialism. Learning about the Philippine experience with the United States is thus an important component of understanding U.S. history as well.

Without further ado, let us begin our study of the Philippines with a survey of the geography of the Philippine archipelago.

THE STORY
OF THE
PHILIPPINES

Luzon Strait
South China Sea
Lingayen Gulf
Baguio
Luzon
Philippine Sea
Mount Pinatubo
Quezon City
Bataan
Manila
Batangas City
Legazpi
Mindoro
Samar
Visayas
Tacloban
Panay
Leyte
Cebu City
Cebu
Negros
Bohol
Limasawa
Puerto Princesa
Palawan
Sulu Sea
Cagayan de Oro City
Butuan City
Mindanao
Lake Lanao
Zamboanga City
Davao City
Brunei
Basilan
Jolo
Borneo
Celebes Sea

Chapter 1

THE LAND OF MA'I

In the westernmost reaches of the Pacific Ocean there is a group of lush, mountainous islands. Not two or ten or twenty islands, but over seven thousand of them. Some are very large, some incredibly tiny, and a great many in between. These islands are huddled tightly, like a flock of sea birds clustered together atop the vast sea. To their west they face the expansive continent of Asia; to the east the endless deep blue of the Pacific.

The medieval Chinese were the first to write about these islands. They called them the land of Ma'i. A Chinese merchant of the Middle Ages wrote, "The people of Ma'i live in large villages on the opposite banks of a stream. Its mountain range is flat and broad, the fields are fertile, and the climate is rather hot." A rather simple description for a very complicated land!

The Chinese called the islands Ma'i, but they have gone by many other names over the centuries. They have been called Lei,

Lusong, and Celebes. The Spanish had several names for them as well. The explorer Magellan called them the St. Lazarus Islands. Others referred to them simply as Islas del Poniente, "Islands of the West." One explorer wanted to call them Caesarea Caroli, after the Holy Roman Emperor Charles V. However, the name that stuck was the one given by the explorer Ruy López de Villalobos, who visited the islands in 1543 and called them Las Islas Felipinas after prince Philip of Asturias, the future King Philip II of Spain. Today, the islands are known by the name given by López de Villalobos—the Philippines. The people who live there are known as Filipinos.

The Philippine islands are an *archipelago*. What is an archipelago? An archipelago is a group or cluster of islands. As we said above, the Philippine archipelago is made of over seven thousand islands. Of the Philippines' seven thousand or so islands, only one thousand have people living on them. The rest are too small or too remote to support a human population. But those one thousand islands support a thriving population of 113 million people.

With so many thousands of islands, how do the Filipinos keep track of where every island is? Well, probably most Filipinos aren't even sure! However, they do have a system of organizing their islands by lumping them together into three main island groups. In the north is the Luzon group, named after the biggest island in the Philippines, Luzon. In the center of the archipelago is the cluster of smaller islands known as the Visayas. Furthest south is the Mindanao group, named after Mindanao, a very large island that makes up the southernmost part of the Philippines. All of the thousands of islands of the Philippines are part of either the Luzon, Visayas, or Mindanao island groups. This makes it easier to keep track of where things are. Today, the flag of the Philippines has three yellow stars symbolizing the three island groups which make up the nation. Throughout this book, we will use the three island group system to reference where the places are that we will be discussing.

This book is about the history of the Philippines. But before we dive into the history of this rich and complex land and the Filipino

Chapter 1: The Land of Ma'i

people, we should learn a little bit more about the islands themselves, the place the Filipinos call home.

The Philippine islands have a tropical climate. This means it is warm and moist most of the time with lots of tropical plants and animals. The tropical climate also means the Philippines do not have four seasons, but only two: a rainy season and a dry season. The rainy season begins in June and lasts until October. During the rainy season there are frequent, heavy rains throughout the islands. Sometimes in September and October there are very powerful storms called typhoons. A *typhoon* is like a hurricane in the Pacific. November to May is the dry season.

The Philippines are a mountainous and rugged place. They are located on something called the Pacific Ring of Fire, an area in the western Pacific known for its volcanoes and earthquakes. The Philippine islands were formed long ago when plates of the earth's surface collided, forming volcanic pockets. As the volcanoes erupted, molten lava cooled and became the many islands of the Philippines. Eventually those rocky volcanic islands became covered in lush trees and grasses, filled with a variety of animals, and eventually cities teeming with people. But we are getting ahead of ourselves.

What are the islands of the Philippines like? Suppose we are standing on the coast of China at the city of Hong Kong, looking east into the Pacific Ocean. We are going to take an imaginary flight from here to the Philippines so we can look at the islands from above and get an idea of what they are like.

To get to the Philippines we would have to fly southeast from Hong Kong for quite some time. We would have to travel for almost eight hundred miles over the bright blue waters of the South China Sea. Eventually, however, we would see a massive green island emerging on the horizon. This is the great island of Luzon. Luzon is the northernmost island in the Philippines, and also the biggest. In fact, it is one of the biggest islands in the world. The Luzon island group takes its name from this great island.

As we get closer to Luzon, we can see broad fields spreading out before us. Farmers grow rice, sugarcane, corn, and fruit in these lush fields. Others use them for grazing pigs, chickens, goats, and water buffalo.

Going east, the fields give way to a massive and rugged range of mountains, the Cordillera Central. Luzon's highest mountain, Mount Pulag, towers over the Cordillera at a height of over 9,600 feet. The Cordillera Central mountains are steep and treacherous, but dozens of different peoples with their own dialects and customs call these mountains their home.

Moving on from the mountains we come to the vast central Luzon plains. The flat plains of central Luzon are almost entirely used for growing rice. As we fly over them we can see the Filipino rice farmers hunched over working in their water-logged rice plots. These plains are watered by two great rivers, the Cagayan in the north and the Pampanga in the south. In the center of the Luzon plains we can see the region's one solitary mountain, Mount Arayat, looming over the plains like a lone sentinel standing guard over central Luzon.

Southern Luzon is dominated by two bodies of water: Manila Bay on the west, which opens out into the South China Sea, and Laguna de Bay, the biggest lake in the country. This area is heavily developed with many cities. The Philippine capital city of Manila is nestled against Manila Bay with its back to Laguna de Bay. Manila is a modern city, complete with glittering lights, skyscrapers, traffic jams, and everything we associate with big cities. Manila is home to almost two million people.

Moving south past Manila, the island of Luzon stretches away to the east into a narrow peninsula called Bicol Peninsula. A *peninsula* is a piece of land almost entirely surrounded by water. The Bicol is a long, thin strip of land that juts off of southeastern Luzon like a bony finger pointing out into the Pacific. It is a rugged, mountainous area full of looming, solitary mountain peaks and several active volcanoes. Though rugged, Bicol is full of cities, towns, and villages clustered around its many bays and gulfs.

If we continue to move south, we leave the island of Luzon and

Chapter 1: The Land of Ma'i

pass over to the great island of Mindoro. Mindoro is part of the Luzon island group and one of the biggest islands of the Philippines. It is home to over one million people. The name Mindoro comes from the Spanish *Mina de Oro*, which means "gold mine," as the Spanish used to extract gold from its hills. Today most of the people on Mindoro are farmers. In the waters east of Mindoro there are many other islands that belong to the Luzon island group, places such as Marinduque, Tablas, Burias, and many others.

If we continue our imaginary flight southeast from Mindoro, we pass over the second of the Philippines' three island groups: the Visayas. The Visayas are a cluster of six large islands surrounded hundreds of smaller islands. These islands sit in a body of water known as the Sulu Sea, which stretches from the Visayas down to the island of Borneo. The six great islands of Visayas are Bohol, Cebu, Leyte, Negros, Panay, and Samar. Do these names sound strange and foreign to you now? Don't worry; by the time you are through with this book you will become very familiar with a lot of these place names.

The people of the Visayas are of a different ethnic group than those of Luzon. We mentioned the island of Borneo on the southwestern edge of the Sulu Sea. According to Filipino legend, the peoples of the Visayas originally came from Borneo centuries ago to escape from a tyrannical prince. To this day, the peoples of the Visayas still observe festivals celebrating the arrival of their ancestors in the region.

The islands of the Visayas are arranged in a semicircle, as if they are an audience looking up attentively at the great island of Luzon. Most of them are mountainous and full of tropical plants. The climate here is very nice and the air is fresh. In olden times, people used to come to the Visayas to recover from sickness. These islands are brimming with people—18 million Filipinos live and work in the Visayan islands. The biggest city here is Cebu City, on the long, narrow island of Cebu. Cebu was founded by the Spaniards and is the oldest city in the Philippines. If we were to walk through its busy streets we would see lots of beautiful old Spanish architecture. This important city was once the capital of the Philippines. It is considered the heart of Filipino Catholicism. The first Filipino converts were from Cebu. It was near Cebu City that the Spanish explorer Magellan was killed. It is a very historic, important place.

Continuing our flight southeast, we come to the last of the Philippines' three island groups, the Mindanao islands. The Mindanao group is named after the largest island, Mindanao. Mindanao is a strange, irregularly shaped island. It looks like a big blob with an elephant trunk jutting off west into the waters of the Sulu Sea. A cluster of hundreds of small islands trails off of the trunk-like peninsula going southwest towards Borneo.

Though there are thousands of islands in the Mindanao group, 92% of Mindanao's population (about 22 million people) live on the main island of Mindanao. Mindanao island is very large—larger than many countries and among the biggest islands in the world. The island has an incredible diversity of landforms. Rugged mountain ranges, rolling plateaus and grasslands, isolated volcanoes, and swampy plains can all be found throughout Mindanao. The tallest mountain in the Philippines is found on Mindanao. Mount Apo, an inactive volcano, towers over the southern coast of the island at an elevation of nearly 10,000 feet.

The people of Mindanao do all sorts of different things for a living. Some farm bananas. Some raise cattle. In northern Mindanao, there is a thriving tourist industry as millions of people come there every year to see the beautiful scenery. The most important city in Mindanao is Davao. Davao sits on the Davao Gulf, a great bay that cuts into the island of Mindanao on the south. Davao is a sprawling, modern city that is home to 1.6 million people.

To the southwest of Mindanao is a string of islands called the Sulu Archipelago. Many of the Filipinos who live here are Muslims; there are many Muslims in southern Mindanao as well.

As you can see, there are so many different types of lands and peoples in the thousands of islands of the Philippines—it is actually remarkable that such a diverse place is even one country! Now we understand why this land has gone by so many names throughout history. There are so many different aspects to the Philippines—so many peoples, so many islands, so many languages. And so much history! In our next chapter, we will begin our study of the Philippines by going back before history was written to learn about how the first people came to the Philippine archipelago.

Chapter 2

COMING TO THE PHILIPPINES

There are a lot of mysteries about the world, especially about how things got to be where they are. For example, there are very tall mountains with lakes atop them full of fish. How did the fish get into those mountain lakes? Or sometimes we may be walking outdoors and see an enormous rock or boulder and wonder how such a massive stone got there. Was it originally part of a larger mountain that got eroded away? Did a glacier put it there thousands of years ago? Is it a meteor that fell from the sky?

Historians ask similar questions when trying to figure out how ancient people got places. The Philippines are a group of islands, so we naturally wonder how the first people crossed the sea and settled there. Did they come across in primitive boats? Perhaps the sea levels were lower back then, enabling them to walk across on the exposed sea bed. And if they did come, where did they come from? Did they come from China or Japan? Or maybe they came from Malaysia or Indonesia. Nobody is sure.

Perhaps people didn't come to the Philippines from elsewhere at all. Perhaps the Philippines used to be connected to mainland Asia, but at some point the ocean levels rose, cutting the islands off from the mainland and stranding the people there.

As you can see, there are a lot of questions! However people came to the Philippines, and wherever they came from, it happened a very long time ago, before written history. The truth is lost in the mists of time.

However, there are a few things we do know. Scientists have discovered the remains of people in the Philippine islands dating back thousands of years, to the very dawn of human settlement in Asia. We know that there were primarily three different groups of people who came to the Philippines in ancient times: the Negritos, the Malays, and the Indonesians.

The Negritos were a people of very short stature, dark skin, and scant body hair. They may have originally come from India. The second group, the Malays, were a numerous people who inhabited southeastern Asia, specifically the Malaysian peninsula, and the islands of Sumatra, Borneo, and Taiwan. They were fairer than the Negritos and somewhat taller, with straight, black hair. The Indonesians were the third group of settlers. They came from a large cluster of islands to the south of the Philippines known as Indonesia. Darker than the Malays but not quite as dark-skinned as the Negritos, the Indonesians came north and made their way to the Philippines by way of the Sulu Archipelago, eventually settling throughout Mindanao and the southern Philippines islands.

The Negritos, Malays, and Indonesians would eventually mix together and give rise to the Filipino people, though that was still a long time in future. And many other groups would arrive after them as well.

For now, we shall concern ourselves with how these peoples got here. One popular theory is that the ancient people took advantage of ocean currents that enabled them to ride rafts to the Philippines. Nobody knows if this is true or not—it happened long before written

Chapter 2: Coming to the Philippines

history. But let us use our imagination to follow the journey of Hari, a Malay chief, and his people as they cross the sea in search of a new home.

The sun beat down upon the endless blue waters of the ocean. It was a nice day, breezy with clouds massed upon the horizon, but still clear and warm. We hear no sound from motor boats or airplanes or any machines anywhere, for we are thousands of years in the past, when the technology of man was limited to what he could chisel in stone or fashion from wood. All we can hear is the whirring of the ocean breeze and the endless lapping of the waves upon the open sea.

Yet on the horizon we catch our first glimpse of man. Several dark objects appear floating on the waves. They look like pieces of driftwood from a distance, but as they float closer we can see they are large rafts. They are made of carved wooden planks lashed together. Some of them have crude sails made of animal hides flapping in the breeze.

And they carry people! Each raft is occupied by anywhere from five to twenty people. Their arms and legs are thin and wiry from a life of hard work. Their hair is dark and matted from days and nights exposed to the spray and wind of the sea. Their skin is tanned and leathery from a lifetime lived outdoors. Men and women alike are clothed in scanty tunics of woven reed. Children nestle in their parents' arms, naked as the day they came out of the womb. Some—perhaps the chiefs or elders—have paint on their faces. Others have tattoos—dark, swirling designs that remind one of the ocean waves.

They squint into the sun as they scan the horizon, looks of determination on their faces. This is a hardy and courageous people. They have crossed the sea seeking a new home. From whence did they come? What drove them to the sea? We do not know. But what a sight it is to see their flotilla of rafts drifting on the sea! At first we see only a few rafts, but gradually more emerge over the horizon. Ten, then twenty, then more, carrying hundreds and hundreds of people.

Today the wind is strong. The little navy of rafts drift briskly across the rolling waves. The flotilla seems to be moving with the current and making very good speed. Many of the men and women perch on the edge of the rafts, their legs cutting into the water and cooling their sun-beaten skin. At the head of the group is a larger raft topped with a crude mast and rawhide sail billowing in the driving wind. This raft belongs to the chief, Hari, and his band of warrior lords. Hari is a proud, strong man, probably around thirty years of age. He is not tall (most of the people of this tribe are quite short), but his lean body is all muscle. His hands are rough from a lifetime of labor and battle. He squints his wrinkled face, scanning the horizon. His eyes are narrow and beady, but they are keen and sharp as a hawk's. He covers his eyes with his hand, looking intently eastward and trying to block out the glare of the noontide sun above.

The top of the Manunggul Jar, found in a cave near an ancient burial site. Discovered on Palawan, the jar has been dated to about 800 BC.

Chapter 2: Coming to the Philippines

Nearby, his twelve year old son Anak notices the look on his father's scrunched up, red-painted face. Anak has seen that look before. It is the look that falls across his father's face before he casts a spear at a gazelle or traps a hare. He sees something!

Sure enough, Hari raises his hands and shouts to his companions. A small troop of warriors comes running. Hari grips his spear—a long, wooden shaft carved to a point—and gestures towards the horizon. The other warriors gather about and stare off into the distance. Anak stands up and stares as well. He doesn't see anything. Or does he?

The men start murmuring. Can it be? Yes, it's true! A small black dot on the horizon. It's land! Hari and the warriors laugh and slap each other on the back. Two warriors dash over the planks of the raft towards the sides. They pick up two long poles with bright, red banners on the ends. They heave the banners aloft with excitement and wave them in the air. This is the sign to the other rafts that land has been spotted. Other banners are lifted from the following ships, and before long the joyful message has been spread through the entire flotilla.

Anak feels a soft hand on his shoulder. It is his mother, Koa. She smiles tenderly at the boy and tousles his hair. Anak smiles back. They have been out at sea for weeks. What will this new land be like? Will they be able to live there? Anak hopes they will be able to settle down. He is weary of floating on the sea.

More land comes into view. The little black dot on the horizon becomes a broad green strip. A chorus of whooping and hollering goes up from the men and women of the flotilla. It is a sign of rejoicing. However, the people soon fall quiet as they drift closer to land. By now the sun is starting to sink in the west behind them and the sky is turning a gentle pink. The land gets bigger and bigger. Soon it fills their line of sight entirely. Hari looks concerned. This island is not little, it is massive. The other warriors seem to share Hari's concern.

Anak is confused. Why would father look concerned? Shouldn't he be happy that they have found their home? Koa explains things to the boy. With an island so large, it is very unlikely that they are the first ones to find it. There very well may be other people there. Hari and his people will have to be on guard. Anak shudders and looks at the island, now looming over them with trees and mountains visible in the distance. It suddenly looks foreboding.

The rafts begin to come ashore shortly after dark. They wash up on the sandy beach in silence, the men and women disembarking softly without a sound. The sand feels strange under Anak's feet—he has not walked on solid earth for almost a month. Even though he is now standing on the ground, it seems that he can still feel the waves lurching in his blood.

The tribe encamps on the beach that night under the stars, their backs to the sea, their warriors taking watches and scanning the deep forest for any signs of danger. But the night passes uneventfully and Anak drifts off into a deep sleep, nestled up against his mother on the sand.

He is awakened to the sound of his father Hari deliberating with the other warriors. His mother explains that they are debating whether to walk up the beach some or to go exploring into the forest. Anak blinks and rubs his eyes. The forest is bright green, a brighter green than he's ever seen. Boys from the tribe are already scrambling up the coconut trees to find food. Women are dragging belongings from the rafts.

Hari sees his son and smiles. He motions for Anak to join him. He and some men are going to walk up the beach a ways and scout out the area. Anak smiles and dashes off to join his father. His father hands him a spear, which Anak clutches securely. At twelve, he is considered a warrior, too. The party sets off.

Are there people on this island already? If so, are they hostile? Will this place be a good home for Hari, Koa, Anak and their people? Anak isn't sure, but one thing he does know is that he feels much safer beside his strong father and their warrior friends. In an uncertain world, there is always safety in numbers.

Chapter 2: Coming to the Philippines

We don't know when this happened. It could have been 6,000 years ago or maybe longer. It's hard to say. Waves of peoples continued coming to the Philippines throughout those earliest centuries of human civilization. Did the Negritos, Malays, and Indonesians get along with each other? Or did they war continually? Nobody knows for sure. Historians do not know much about the early Philippines. Probably the three groups were aware of each other and fought or intermarried occasionally, but most likely they kept to themselves in their own little kingdoms. Left to themselves, they began to develop unique cultures.

In our next chapter, we will learn about one of the early cultures of the Philippines: the Jade Culture of Luzon and the Visayas.

Chapter 3

THE JADE CULTURE

You have probably heard words like *society* and *culture* before. But have you ever given any thought to what these words mean exactly? Are society and culture the same thing? If not, how are they different?

Human beings are social creatures. This means we naturally live together in communities instead of apart on our own. This was part of God's design for humanity. In designing us to live together, God intends for us to learn to look beyond ourselves and practice charity towards our fellow man. When humans live together in community it is called *society*. To be human is to live in society.

But oftentimes societies will develop differently depending on when and where they live or what their environment is like. They develop their own unique languages, their own art, beliefs, and ways of living. When societies start distinguishing themselves this way, we now have the emergence of different cultures. A *culture* is the shared beliefs, arts, and intellectual activity of a specific group of people. In this chapter, we will learn about one of the first cultures of the Philippines, the Jade Culture.

Back in the 1930's, American archaeologists in the Philippines started digging up mysterious artifacts made from a substance known as jade. *Jade* is a type of rock found throughout Asia, known for its green coloring. It is a relatively soft rock that can be carved and polished. Many Asian cultures made beautiful artwork out of jade.

What sort of jade artifacts did the archaeologists find in the Philippines? All kinds! Beautiful earrings and pendants in the shapes of animals, ornate bracelets, bead necklaces, and all sorts of jewelry. They also found chisels and tools made out of jade. They were carved and polished with exquisite skill. Whoever created these jade pieces, they were expert artisans.

Tens of thousands of these jade pieces were found throughout the Philippines, but especially in the region of Batangas, in southern Luzon. This led archaeologists to think that southern Luzon was once home to a culture that specialized in jade artwork. They began to refer to these people as the Jade Culture.

How old were the jade artifacts? It's always tricky dating something like a piece of jewelry, but scientists think the jade artifacts were made between 2000–1500 BC. This makes the Jade Culture the oldest known culture on the Philippines.

Unfortunately, there is little else we know about the Jade Culture. They left no writings behind. Their homes—probably rough structures of wood or bamboo—have long since rotted away. The only other remains left by the Jade Culture were some fragments of pottery. Not very much to go on! The identity of these skilled jade workers has been lost to history. We only know them through their fantastic jade carvings.

The interesting thing about the Jade Culture is that the jade they worked with is not found on the Philippines. This means they must have imported it from somewhere else. Where did the Jade Culture get their jade?

Chapter 3: The Jade Culture

Scientists have determined that the jade used to create the artifacts found in the Philippines originally came from the Niaosung people who inhabited Taiwan, a large island off the coast of China that was the center of an ancient culture of merchants. The jade must have come from Taiwan through some sort of ancient trading network.

One of the most frustrating things about studying prehistoric cultures is there is so much speculation. We know so little! How did the people of Taiwan and the people of the Jade Culture come into contact? What did they trade with the Taiwanese to get the jade? Where did the artists of the Jade Culture learn their skills? We can only guess.

However, it might have looked something like this.

Joyo watched grimly as three black-sailed ships moved closer to the shore. "Who are they papa?" his little son Ajij asked.

"Niaosung traders," Joyo responded.

"Are they…bad?" Ajij said, looking at the gloomy black sails of the Niaosung ships.

"That depends on what they are here for," Joyo said. "Usually they just want to trade. But sometimes they want to plunder."

"Should I alert the village?" Ajij asked excitedly. "Should we call out the warriors?"

"No, son," said Joyo, tousling the boy's hair. "Let's wait and see what they want. We should not provoke them needlessly. But why don't you run back home and tell your mother and sister to bring out the copper?" Ajij nodded and dashed off into the fields that sloped up from the coast.

By the time Ajij and his family had returned from the village, the three Niaosung ships had beached and their crews were beginning to disembark. They were grim, stocky men armed with curved swords of bronze strapped to their sides. The Niaosung, dressed in black tunics, eyed Joyo and his family suspiciously. Some of them fingered their swords.

"I'm scared, Papa," said Ajij.

"Peace, son," said Joyo nervously. This was the moment of truth. Would the Niaosung attack and slaughter them all, or were they interested in trade? "Dewi!" Joyo called to his daughter, who stood a ways off with her mother. "Bring the cart here. Let's show them what we offer."

Dewi, a girl of eight, approached cautiously, pushing a wooden cart. "Here," Joyo gestured to the Niaosung. "Copper, which we have recovered from the hills of our island." The Niaosung walked up to the cart and inspected it carefully. Joyo and his family had spent the summer collecting lumps of copper from the hills of Luzon. Joyo had heated the copper in an oven to make it soft and beaten it into long strips.

The Niaosung held up the copper strips and nodded. Joyo smiled. "They mix our copper with other metals from their own land to make their bronze swords," Joyo explained to Ajij as the Niaosung traders discussed among themselves what they would offer Joyo for his copper. One of the Niaosung produced large cloth. Unwrapping it on the ground before Joyo, it contained a dozen hunks of stone. The stone was green and had a creamy look to it.

Joyo's eyes widened. "Ah! Jade!" By this time other villagers had begun making their way to the shore to offer their own wares. The Niaosung had relaxed and were negotiating with the villagers for their goods. All payment was made in jade.

Joyo had parted with his entire cart of beaten copper in exchange for the twelve hunks of jade stone. By sunset, the Niaosung had departed to trade elsewhere, and Joyo and his family were back inside their hut. Dewi slept while her mother mended garments. Joyo and Ajij examined the jade by the flickering light of an oil lamp. "Well son, let's see what we can do with this, shall we?" said Joyo. "

Ajij handed his father a small copper chisel. His father held the lump of jade in his rugged hands and began working it with the tool. Ajij had seen his father do this hundreds of times. Joyo, like many in the village, was an expert jade worker. Sweat beads formed on Joyo's brow as he patiently chiseled away minute flakes of jade. Sometimes

Chapter 3: The Jade Culture

he turned them into bracelets, sometimes ornate earrings shaped like little animals. This particular piece would become a turtle pendant, his father told him, meant to be worn around the neck as a charm. "We can trade these with the people of the southern isles when we go there next spring," said Joyo.

Joyo would have much more work to do before the pendant was done. After the rough shape of the jade was carved, he would have to polish the piece for days by rubbing it with sand. Then he would use much smaller chisels and knives to bring out the detail he desired.

Thousands of artists just like Joyo must have been behind the marvelous work of the Jade Culture. Clearly their art was valued all throughout the archipelago, for the works of the Jade Culture have been found throughout the Philippines.

However, by 1000 BC another group of people were starting to outdo the Jade Culture in the quality of their work. The Sa Huynh were a people from mainland Asia, from what is now known as Vietnam. Like the Niaosung in the story above, they were merchants and traders. They, too, learned the art of working in precious stones, perhaps from observing the work of the Jade Culture. They began making beautiful beads from things such as glass, carnelian, agate, zircon, gold and garnet.

People wanted their exquisite beads. Before long they had established their own trading networks around the South China Sea. The Sa Huynh came to the Visayas in the central Philippines and began trading there, disrupting the trade of the Jade Culture. Before long, the Jade Culture and their wondrous artifacts disappeared from history, never to be seen again until American archaeologists in the Philippines started digging up their jade artifacts in the 1930s, over three thousand years after they were made.

What happened to the people of the Jade Culture? Did the Sa Huynh conquer them? Did they intermarry with the Sa Huynh or other groups and lose their identity? Did they take to their ships and leave the Philippines to find another home? Nobody knows. It's one of the frustrating things about studying ancient history. There are so many unanswered questions.

In our next chapter, we will start learning about one of the first historic kingdoms of the Philippines, the Kingdom of Butuan.

Chapter 4

THE RAJAHS OF BUTUAN

In our last chapter we learned about one of the earliest cultures of the Philippines—the Jade Culture—and their marvelous jade artifacts. We also learned how the Jade Culture was displaced by the Sa Huynh people sometime around 1000 BC.

This is how it went in the Philippines for a very, very long time. New people constantly arrived from places like Taiwan, Malaysia, and Indonesia, one group displacing another, sometimes by conquest, sometimes by intermarriage. Various cultures formed in different parts of the archipelago, creating their own unique art, tools, and beliefs, only to give way before a newer, more vibrant culture. Just like the Jade Culture, each wave of people left little behind except their artifacts. They left no writing, no histories, and no literature. But they did bring their own distinct cultures, religions, and stories, which have often been preserved.

This coming and going of peoples went on for almost two

thousand years. Consider how long that is and all that passed in that time! The rise and fall of the Kingdom of Israel, the conquests of Alexander the Great, the reign of the Caesars, the barbarian invasions and the collapse of the Roman Empire—and the coming of our Lord Jesus Christ and the spread of the Christian faith. These momentous things all occurred without the peoples of the Philippine archipelago having the least idea about them. This is not surprising—they were on the other side of the world. For the early people of the Philippines, the world pretty much consisted of the archipelago and the bright blue sea.

But this all began to change towards the end of the first millennium AD. From the disjointed tribes and cultures of the archipelago, distinct kingdoms began to emerge. They began to have more contact with the outside world—places like China, Sumatra, and Malaysia. We will learn about some of these kingdoms throughout the next few chapters. In this chapter, we will begin with the Rajahs of Butuan.

What on earth is a *rajah*? Well, before we get to that, let's talk about Butuan.

In the northeast corner of the great southern Philippine island of Mindanao there is a region called Butuan. It is a heavily forested region full of many rivers. But the rivers of Butuan are special, for since ancient times the Butuanese have mined for gold along these river banks. This gold made the Butuanese wealthy. In time, many people came from different kingdoms to trade in Butuan and exchange things for Butuanese gold—things such as fine clothing and jewelry, chinaware, cosmetics, and much more. Items have been found in Butuan from China, India, Cambodia, Thailand, Vietnam, and other Asian countries. Because of its power, wealth, and influence, Butuan is considered the first true Philippine kingdom. To this day the Butuanese have a saying, "In the beginning there was no Philippines, but there was Butuan."

The rulers of Butuan were called *rajahs*. A rajah is essentially like a tribal prince. From around AD 900 to 1400 the Rajahs of Butuan

Chapter 4: The Rajahs of Butuan

Examples of Butuanese goldsmithing dated to the 10th through 13th centuries AD.

were the most powerful men in the Philippines. They won the respect of all the peoples around them, even the mighty emperors of China. In fact, the first written records of the Kingdom of Butuan come not from the Butuanese themselves, but from the court of China's Song Dynasty.

The annals of the Song Dynasty record that ambassadors from a rajah named Kiling showed up at the court of Emperor Zhenzong in the year 1001. The ambassadors from Butuan did not make much of an impression on the fabulously wealthy, powerful Chinese monarch. Rajah Kiling was hoping to enter into an alliance with China, but the officials of the Emperor Zhenzong yawned, made some notes about the Butuanese, took their obligatory gifts, and then shuffled them out the door.

However the Butuanese were not ready to give up. Their kingdom was wealthy and populous, but small and vulnerable. They needed the protection of a more powerful kingdom like China. In 1011 the successor of Kiling, Rajah Sri Bata Shaja, decided to try approaching Emperor Zhenzong again, this time with an ambassador the rajah believed would be capable of getting the emperor's attention. This man was Likan-Hsieh, and the tale of Likan-Hsieh's appearance before Emperor Zhenzong is a very famous episode in Philippine history. Let's stop in and visit the court of Emperor Zhenzong that day in 1011 when Likan-Hsieh made his memorable visit.

It was the eve of an important state sacrifice. Officials from all over China cluttered the great hall where the Emperor Zhenzong would soon perform the customary sacrifices to Heaven on behalf of the kingdom. The ritual was a complicated rite, composed of seven different phases that took the entire evening. Music and dancing characterized the first part of the ritual, preparing for the climax of the night when the emperor himself would arrive from his palace to offer sacrifices of jade, silk, and food on the ornately carved altar to Heaven at the north end of the hall.

Also milling about in the room were several ambassadors from foreign kingdoms. These men hoped to pay their respects to Emperor Zhenzong at the festivities after the sacrifice and perhaps win the emperor's favor. One of these ambassadors was Likan-Hsieh from Butuan in the Philippine archipelago. Likan-Hsieh was adorned in the *barong tagalog*, a long white tunic decorated with ornate embroidery which was the ceremonial dress of the Butuanese. He looked out of place, his white barong tagalog forming a marked contrast to the richly colored silk robes of the Chinese officials. His hair, somewhat unkempt and his beard untrimmed, also caused the austere Chinese to look askance at Likan-Hsieh.

"Who is that barbarian, Zuan?" said one official condescendingly.

Zuan scratched his beard. "Most esteemed Guang, unless my memory mistakes me, that is the ambassador from the Kingdom of Butuan."

"Butu…what?" exclaimed Guang.

Chapter 4: The Rajahs of Butuan

"Butuan, dear Guang. An insignificant island kingdom. They have been trying unsuccessfully to win the attention of Zhenzong for ten years now."

"No doubt they will never win his attention if they send uncouth vagabonds like this fellow!" snorted Guang.

"Yes," chuckled Zuan, "you are correct. After ten years of trying, the emperor is still no more aware of Butuan than he is of the mites on the mane of his steed."

"Very true, Zuan, but say, what do you suppose he carries in that leather pouch?"

Zuan looked at Likan-Hsieh. Indeed, he carried a leather side bag that appeared to be stuffed full of something. "I cannot say," Zuan said shaking his head. "I am frankly surprised the guards allowed him to bring it into the great hall."

At that moment a great clanging of cymbals announced the arrival of the emperor. The room fell silent. The crowd parted, making a broad aisle for the emperor and his retinue to enter the hall. A moment later, Zhenzong himself appeared at the end of a train of servants and officials. At the sight of him all heads in the room bowed. The emperor was glorious to behold. His robes were yellow embroidered with golden threads depicting dragons and colored silken threads forming beautiful images of flowers and ivy. Upon his shoulders was a broad and heavy cloak, black without and red within, fitting for the solemnity of the occasion. The emperor's attendants were clothed in similar splendor.

The procession was set to a piece of formal music, which was painstakingly slow. The emperor took only one step every few seconds. Likan-Hsieh began to huff and rustle about at having to keep his head bowed so long. Zuan and Guang shuffled uncomfortably at the jostling of the Butuanese ambassador.

Presently, Emperor Zhenzong passed by Likan-Hsieh. Likan-Hsieh lifted his head. "Your majesty!" called out Likan-Hsieh. The procession stopped dead in its tracks. The music sputtered out. Zuan and Guang dropped their jaws. "Yes, your majesty! Holy and exalted one!" Likan-Hsieh cried out, stepping out of place and awkwardly making a half-bow before Zhenzong.

"No you fool!" shouted Zuan.

"The impudence!" growled Guang.

"Begging the pardon of the Son of Heaven," stammered Likan-Hsieh. "It's me! That is to say, Likan-Hsieh. My lord, Sri Bata Shaja, Rajah of Butuan, has sent me to petition his Majesty…"

"Guards! Take this fool out and throw him in the river," grunted one of the officials. Immediately a band of guards made their way up and seized Likan-Hsieh roughly. Zhenzong stood motionless and expressionless, biting his lip in an attempt ignore this brash interruption.

In the jostling, Likan-Hsieh's leather bag came opened and a large golden tablet fell out upon the floor. The golden tablet, glistening in the torchlight, drew all eyes to it. Likan-Hsieh took advantage of the momentary distraction. He seized the tablet and presented it to Zhenzong. "A gift from the Rajah of Butuan to you, O Lord of Ten Thousand Years!" Zhenzong reluctantly took the tablet and read the inscription upon it. It contained tender professions of friendship from Rajah Sri Bata Shaja to the emperor.

"But wait, there's more!" said Likan-Hsieh excitedly. "Camphor oil! Moluccan cloves! Jade pendants!" Likan-Hsieh rattled off, producing each item from his pouch and dumping them in the stunned emperor's arms. The emperor's jaw dropped open at the flamboyant audacity of the Butuanese ambassador. "Well don't you like it, Majesty?" said Likan-Hsieh incredulously. "I mean, look at all this great stuff!"

Zhenzong handed off the pile of gifts to an attendant without taking his eyes off Likan-Hsieh. "Great Son of Heaven," said a guard bowing with sword drawn, "only say the word and I will slay this interloper who has so defiled our sacred ceremony."

Zhenzong cleared his throat and spoke, "What kingdom do you come from, O clumsy one?"

"From Butuan, O Majesty," said Likan-Hsieh, "whose lords have

Chapter 4: The Rajahs of Butuan

sought friendship with your majesty for these ten years."

Zhenzong nodded. "Guard!" he snapped.

"Yes my lord! I will take him out and kill him," said the guard, grabbing Likan-Hsieh by the neck.

"No," said Zhenzong. "Seat him near me at the festivities tonight. I wish to learn more about this kingdom of Butuan and what sort of lord it must have who sends such…eccentric men to negotiate with the Son of Heaven."

"Yes…O Majesty!" the guard said, sheathing his sword.

"Well Likan-Hsieh," said Zhenzong smiling, "if you are now satisfied, may we continue our sacrifice in peace?"

Likan-Hsieh bowed his head and returned quietly to his place, smiling.

Stodgy Chinese officials like Zuan and Guang might have been appalled at Likan-Hsieh's tactics. But whatever they may have thought of the flamboyant Butuanese ambassador, his awkward introduction and gifts worked. Zhenzong was fascinated by what Likan-Hsieh told him of Butuan and entered into a treaty with Rajah Sri Bata Shaja and allowed the Butuanese to trade in China. It was a magnificent honor for the little kingdom of Butuan to be recognized by such a mighty power as Song Dynasty China.

This was the beginning of a golden age for Butuan. As we said above, nations from all over Asia would come to trade for Butuanese gold. The Butuanese themselves would take to boats and travel all over the South China Sea trading their gold. Remains of their massive wooden ships called *balangays* have occasionally been found throughout the region, evidence of the once sprawling trade networks of the Butuanese made possible by the antics of Likan-Hsieh.

As for Butuan, it continued on for several centuries, though eventually surpassed by other kingdoms of the archipelago. The Butuanese rajahs were still reigning when the Spanish showed up in

1521. But we are still a long way off from that. For now, let us leave Butuan and Mindanao to head north to the Visayas, where in Cebu another kingdom was flourishing.

Chapter 5

THE KINGDOM OF CEBU

We keep speaking about the Philippines or the Philippine Archipelago, but hopefully you are realizing that, at least up until now, the term "Philippines" is just a geographic expression, the same way we would say "New England" or "the Midwest." For most of its history the Philippines was not a single country unified under a single government. Rather, it was scores of tiny tribal territories and petty kingdoms with ever shifting borders. It's questionable whether people like the Butuanese even thought of themselves as dwellers of a single community of islands. Probably they thought of themselves as Butuanese and nothing more. The other kingdoms of the archipelago were probably as foreign to them as a country on the other side of the planet would be to us.

One of these other kingdoms was the Kingdom of Cebu. Cebu is a long, narrow island in the midst of the Visayas. In case you don't remember, the Visayas are second of the Philippines three island groups. They are the cluster of six large islands that sit between Luzon and Mindanao.

Though people had dwelt in Cebu since the dawn of history, it was not until the 13th century that the first real civilization arose on the island. And it came from far over the sea.

Far to the west of the Philippines—over 1,700 miles away, in fact—is the Indonesian island of Sumatra. Since time immemorial Sumatra had been settled by peoples who had originally come from India. Like the Indians, they were either Hindu or Buddhist and continued many of the cultural traditions of India. The ruler of Sumatra was the *Maharajah*, or "High King."

In the 13th century, the Maharajah of Sumatra ruled over a vast empire that stretched from the islands of the Maldives in the south to as far north as the banks of the Godavari River in eastern India. Wanting to extend his reign even further, the Maharajah sent his son Sri Lumay to lead an expedition east to establish military bases in the Visayas. Sri Lumay led his father's navy to the Visayas and landed on Cebu around the year AD 1200.

Cebu, however, was a very lovely island and Sri Lumay was hesitant to give it up to his father. Full of rolling hills, broad coastal plains, and a good deal of arable land, Sri Lumay decided Cebu was too splendid a place to give up. Instead of founding Sumatran bases there, he rebelled against his father's rule and proclaimed Cebu its own independent kingdom. Sri Lumay took the title of rajah and became the first Rajah of Cebu.

Sri Lumay was a kind and just ruler. Under his reign his people spread out to farm the great island of Cebu and populate it with towns and villages. He was such a kind ruler that during his reign not a single one of his many slaves tried to escape, preferring to stay in servitude to their loving master than risk freedom.

This is not to say Sri Lumay couldn't be fierce. He was a determined opponent and in war he was ruthless. His enemies would soon find this out.

South of Cebu was the great island of Mindanao. In the early 13th

Chapter 5: The Kingdom of Cebu

century Mindanao was inhabited by Muslims from the Sultanate of Borneo. We will discuss how Islam came to the Philippines in Chapter 7, but for now it is sufficient to know that these Muslims of Mindanao were notorious pirates and slave traders. Each year they sailed forth from Mindanao to plunder and terrorize the peoples of the archipelago, taking thousands of prisoners for galley slaves. These Muslim pirates were called Moros, but around the Philippines they were known as *Magalos*, which means "destroyers of peace."

Sri Lumay was just beginning his reign in Cebu when the dreaded Moro pirates arrived on his shores. They struck without warning, burning villages, slaying without pity, and carrying off Sri Lumay's people into slavery. Sri Lumay was bitter and swore he would never allow his people to be so vulnerable again.

Let's visit Sri Lumay's kingdom to see how he dealt with these Magalos who would dare lay violent hands on his people.

It was an overcast day on Cebu. The tall, island grasses rippled in silvery waves as the wind swept overland from the sea. But the breeze was not the only thing that rustled the fields this day, for trudging upland from the coast were a party of Moro raiders from Mindanao. Draped in cloaks of black or deep blue, the Moro raiders looked like spectral ghosts gliding through the fields. They carried deadly *kalis* swords, cruel weapons with wavy blades designed for thrusting or slashing. Other Moros hauled lengths of rope and netting up from the shore. These would be used for restraining the Cebuano slaves they hoped to capture.

"How far is the village, Amir?" growled one of the Moros. "We've already come some ways inland and found no signs of anything."

"It is strange, Bakil," said Amir, the captain, stroking his grizzled beard. "We should have encountered the Cebuano by now. But the village is only a half hour more. By Allah, we shall certainly find our slaves there."

The Moro raiders continued inland in a long line, some two hundred in number. They passed several huts on their way, but to their disappointment found them abandoned. "They've gotten word of our coming!" snarled Bakil. "We should be on our guard."

"You're afraid of these men of Cebu?" chuckled Amir. "Remember how easily we slaughtered them last time? No doubt they are cowering in the village. But all the same, keep your weapons drawn, men."

After sometime the Moros crested a small slope and saw the Cebuano village in the distance. But to their surprise they saw it smoking. "What's this devilry?" said Amir. The troop set off at a jaunt and came down to the village to investigate. Sure enough, the entire village had been set on fire. Only the smoldering foundations of the buildings remained, which curled wisps of black smoke into the gray sky. The Moro warriors threw themselves on the ground to rest, wearied from their walk and frustrated at the lack of Cebuanos to capture.

"Bakil, draw some water from the well," said Amir. "At least we can slake our thirst." But a moment later, Bakil returned with a scowl on his face.

"No water," he said. "They've filled the well with stones." This was overheard by the rest of the Moros, who groaned and complained.

"Everybody up!" shouted Amir. "We must press on! They mean to make it hard for us. Well, we shall make it hard for them. An even larger town is only another two hours inland. Let us press on."

The men grumbled but did as Amir ordered. But as they pressed on inland, it became clear what was happening. The papaya and mango trees which were usually found in abundance outside Cebuano villages were cut down and stripped of their fruit. Rice paddies on the hillsides had been plowed up. Wheat fields were smoking from recent fires. All along the road the Moros found the dead and decaying bodies of ducks, swine, and other animals that had been killed and left to rot.

"By Allah, we could not have devastated the place worse if we'd done this ourselves!" marveled Bakil.

"Captain Amir," said Farouk, one of the Moro war-leaders, "the

Chapter 5: The Kingdom of Cebu

men are weary. They've neither eaten not tasted a sip of water all day. And they are unhappy with what we've found here and wish to return to the ships."

"Cowards!" shouted Amir, slapping Farouk across the cheek. "How can I return to Mindanao and show my face without Cebuano slaves? I'll be dishonored! No, Farouk, we continue on to the next town."

But the next town was an even bigger disappointment. Though the town was not burned, it was deserted. Again, all the wells had been filled up with sand or stone, depriving the Moros of water. All the livestock had been killed, and the fruit trees cut down and stripped. Amir raged and stomped in anger, but the other Moros just watched in silent dejection.

"Amir, we return to the ships," said Bakil stoically.

"I am in command!" shouted Amir. "You will heed me!" he demanded, grabbing Bakil's shoulder as the latter began to walk away. In an instant, Bakil turned and unsheathed his curved *kalis*, pressing the blade to the flesh of Amir's chin.

"We return to the ships," repeated Bakil coldly. "And you will not lay hands on me or any of us again."

Amir grinned a murderous grin. "Very well, Bakil. Very well. We shall see what Datu, our lord, says when I tell him we returned to Mindanao empty handed because of your cowardice."

Bakil sheathed his sword. "Let's just focus on returning first, Amir, then we will worry about what Datu thinks."

The band of Moros, now tired, hungry, and parched with thirst, began a weary march back to the shore, some three hours distant. The sky was still gray, thunder rolled somewhere in the distance. "If only it would rain," mumbled Farouk to Bakil. "Then we could at least have some water."

"The cursed island is going to be the death of us!" said Bakil.

"You're right about that," said a strange voice from the trees beside the road. The Moros turned to see a noble looking Cebuano man standing before them, holding a spear. It was Sri Lumay, the lord of Cebu. "It will not only be your death, you Magalos, but also your tomb," he said.

At that word, scores of Cebuano warriors leaped from hiding and dashed out of the trees beside the road. A Cebuano spear thudded into Farouk's chest and sent him toppling onto the dusty road. "Ambush!" shouted Bakil, drawing his *kalis*. "For Allah!" he cried, warding off the long knives of the men of Cebu who were already upon him.

The Moros were not only surprised, but famished and tired. They were no match for the fighters of Cebu. Every moment more Moros were struck down. Bakil fell with multiple knives stuck in him. His *kalis* fell useless to the dirt.

The skirmish was over in a few minutes. The majority of the Moros had been slain, but a dozen or so had been rounded up and taken prisoner, including Amir, the captain of the expedition. "Kneel before the rajah, Sri Lumay!" called the Cebuano warriors, forcing the Moros to their knees.

"Well Magalos," said Sri Lumay, "you thought the men of Cebu would fall before you easily as before. Not so. We would sooner destroy our own livestock and crops than let them give aid to you."

"What shall we do with them, my king?" asked one of the Cebuano warriors.

Sri Lumay furled his brow. "Rightly are they Magalos, 'destroyers of peace,' for they came to pillage and take our people away. But this day, we will destroy their peace. Put them all to death. Leave none alive." Without hesitation the Cebuano warriors plunged their long knives into their prisoners. Amir muttered some prayers to Allah as he met his doom under multiple blades.

It was over in an instant. The dead Moros littered the road. "Clean up the bodies of these Magalos," ordered Sri Lumay. "And tell our people it is safe to come down from the hills now." Runners were dispatched to carry news of the victory to the villagers hiding in the hills. As they left, thunder pealed across the sky, and a gentle rain began to fall.

Chapter 5: The Kingdom of Cebu

Sri Lumay had many such victories against the Moros. He sired many sons, and his kingdom grew prosperous. But the Moros eventually came to anticipate his tactics, and eventually the great king was slain in battle with them. He was succeeded by his son, Sri Bantug, who continued to defend the Kingdom of Cebu while working to improve its trade, agriculture, and laws. By the time of Sri Bantug, Cebu was a very powerful kingdom, despite constant harassment by the Moros.

The descendants of Sri Lumay would continue to rule the kingdom of Cebu for the duration of its existence, growing the region until it was powerful enough to engage in trade with Japan and many other kingdoms.

As we mentioned at the start of this chapter, the Philippines in these days were divided into many different kingdoms. We have already visited Butuan and Cebu. Next let us go north to Luzon to learn about another, the Kingdom of Tondo.

Chapter 6

THE KINGDOM OF TONDO

We have spent the last two chapters learning about the kingdoms of Butuan and Cebu. In this chapter we shall learn about the third of the great Philippine kingdoms of old, the dominion of Tondo.

But before we can learn about Tondo, we must meet the Tagalog people. As we have mentioned, the thousands of island of the Philippine archipelago were settled by many different ethnic groups. For example, recall that the people of Cebu had migrated to the Visayas from Sumatra? The people who would build the Kingdom of Tondo were called Tagalog. The Tagalog lived on Luzon and in the northern Visayas. They had been in the Philippines for a very long time. The Tagalog came to the archipelago some time during the early 1st millennium AD. They seem to have come from Indonesia. The old Tagalog language was a blend of Malay, Javanese, and Sanskrit (the ancient script of India).

By the late 8th century, the Tagalog had established a kingdom along the Pasig River in Luzon. This was called the Kingdom of Tondo. Tondo was not really a kingdom in the strict sense, though. It was more of a federation of city states called *Barangays*. Each Barangay was governed by a *Datu*, who was a kind of senior chief or prince of the settlement. The Datus in turn all recognized one of their number as a first among equals, a chief-of-chiefs. This was the *Lakan*. The Lakan of Tondo was like a ceremonial head of the Barangays of Tondo, but historians still debate what his powers were. The Spaniards would later think of the Lakan as a king, but this might be inaccurate.

At any rate, the Barangays of Tondo were well protected. Situated at the delta of the Pasig River, Tondo was surrounded by water: Manila Bay to the west and the Pasig to the south, but it was also bounded by several other rivers on the north and east. Anyone seeking to invade Tondo would face the difficult challenge of bringing their armies across several rivers and marshes. This made Tondo easy to defend. In their secure homeland, the Tagalog

Chinese traders show their wares in the Kingdom of Tondo.

Chapter 6: The Kingdom of Tondo

grew rice, raised duck—the staple meat of Tondo—and made wine. Tondo was thus a secure, prosperous little kingdom.

The religion of the Tagalog was based on the belief that the world was inhabited by a multitude of spiritual beings—some powerful, others petty; some good, others evil—who must be honored through worship and sacrifice. Every place and natural phenomenon had its own nature spirits. Families and clans had their own special guardians, and ancestors were paid homage as spiritual mediators with the mysterious powers that governed the universe.

By AD 900, Tondo had a very sophisticated society, with their own language, religion, art, and literature. They had alliances with other Barangays on Luzon, such as the powerful Rajahnate of Maynila on Manila Bay. Like Butuan, Tondo was rich in gold. The Tagalog excelled in gold working. They fashioned many excellent coins and jewelry in gold. Years later when the Spanish arrived in Tondo, one Spaniard wrote of the Tagalog, "The people of this island are very skillful in their handling of gold. They weigh it with the greatest skill and delicacy that have ever been seen. The first thing they teach their children is the knowledge of gold and the weights with which they weigh it, for there is no other money among them."

Many nations sought the gold of the Tagalog of Tondo. One kingdom who wanted to trade with Tondo was China. Do you think this would make Butuan jealous? The Butuanese tried desperately to catch the attention of the Chinese emperors while China was eagerly seeking trade with Tondo. Under the Chinese Ming Dynasty (1368-1644), the Tagalog became important trading partners. The Chinese received gold and other goods from Tondo, and in exchange, the Chinese sent the Tagalog silk and porcelain. The Chinese and the Tagalog became very close. The people of Tondo adopted many Chinese customs. In later years, when China closed its sea ports to trade from outside kingdoms, Tondo alone was exempted and allowed to continue shipping goods into China.

One people who were definitely jealous of Tondo were the Japanese. The Japanese envied Tondo's favored trading status with

China. The Ming Emperors of China allowed Tondo to come trade in China once every two years. By comparison, Japan was only allowed to trade once every ten years. This angered the Japanese. They thought they were worthier trading partners than the Tagalog and should be given better treatment. They coveted all of the silk and porcelain that the Chinese regularly shipped into Tondo. Sometimes, the Japanese resorted to piracy to obtain the precious Chinese goods.

Here's what one of these encounters might have looked like. Our Tagalog captain, Magtanggol, is returning from a trading expedition to China bearing rich silks. His ship has passed the straits between China and Taiwan when it encounters a Japanese pirate ship. Let's see what happens.

"Bayani!" called Captain Magtanggol. "Guard the silks! If they are taken, we will lose a fortune!"

The ship's second-in-command, Bayani, wasted no words. He and his men formed a square around the precious cargo of silks. The brightly colored Chinese silks were stacked upon deck, roll upon roll, and almost six feet high. They were worth an entire year's pay for Magtanggol and his men. Now surrounding the cargo, Bayani and his men raised their elongated wooden shields, each one as tall as the warrior who stood behind it.

Their shields were raised not a moment too soon. The Japanese ship was now within firing range. Japanese archers began firing from an elevated platform. Arrows rained down on the Tagalog ship. Fortunately Bayani and his men were prepared. The arrows thudded into the men's shields.

"Safe for now," Captain Magtanggol said, ducking behind some crates. "But how long can we hold them off? Hopefully the wind will pick up and we can outrun them!"

Alas, the weather was not with Magtanggol. The sun was hot in the sky. The wind was only a light breeze. The Tagalog ship drifted infuriatingly slowly, the sails limp. Meanwhile the Japanese

Chapter 6: The Kingdom of Tondo

ship continued to close on them, propelled by rowers adding extra momentum. Another volley of arrows swept over Magtanggol's ship. This time a few of them found their marks and some of the Tagalog warriors crumpled over, arrows protruding from their necks or backs.

"Bayani!" cried Magtanggol, "do you recognize that blue flag on the Japanese ship? Is that what I think it is?"

Bayani squinted, shielding his eyes from the sunlight with his hand. "Yes, captain," he said dejectedly. "That blue flag bears the emblem of Fūma Kotarō."

"Fūma Kotarō!" Magtanggol repeated. "The most dreaded of all Japanese pirates!"

"My captain," called Bayani, "if that is the ship of Fūma Kotarō, we have neither the men nor the skill to stand up to him. We have but a dozen men, most merchants, not warriors. That ship is twice our size and probably carrying three times as many—and all hardened cut-throats."

"What are you suggesting, Bayani? That I just hand over all of our goods? Enough wealth to hold us over for a year?" demanded Captain Magtanggol angrily. As soon as he said this, another barrage of arrows tore across the deck. One struck the mast only two feet from Magtanggol's head.

"Well sir, it depends on how much you value your life," said Bayani stoically.

Magtanggol looked down, deep in thought. A look of resignation came over him. "Lower the sails!" he called to his deck hands. "Bayani, command your men to lower their shields and raise their hands in surrender."

Bayani nodded silently. The Tagalog laid down their shields and raised their hands in the air. The sails were lowered. Magtanggol stood aloft, waving to the Japanese ship and signaling that they had no intention to fight or flee.

Within minutes the Japanese ship drifted beside Magtanggol's craft. Gang planks were dropped from the pirate ship, allowing several burly Japanese warriors to board Magtanggol's ship. The pirates were armed with deadly *naginata* spears, long poles with curved, single edged blades affixed to the end. The pirates went from man to man on Magtanggol's ship, relieving the merchants of all of their possessions and anything of value. Captain Magtanggol was humiliated as the pirates ripped his shirt apart and cut slits down the sides of his trousers looking for hidden pockets that could contain pouches of gold. But the pirates were disappointed—Magtanggol had traded all his gold in China.

After the merchants had been thoroughly plundered, a tall man with long, flowing brown hair stepped on to the ship. His leather armor and red sash about his waist identified him as the leader of the pirates.

"Fūma Kotarō, I presume," said Captain Magtanggol, bowing ceremoniously.

"You did wisely to surrender," Fūma Kotarō laughed, clasping Magtanggol. "We were just about to start shooting flaming arrows. In choosing wisely, you've saved your own life." Fūma Kotarō turned and walked over to the large pile of silk rolls. He ran his hand over them delicately, smiling at the quality of the Chinese silk. "Yes," he said, "you've saved your life – but not your cargo!"

"I beg you, Fūma Kotarō! Do not deprive me of my livelihood!" Magtanggol demanded.

Fūma Kotarō turned to Magtanggol. A sarcastic smirk flashed across his face. "Perhaps next time you go to China, you can tell the emperor to grant us Japanese the same trading rights as Tondo. Then we would have no need to steal. But, given that things are what they are, we cannot stop you from trading in Chinese silks"—then, slapping Magtanggol on the back and grinning—"and you cannot stop *me* from making them my own! Ha!"

"But you've bankrupted me!" shouted Magtanggol.

Fūma Kotarō snapped his fingers. His men immediately began lifting the heavy silk rolls and removing them to the Japanese ship. Magtanggol continued to fume. Bayani tried to calm him down, but

Chapter 6: The Kingdom of Tondo

Magtanggol was shaking in anger. "Peace, my captain. Let us live and trade another day," said Bayani.

Magtanggol's anger turned to despair. He collapsed on the deck of his now empty ship and wept. By now most of the pirates had returned to their vessel. Magtanggol was a pathetic sight: trousers ripped, shirt torn off, weeping on his knees. Before Fūma Kotarō left, he turned to Bayani and said, "Calm your captain down, man! Life is a gamble. Sometimes you win, sometimes you lose. Today you lost. Tomorrow it may be me who loses. Farewell!"

Despite being occasionally harassed by Japanese pirates, Tondo remained powerful for many centuries. Tondo's most important ally was the Rajahnate of Maynila, a large city-state across the Pasig River. Both kingdoms were Tagalog and shared the same culture. For many years Tondo and Maynila enjoyed friendly relations. The Lakans of Tondo intermarried with the ruling class of Maynila, so that by the 1500s both kingdoms were ruled by members of the same family.

That harmony was destined to be broken, however. In the early 1500s, Maynila was governed by a good queen, a widow, whose name tradition has forgotten. But her son is remembered as Young Prince Ache. Young Prince Ache was of noble character and beloved by his people. Because the ruling houses of Maynila and Tondo were related, his cousin Dula was the Lakan of Tondo. Young Prince Ache and Lakan Dula were raised together, both trained to rule. They trained and were schooled in the arts of diplomacy, war, and government.

But as Ache's mother grew older, her mind darkened and her resolve wavered. Lakan Dula took advantage of the weakness of Ache's old mother and began claiming some of the lands owned by Maynila. Young Prince Ache was heart-broken by his cousin's treachery. He went to his mother and told her what Lakan Dula was up to and begged her to grant him leave to confront his cousin. His mother, however, refused and begged Ache to keep the peace.

Young Prince Ache, however, was unwilling to simply let his kingdom be eaten away by his greedy cousin. If his mother would not give him permission to fight, he would fight under another banner. He sailed to the court of the powerful Sultan of Brunei on the island of Borneo. Brunei was a Muslim kingdom, and the Sultan was a relative of Young Prince Ache. We will learn more about the Sultans of Brunei in Chapter 8. Young Prince Ache told the Sultan about the aggression of Lakan Dula. The Sultan of Brunei agreed to give Ache command of his navy if he would first enter the Sultan's service and fight on his behalf elsewhere.

Young Prince Ache agreed and pledged fealty to the Sultan. He led the Bruneian army to many great victories in and around Borneo. After some time, he said to the Sultan, "Let me return now to my homeland and settle affairs with my cousin, Lakan Dula, as we agreed." The Sultan gave Ache permission to take the Bruneian fleet and return to Luzon to attack Tondo and his cousin Lakan Dula.

However, on the way to Tondo, something happened that Young Prince Ache did not expect: he encountered a Spanish fleet.

We will meet up with Young Prince Ache and the Spanish again in Chapter 12. But before we can get there, we have to spend some time discussing a very important factor in Philippine culture: the coming of Islam to the archipelago.

Chapter 7

THE COMING OF ISLAM

By the time of the high Middle Ages in Europe, the Philippine archipelago was home to three thriving kingdoms, each in one of the Philippines three island groups. On the northern island of Luzon, the people of Tondo worked their gold happily, enjoying their favored trading status with imperial China. In the central Philippines, the descendants of Sri Lumay were ruling the powerful little kingdom of Cebu in the midst of the Visayas. In the southern island group of Mindanao, Butuanese merchants were traversing the Sulu Sea in their vessels, trading with far flung places like Sumatra, Brunei, and even China.

And these were only the major kingdoms. There were many more. Luzon, for example, was home to several kingdoms besides that of the Tagalogs of Tondo. The Tagalogs shared the island of Luzon with two other peoples, the Kapampangan and Pangasinans. In the early 15th century, part of the island was even under Chinese administration and had a Chinese governor. Luzon was a mishmash of all different tribes, cultures, and political powers.

This was the case all over the archipelago. The Philippines had been visited and settled by so many different people that it was really a melting pot of hundreds of cultures. As you can imagine, these different cultures all had different religious practices. In some areas, like among the Tagalogs of Tondo, religion was very much centered on the worship of nature spirits. Among the people of Cebu, religion was very much influenced by the Hindu and Buddhist religions of India. The Butuanese shared religious ideas with the peoples of China and Taiwan. And of course, just as the Philippines were a mixture of peoples, religious ideas all mixed together as well. Sometimes all these different religious ideas and practices might be found together among a single people.

Throughout the early Middle Ages, the Philippines knew little of the great religions of the west. The inhabitants of the archipelago had most likely never heard of Christians. If they had, it would have been hearsay—some gossip about strange foreigners brought back from the Chinese imperial court. Filipinos would not encounter Christianity until the arrival of the Spanish in the 16th century.

Islam was a different story, however. Islamic merchants from the Middle East had traveled around the Indian Ocean for centuries, founding trading outposts and gradually working their way east. By the high Middle Ages they were present in Malaysia, where they came in contact with some of the peoples of the Philippine Archipelago.

The Islamic religion was founded in Arabia in the early 7th century by the merchant-turned-prophet, Mohammed. Mohammed claimed to bring a new revelation from God, delivered by the Archangel Gabriel. This final revelation was claimed to complete the earlier revelations God made through Christ and to the people of Israel.

Islam as a religion is very syncretistic, which means it took elements from various religions and blended them together:

Chapter 7: The Coming of Islam

Christian theology, Jewish legal concepts, pagan myths lifted from ancient Arabia, and the personal sayings and traditions of Mohammed were all part of Islam. The central idea behind Islam was that Mohammed was the supreme prophet of God, or Allah as the Muslims call him. One pleases God by submitting to the teachings of Mohammed as found in the Koran, the holy book of Islam. The word *Islam* means "submission." One demonstrates their submission to Allah by various practices, such as Friday prayers, almsgiving, periodic fasting, pilgrimages to Islamic holy sites, and professing faith in the revelation of Mohammed.

In 1380, a merchant vessel from Arabia brought the new religion to the Philippines. This vessel was commanded by Karim Al Makhdum. The Arabians had never ventured that far east before. Karim skirted along the islands of the Sulu Archipelago before landing on the little island of Jolo, part of the southern Philippine Mindanao island group. Karim was a Muslim, and his arrival in Jolo marks the beginning of Islam in the Philippines. Karim stayed in Jolo for several years trading throughout the area and spreading Islam.

A few years later, the Muslim Prince Baguinda Ali came from Sumatra to the Philippines to organize the isolated Muslim peoples living there into a single community. He tried to land on the island of Buansa in Mindanao, but the people of Buansa were very suspicious of him. They tried to sink his ships so as to drown the prince at sea. Baguinda fought back, telling the Buansa he came in peace to live among the followers of Mohammed. The natives relented and allowed Prince Baguinda to come ashore. Baguinda Ali consolidated the Islamic settlers throughout the islands of Sulu and was given the title *Rajah* by the Buansa. Under Rajah Baguinda all the Muslims of Sulu united, and many of the natives converted. This region would later become known as the Sultanate of Sulu.

Another Muslim influence on the Philippines came from the powerful Bruneian Empire. Brunei was a city-state on Malaysian island of Borneo, about five hundred miles southwest of the

Philippine archipelago. Brunei had been an independent kingdom since the 7th century, but in the 15th century the King of Brunei converted to Islam and took the title sultan. Brunei was henceforth known as the Sultanate of Brunei. We will read more about Brunei in our next chapter.

The Sultans of Brunei became powerful. Many of the royal families of the smaller kingdoms entered into dynastic marriages with the house of the Sultans. The Sultanate of Brunei used its influence to spread Islam all around the southern Philippine archipelago. Many of the petty Islamic kingdoms that would grow there were under the authority of the Sultanate of Brunei.

By 1400, Islam had reached the island of Mindanao proper. The first mosque was built in the town of Simunul, followed by many more throughout Mindanao. Word spread of the new Muslim communities cropping up, and Mindanao became the focus of a targeted plan of Muslim immigration. Muslims from Brunei, China, Persia, and India all came to Mindanao. Ship after ship arrived, year after year bringing Muslim settlers. This seems to have happened peacefully—the tribes of Mindanao were disorganized and not inclined to resist. Many of them intermarried with the Muslim foreigners and adopted Islam as well.

Before long, Islam was the dominant force in Mindanao. The Muslims organized their dominion into several kingdoms, each ruled by a prince who took the title of Sultan, an Arabic word meaning "monarch" or "king." The Mindanao island group was divided up amongst three Muslim kingdoms: the Sultanate of Maguindanao, Sultanate of Sulu, and the Sultanate of Lanao. These three Sultanates were under the authority of the powerful Sultanate of Brunei.

Of these three, the Sultanate of Sulu was the most important, for it was the oldest, had the biggest Muslim population, and the strongest government. The Sultanate of Sulu ruled the islands in the Sulu Archipelago, parts of Mindanao, certain portions of the island of Palawan and north-eastern Borneo. The first Sultan

Chapter 7: The Coming of Islam

of Sulu was Sharif Al-Hashim. Al-Hashim was an explorer and religious scholar from the city of Mecca in Arabia. Al-Hashim wanted the Sultanate of Sulu to be a kingdom that combined all the best parts of local culture with the Islamic religion. He did not want his people to feel like they were being ruled by foreigners. He wanted the Muslim and non-Muslim people of Sulu to think of themselves as a single culture. To help this, he married Paramisuli, a princess from the family of Rajah Baguinda, and changed his name to Paduka Mahasari Maulana. The Sultanate of Sulu became the center of Islam in the Philippines.

It was not long before these new Islamic states began sending raiding parties against the other kingdoms of the Philippines. These Muslim raiders were known as Magalos. These Magalos sailed throughout the archipelago attacking villages, plundering, and carrying off slaves. In the Middle Ages, they carried out several attacks against the islands of the Visayas. They were unable to establish a foothold in the Visayas, however, because the powerful King of Cebu, Sri Lumay, fought them off, as we learned in Chapter 5.

By the latter Middle Ages, Islam was the dominant force in the southern island group of Mindanao. The Visayas had resisted Islamic conquest, leading the Magalos to turn their eyes to the northern island group of Luzon, home to the wealthy kingdoms of Maynila and Tondo, whose wealth the Muslims coveted. We will learn more about this in our following chapter.

Chapter 8

THE SULTANS OF BRUNEI

In our last chapter we mentioned the Empire of Brunei, centered on the Malaysian island of Borneo. From the 15th century onward the Bruneians were Muslim and their rulers known as the Sultans of Brunei. The Sultans of Brunei became a powerful influence in the region. They intermarried into many other royal families and used their influence to promote the growth of Islam. In this chapter we will learn about the Bruneian Empire and its impact on the development of the Philippines.

The island of Borneo is not part of the Philippines. It is part of a larger island group known as Malaysia which lies to the southwest of the Philippines in the midst of the Java Sea. Being much further west than the Philippines, Borneo fell under the influence of India and the kingdoms of southern Asia. Not much is known of Borneo's early history. The Chinese knew of the island and called it *Boni*. A

Chinese official visited Boni in 1225 and recorded that the people of Borneo were wealthy from trade and maintained a navy of 100 warships to protect their interests.

The people of Borneo did not long enjoy independence, however. Sometime in the 1400s they became subject to the Kings of Java, another island further west. The Javanese exacted a heavy tribute from the peoples of Borneo. Another Chinese report of 1371 says the people of the island were impoverished and totally controlled by the Javanese.

Borneo thus remained weak under Javanese rule, divided into many petty kingdoms and city-states. The island was fractured, politically and culturally. Some of the Borneans were Hindu or Buddhist, just like in India. Others practiced the pagan tribal religions of old. In many places, especially merchant cities, the population had converted to Islam under the influence of Arabic merchants. One of these Muslim areas was the city-state of Brunei, on the northwestern side of Borneo.

Things changed for Brunei and the island of Borneo in 1389. In that year the powerful Javanese King Hayam Wuruk died. Following his death, the Kingdom of Java was rent by civil war among Wuruk's heirs. This chaos sent Java into decline, but it gave the city-state of Brunei the breathing room it needed to assert itself and shake off Javanese rule.

Shortly after this, the Chinese Emperor Yung-lo invited the people of Brunei to pay tribute to the Chinese court. The Bruneians eagerly ingratiated themselves with Yung-lo, not only paying tribute but collecting tribute from other lands on his behalf. This was lucrative work, and the Bruneians grew rich because of it.

Around this time, the Buddhist Rajah of Brunei, Awang Alak Betatar, converted to Islam. He was the founder of the Sultanate of Brunei. As we shall see, Betatar had some new ideas about the influence of Brunei in the region.

Chapter 8: The Sultans of Brunei

Hosho and Banko were two prominent Buddhist monks who served in the Buddhist temple of Brunei. They had occasionally served as advisors in the court of Rajah Betatar. Today they have been summoned to a special meeting. Their footfalls on the flagstone courtyard of the Rajah's fortress are hurried with anxiety.

"Has the Rajah really adopted the religion of the Mohammedans?" Hosho asked his companion.

"That is the word, my brother," replied Banko. "He has been spending a lot of time with the Muslim merchant class of the city as of late. I fear they have infected his mind with their doctrine."

"Hmm, the situation may be grim indeed then," said Hosho. "Our monastery could lose its influence. We must prevent that from happening!"

The two monks approached the sturdy wooden doors of the fortress citadel and are shown inside. The reception area of the fortress was a pillared hall about twenty yards long. Dull light filtered in through window shafts aligned along the western wall. Rich Chinese tapestries hung about. At the far end of the hall sat the Rajah on a gold encrusted throne on an elevated dais, draped in a robe of green silk and flanked by attendants. Dim candles flickered, casting eerie shadows about.

The two monks approached slowly. "I do not recognize these attendants," Hosho whispered.

"I do," said Banko. "They are of the Al-Danesh clan. Muslims, all of them."

"Allah be gracious to you, my fair counselors!" said the Rajah, extending his ringed hands to the monks.

Hosho and Banko bow deeply. "*Amitabha.* Greetings, most powerful Rajah Betatar," said the monks in unison.

"Ah," laughed the lord, standing up and stroking his curly black beard. "That is the first thing we shall have to remedy, for I no longer go by the name of my fathers. As you know, I have adopted the religion of the Muslims and professed faith in the Prophet Mohammed, whose name I have taken. Henceforth I shall be known as Mohammed Shah."

Hosho and Banko looked at each other. Hosho bowed "As you wish, Rajah Mohammed—"

"And no longer call me Rajah," interrupted Mohammed Shah. "Call me *Sultan*, for such are the great lords among the Muslims called."

"Sultan Mohammed Shah"—the words sounded awkward and foreign coming out of Banko's mouth—"why have you summoned us from our duties at the monastery to attend to your august presence?"

"My good monks," began the Sultan, "for too long has Brunei been content to play the middle man between the Chinese and the peoples of the isles. We run our ships to and fro collecting tribute from the island nations to deliver them to the Ming emperors in China."

"Yes, and it has brought us peace and prosperity," said Hosho.

"But there is more than peace and prosperity," grinned the Sultan, rubbing his hands together. He looked to his attendants. "I have taken as my counselors the merchants of the Al-Danesh clan. They tell me that in other Muslim lands, lords such as myself are masters of vast trading empires and are revered as kings."

"You already are very wealthy," said Banko coldly.

"Yes, yes, but there's even more wealth to be gained, and power as well," said the Sultan excitedly.

"The Buddha says that it is desire which leads to suffering," Hosho said, somewhat agitated. "Seeking delight and lust, seeking delight here and there—that is, craving for sensual pleasures, craving for becoming, craving for empty, vain honor—it brings only suffering."

"Do not speak to me of the Buddha's teaching!" yelled the Sultan angrily. "The Prophet Mohammed (peace be upon him) hath said, 'Fight and slay the Pagans wherever ye find them, and seize them, beleaguer them, and lie in wait for them in every stratagem of war.'" His attendants nodded approvingly at the Sultan's citation of this passage from the Quran. "I will use our ships and our networks and

Chapter 8: The Sultans of Brunei

I will make war, my good monks. And I will build an empire in these lands throughout which I will spread the religion of Mohammed." The Sultan was almost shouting now, his eyes possessed with a wild, fiery zeal.

"My lord Sultan," said Hosho after a long pause, "what will become of our monastery, and of your subjects who still follow the doctrines of the Buddha?"

"Or of the Hindus, or the pagan gods?" added Banko.

One of the members of the Al-Danesh clan leaned over and whispered in the Sultan's ear. The Sultan nodded. The attendant backed away slowly and deferentially, and the Sultan again spoke: "Your monastery will remain in place—for now—and you will continue to worship as you have been accustomed. However, the annual donative you have been accustomed to receiving from me shall now be given instead to the mosque of Brunei."

The monks gasped. "But, Lord! That donation amounts to half of our annual revenue! Our monastery cannot do without it!"

"Yes!" pleaded Hosho, "we depend upon that money, my Lord."

A long grin spread across the Sultan's face. He twirled his black moustache playfully between his fingers. "My good monks, desire leads to suffering. Let go of your desires, and you will be much happier men, I assure you."

Mohammed Shah carried out his plan. The Sultans of Brunei spread their influence through their naval strength, forging together an empire made up of a far-flung collection of coastal cities and islands. Their multitude of territories was known as the Bruneian Empire. Wherever the Bruneians went, they brought Islam.

The Bruneian influence eventually spread to the Philippine archipelago. They came to Luzon and founded a city called Selurong, which served as their port of influence in the Luzon island group. From there they fanned out across the archipelago to trade, make war, and spread Islam.

Selurong would eventually become the city of Maynila. Maynila and their Bruneian allies had a tense relationship with the neighboring Kingdom of Tondo. As we saw in Chapter 6, the Maynilan Prince Ache used Bruneian forces in his war against Lakan Dula of Tondo. But that brings us right up to an event that would have drastic consequences for the various petty kingdoms of the archipelago—the arrival of the Spaniards.

Chapter 9

MAGELLAN AND THE SPANIARDS

Thus far, we have had the luxury of keeping our story focused on the relatively limited adventures of the kingdoms and city-states of the Philippine archipelago. But we have come to the time when the story of the Philippines blends with the narrative of a very different people—the Spanish—and the arrival of the Catholic faith.

Columbus's discovery of the New World in 1492 meant new wealth and scores of colonies for Spain, but it also proved an obstacle. Remember, Columbus's original plan was to get to the Orient by going west. Spain was still interested in this proposal, but it seemed much more daunting now that they realized there were two continents in the way.

Even so, a Portuguese captain, Ferdinand Magellan, was convinced it was still quicker to get east by going west around the southern tip of South America than it would be to go around the coast of Africa. Magellan's plan was rejected by the King of Portugal, so like Columbus, Magellan went to the King of Spain. In October 1517—the same month Martin Luther was posting his 95 Theses that would inaugurate the Protestant revolution—Magellan presented his plan to King Charles I of Spain. Charles was intrigued by the proposal and agreed to fund Magellan's expedition. He granted Magellan five ships (*Trinidad, Concepción, San Antonio, Victoria*, and *Santiago*), enough provisions for two years, and the rights to many other revenues and titles should the voyage prove successful.

Magellan's crew consisted of 270 men from many nations, but mainly from Spain. The expedition left Spain in August of 1519. They reached Brazil by December and wintered over at a place called Puerto San Julian in what is now Argentina. While spending the winter of 1520 at Puerto San Julian, Magellan faced a mutiny from three of his five ships' captains. Magellan acted swiftly and killed the lead mutineers, having them drawn, quartered, and impaled on the beach. This quelled any further challenges to his authority.

The ships resumed their voyage and passed the southern tip of South America in November (recall that in the southern hemisphere, November is in the spring) and passed into the South Pacific. Not all was well though—the *Santiago* was destroyed in a storm and the captain of the *San Antonio* deserted and sailed back to Spain, leaving only three ships to continue on to Asia.

After stopping at several smaller islands to gather provisions, Magellan's ships sighted the Philippine island of Homonhon in the Visayas. By this time Magellan had a mere 150 crew members left and was in desperate need of supplies. The Spaniards landed at Homonhon on March 16, 1521 and scavenged unsuccessfully for provisions on the uninhabited island. This inauspicious expedition for food was the first landing of Europeans in the Philippines.

Their landing did not go unnoticed, however. As their boats sat anchored off Homonhon, they were sighted by vessels belonging to the Rajah Colambu of Butuan. The Butuanese saw Magellan's men in desperate straits and led them to the nearby island of Limasawa

Chapter 9: Magellan and the Spaniards

The first Mass in the Philippines, celebrated on Easter Sunday, AD 1521.

where Magellan was given an audience with the Rajah Siaiu, an ally of Colambu. Rajah Siaiu, Colambu, and Magellan became friends. They formalized an alliance by a blood compact, becoming blood brothers, and putting Magellan into a formal alliance with Butuan and Limasawa.

It being almost Easter, the Spaniards decided to stay until after the Holy Day. The first Mass in the Philippines was celebrated on Easter Sunday, March 31, 1521, by Father Pedro Valderrama, the Andalusian chaplain of the fleet and the expedition's only priest. The Rajahs Colambu and Siaiu both attended Mass with Magellan, marveling at the mysterious ceremonial and the beautiful Latin hymns. The Mass was said near the shore of Limasawa and marks the birth of the Catholic faith in the Philippines.

That same day, Magellan instructed his men to erect a massive wooden cross atop the hill looking down upon the beach near where the Mass had been said. After the cross was erected, the men of the expedition assembled before the symbol of the Christian faith and repeated the *Pater Noster* and *Ave Maria*, followed by heartfelt prayers of adoration kneeling before the cross. Rajahs Colambu and Siaiu participated in these prayers and devotions as well. The island was formally claimed by Magellan in the name of King Charles I of Spain.

After the conclusion of the Easter celebrations, Rajah Siaiu told Magellan that he himself was vassal of a more powerful lord, King Humabon of Cebu. We have already learned about Cebu in Chapter 5. It was a powerful kingdom that dominated the Visayas and whose Rajahs commanded an impressive trading network that stretched as far as Japan. Rajah Siaiu offered to lead Magellan to the court of King Humabon, whom Siaiu promised would be a formidable ally.

Magellan arrived in Cebu in early April, and the Spaniards found a warm welcome there. King Humabon entertained Magellan on several occasions, questioning him about his religion and the mission of the Spaniards in the archipelago. So impressed was Humabon with the Spaniards, their religion, and their might that he and his wife Hara Amihan converted to Christianity and accepted baptism, becoming the first Catholic converts in the Philippines, taking the names Carlos and Juana. To show his gratitude, Magellan presented the king and queen with an image of the Child Jesus. This image has

Chapter 9: Magellan and the Spaniards

been preserved in Cebu and today is housed in the Basilica of Santo Niño. Over five hundred and forty others also accepted baptism, including Rajah Colambu, who took the Christian name Juan.

After the solemnities had ended, King Humabon and Magellan began to discuss the Spanish aims in the Philippines and how they could be brought to serve the interests of the Kingdom of Cebu. Humabon suggested that Magellan should attack Cebu's rival, the Rajah Lapu Lapu of the island of Mactan.

Magellan was hesitant to get involved in the petty squabbles of the local rajahs. Initially, he sent envoys to Lapu Lapu in hopes of converting him to Christianity and making him an ally, as he had of Humabon. Lapu Lapu angrily rejected Magellan's messengers, however. Seeing that Lapu Lapu would prove a threat to Spanish ambitions in the area, Magellan decided that perhaps attack was the best option.

On the morning of April 27, 1521, Magellan and his men landed on the shores of Mactan and began their assault on Lapu Lapu's domain. The battle did not go how Magellan had hoped.

"Santiago y cierra, España!" shouted the Spanish conquistadors as they leaped from their ships into the briny, knee-deep water. About fifty in number, the Spanish waded through the foamy surf towards the shores of Mactan.

"Hold close, men!" shouted Magellan, waving his sword aloft.

On the shore, some hundred yards away, natives were forming up on the hillsides preparing for a fight. They came swarming out of the forests by the dozens.

"Don't fear," Magellan called to his men. "They outnumber us, but we have crossbows and muskets, which terrify the natives."

"Aye! And we have our Spanish steel!" shouted Juan Elcano, one of Magellan's officers.

The last few yards of sea were rocky and difficult to negotiate. Several Spaniards stumbled or cut their shins on the jagged stone. By this time the warriors of Lapu Lapu had swelled to over 1,500 men and formed up into three companies. They roared frightening battle cries and charged down upon the Spaniards.

"Give them a taste of musket fire, men of Spain!" cried Magellan as he reached the shore. The Spanish musketeers began firing up the ascent at the charging natives. They appeared to do little damage, however. Crossbow arrows similarly seemed useless. "What's wrong? Why are we missing?" demanded Magellan.

"We fired too early," growled Elcano. "We're still out of range!"

"Stop shooting!" cried Magellan. "Hold your fire!" But his commands were ignored in the tumult. The musketeers and crossbowmen continued to fire uselessly until almost all of their ammunition was used up.

Meanwhile the natives began to rain arrows down on the Spaniards. Their helmets and breast plates deflected the arrows harmlessly, but the uncovered legs of the Spaniards were dangerously exposed. An arrow struck Magellan in the thigh. "Argh!" cried the captain, clutching his leg in pain. Other Spaniards took similar wounds.

Magellan meets his end in battle against Lapu Lapu's warriors.

Chapter 9: Magellan and the Spaniards

"Are you alright captain?" called Elcano.

"The Mactans poison their arrows, Juan," said Magellan grimly, looking at the shaft protruding from his bloodied leg.

"We'll worry about that later, sir. Right now let's just take this hill!" said Elcano.

Magellan steadied himself on his wounded leg and roared. "Let's give them steel!" he called. The Spanish drew their swords and axes and charged the natives. Those who closed with the Spanish were no match. The cold, hard steel of the Spanish weapons cut through their bamboo spears effortlessly and sliced into the natives' bodies. Limbs dropped, heads went rolling into the sand, and torsos were hewn asunder.

But Lapu Lapu's men were resilient. They put some distance between themselves and the Spaniards to escape their biting steel. Once reformed, they let loose a barrage of projectiles: bamboo spears, arrows, stones, knives, darts and more came flying down the slope. The cloud of projectiles was so dense the Spaniards could do nothing but scramble for cover.

A stone struck Magellan in the head and knocked his helmet off. "That was close!" he said, making the sign of the cross and picking his helmet up off the beach. He was fastening it on his head when a second stone struck him, somewhat harder. Magellan tumbled into the sand and his helmet came flying off again. He dropped his sword.

"They are intentionally targeting the captain!" shouted Juan Elcano. "Protect him, men!" Several Spanish fighters came to close around Magellan. But before they could reach him, a native warrior lunged out at Magellan and thrust a bamboo spear at his face. Magellan quickly pivoted away from the blow, grabbed a nearby lance from a dead Spaniard and thrust it through the native's belly. He howled in pain and collapsed in the sand.

Magellan scrambled for his sword but as he was picking it up another native leaped upon him and thrust a bamboo spear into his shoulder. Magellan cried out. The native grinned cruelly and pressed the spear in, crushing bone and muscle. Magellan howled.

The Spaniards rushed to his aid. The native was pierced with multiple swords and fell, but it was too late. The rest of the natives had realized who Magellan was and were closing in on him. The entirety of the native force swarmed upon Magellan. Those who defended him fell one by one.

"Retreat!" Magellan cried to Elcano as he struggled.

"Run, men! To the boats!" Juan Elcano shouted. The Spaniards began withdrawing.

Magellan grunted and roused himself to his feet. Crying a fearsome battle cry he struck out with his sword at the natives swarming over him in a final, desperate act of defiance. The natives closed in. A spear passed through his belly. A crooked, iron blade broke his shoulder blade and sunk into his back. His hands went numb and the gnarled fingers of the conquistador dropped his blade—the sword fell uselessly into the sand. The rest of the men around him were slaughtered.

Elcano and the remainder of the force had made it to the boats and were pushing off from shore. Juan turned back to see what had become of the captain. Magellan had fallen on his stomach in the sand. He was still alive, gazing blankly out at the boats as the natives thrust him through again and again. Tears filled Elcano's eyes. "Our captain. Our light," he murmured, crying gently.

Magellan weakly lifted his hand from the sand and waved faintly. That was the last Elcano saw of him before the natives completely surrounded him, further slicing and mutilating his body.

Ferdinand Magellan was dead. He had scarcely been in the Philippines for three weeks. King Humabon was heartbroken. He offered Lapu Lapu a significant sum of money for the return of Magellan's body, but Lapu Lapu refused, wanting to keep his remains as a trophy of victory.

Chapter 9: Magellan and the Spaniards

Fourteen Spaniards had been killed in the battle on Mactan. The expedition was taken over by Juan Elcano. Elcano decided the remaining Spanish force was too small to man the three remaining ships, and thus ordered one of them, the *Concepción*, burned. The two remaining ships, *Trindad* and *Victoria*, pulled anchor and sailed west away from the Visayas as quickly as they could.

The initial Spanish contact with the peoples of the Philippines had been reckless and deadly. Lapu Lapu celebrated and boasted of his victory over the strange foreigners, but he had not heard the last of the Spaniards. He—and all the people of the archipelago—were about to learn that the Spaniards were a people not easily frightened off.

Chapter 10

THE SPANISH CONQUEST OF THE PHILIPPINES

After the death of Magellan, there was a disagreement among his men over what to do next. The *Victoria* and *Trinidad* would eventually go their separate ways. The *Trinidad* tried to sail back east to South America but met only with disease and shipwreck. Most of the men died.

The *Victoria*, now under the command of Juan Sebastián Elcano, continued westward towards Borneo and the Spice Islands. While the *Victoria* was passing the coast of Borneo in 1521, they came upon a fleet in service of the Sultan of Brunei. This fleet was commanded by none other than Young Prince Ache, whom we met in Chapter 6. Ache was on his way to Luzon to make war on his cousin, Lakan Dula of Tondo, in vengeance for Lakan Dula's exploitation of Ache's mother.

Young Prince Ache and his men were in awe of the *Victoria*.

They'd never seen such a vessel. They knew nothing about Elcano, the Spaniards, or the Magellan voyage, but Prince Ache immediately thought to himself, "If I can capture this remarkable ship and bring it captive to Maynila, I will have great glory and be exalted above my cousin, Lakan Dula." Young Prince Ache gave the command for his vessel to attack Elcano and the *Victoria*.

Young Prince Ache was in for quite a surprise, however, as he and the navy of Brunei were about to get a brute introduction to European gunpowder. Though using his shot sparingly, Elcano was able to unleash enough firepower to disable Ache's ship and sufficiently terrify the rest of Bruneians into falling back. The Spanish boarded the Bruneian vessel and took Young Prince Ache captive.

Elcano sent some of the Bruneian captives back to the Sultan's fleet with word that they would return Ache—in exchange for a sizable ransom. The Bruneians collected the ransom and paid Elcano an impressive sum in gold and spices. Elcano released Ache back to them with a stern warning to not test Spanish power again. Young Prince Ache would eventually go on to rule Maynila in place of Lakan Dula and took the name Rajah Matanda. In his old age would deal with the Spaniards again, though that was still a long way off.

As for Elcano, the *Victoria* would successfully land in the Spice Islands in Indonesia. There the men rested, the *Victoria* was resupplied and repaired, and the Spanish took on a hefty cargo of cloves and nutmeg. He would successfully return the *Victoria* to Spain in September of 1522, a little over three years after Magellan's departure. Elcano was awarded a special coat of arms by King Charles of Spain, featuring a globe with the motto: *Primus circumdedisti me*, which in Latin means, *"You went around me first."*

The stories told by Elcano were enough to get the Spaniards curious about the "Islands in the West", as the Philippines were then known. The hostility of Lapu Lapu and the killing of Magellan was enough to deter Spanish settlement for a time, although the

Chapter 10: The Spanish Conquest of the Philippines

Spaniards returned to the area several times. Most of these early expeditions merely passed the Philippines or stopped at them briefly on the way to the Spice Islands. One notable expedition was that of Ruy López de Villalobos in 1542. Villalobos spent two seasons exploring around the islands of Mindanao. He was eventually captured by the Portuguese and died in prison, but before he did he called the islands Las Islas Filipinas, or the Philippines, after the Spanish Prince Philip II. And thus have these islands ever been known.

The actual conquest of the Philippines would begin with the Spaniard López de Legazpi. Legazpi had come to Mexico after the conquest of Cortez to settle there. He had risen through the ranks of the colonial administration and once served as governor of Mexico City. The Viceroy of New Spain asked Legazpi to find a reliable route to and from the Spice Islands, as previous Spanish explorers had seemed to stumble upon the islands by chance and only after many turn-arounds. Legazpi departed Mexico for the Spice Islands in 1564. He landed, however, not in the Spice Islands but off the coast of the Kingdom of Cebu in the Philippines. Cebu at the time was being ruled by Rajah Tupas, a descendant of Sri Lumay, whom we met in Chapter 5.

The Cebuano people were fierce warriors and hostile to Legazpi. Legazpi decided not to land in Cebu. Instead he traveled to another Visayan island, Samar, where the local Datu, Urrao, welcomed him. Legazpi got on well with Datu Urrao and made a blood compact with him. Legazpi did the same in Limasawa and Bohol, two other Visayan islands. In Bohol, the local lords Datu Sikatuna and Rajah Sigala, both determined enemies of the Kingdom of Cebu and the Portuguese, made a solemn blood pact with Legazpi that the Spaniards and the peoples of Bohol should be allies. To this day, a holiday called *Sandugo* ("one blood") is celebrated every July on Bohol to commemorate the alliance between Legazpi and the two kings of Bohol.

Strengthened with the support of multiple chieftains across three different islands, Legazpi returned to Cebu in 1565. The ruler, Rajah Tupas, was the nephew of King Humabon, the ruler who had made an alliance with Magellan and converted to Christianity back in 1521. After Magellan's death, Humabon and his people had abandoned Christianity and broken the alliance. Tupas wanted nothing to do with the Spaniards. When he heard of the arrival of Legazpi, Tupas gathered his people and fled to the interior of the island.

When Legazpi and his men arrived at the city of Cebu, they found Tupas gone, along with many of the people. Legazpi was not happy that Rajah Tupas had fled. Here's what happened next:

Legazpi and his men trudged into the center of town. The clanking of their swords and tromping of their heavy boots frightened off the few Cebuano who had stayed behind when their leader, Rajah Tupas, had fled.

"Impressive," said Martín, one of Legazpi's captains. "This city of Cebu is solid. They've got sturdy stone buildings, nice even streets, and a broad public square."

"Agreed," said Legazpi, admiring the buildings. "The rajahs of Cebu are the most powerful lords in the region. That's why we're treating with Rajah Tupas first. Too bad he has failed to show us hospitality."

Legazpi had given orders to some of his men to round up any royal officials or town elders left behind and bring them to the city square. Gradually, his soldiers returned, dragging trembling Cebuano officials with them. The royal officials were easy to find by their aristocratic appearance and brightly colored robes.

After some time, when about thirty elders had been rounded up, Legazpi said to them, "Greetings. My name is López de Legazpi. I come in the service of His Most Catholic Majesty, Philip II of Spain."

"We know who you are," grumbled one of the Cebuano officials. "The Spaniard Magellan was here in the days of our fathers. He brought us war with the Mactan in the time of King Humabon."

Chapter 10: The Spanish Conquest of the Philippines

"Ah, then you acknowledge you once had an alliance with us?" said Legazpi. "Excellent. I have come to speak with your lord, Rajah Tupas about this alliance, and the terms upon which it could be renewed. However, since Tupas has refused us hospitality and fled, I declare that he has abdicated his rule."

The Cebuano officials murmured in alarm when it was explained to them what this meant. "My lord Legazpi," begged one of the men, "Rajah Tupas has not given up the throne. He has fled because he feared battle with the Spaniards."

"And why would he fear battle unless he had broken his allegiance?" said Legazpi. "In fact, he and all you Cebuano are traitors. You abandoned the alliance you made with Spain in the days of Magellan and are rebellious Spanish subjects."

He then unrolled a parchment he had been carrying in his vest. This was the *Requerimiento*, a legal document issued in the name of the King of Spain authorizing Legazpi to take possession of a territory in the king's name. Legazpi began reading. The document declared the entire island of Cebu to belong to Spain. It admonished the Cebuano to serve the Spanish loyally and accept the Catholic faith, and warned them that if they resisted they would face war.

Even as Legazpi read the document to the stunned officials, Spanish soldiers began looting the empty buildings of the city. The Cebuano couldn't believe what was happening.

And just like that, the Spaniards took control of Cebu. Legazpi build a stockade camp within the town and sent word through his native allies that the entire island of Cebu was to submit to Spanish rule. A few weeks later Rajah Tupas came out of hiding and formally surrendered to Legazpi. Despite losing his kingdom to Legazpi, Tupas would come to have a grudging respect for his Spanish master. He helped him to pacify the other chieftains of Cebu. Three years later, Rajah Tupas converted to Christianity and was baptized.

In 1569, Legazpi founded a second Spanish settlement on the Visayan island of Panay, whose people had welcomed him. The Panays hoped Legazpi would defend them against the dreaded Moros, Muslim pirates who came from Mindoro and raided the Visayas. Legazpi sent his grandson, Juan de Salcedo, to Mindoro to punish these raiders. Salcedo slaughtered the Moros he found and burned their forts.

Legazpi's greatest victory would come in Luzon, however—and it would not come by war, but by diplomacy. Legazpi had heard for some time of the natural resources of Luzon and the fabled wealth of Islamized kingdoms of Maynila and Tondo. He sent his faithful captain, Martín de Goiti, to land in Luzon and make contact with the powerful lord of Maynila. The ruler of Maynila at this time was none other than Rajah Matanda, the regnal name of Young Prince Ache—though by now he was no longer young. He was in fact about 90 years old!

Rajah Matanda had vowed never again to fight the Spaniards. De Goiti wanted Rajah Matanda's permission to set up a trading post in Maynila. Matanda was inclined to grant de Goiti's request. The Rajah's allies, however, did not like this. They begged Rajah Matanda to fight Legazpi and de Goiti. They even offered to kill 50 Spaniards as evidence of their willingness to fight.

Rajah Matanda and de Goiti did their best to calm the situation, but another prince, Rajah Sulayman, attacked the Spaniards. In the scuffle, the Spanish fortifications caught fire and were burned down. De Goiti fled back to Legazpi and returned with reinforcements in the spring of 1571. Rajah Sulayman realized he could not persuade Rajah Matanda to lift a finger against the Spaniards and bowed out of the fight.

Legazpi, de Goiti, and Matanda were thus left to themselves to negotiate the Spanish use of Maynila Bay. In the end, Legazpi got the Rajah Matanda and the Rajah of neighboring Tondo to agree to the creation of a Spanish fortification within Maynila (which would henceforth be known as Manila). Both Rajah Matanda and the

Chapter 10: The Spanish Conquest of the Philippines

Spanish agreed to organize a city council, consisting of two mayors, twelve councilors, and a secretary, representing both Spaniards and Maynilans, though in reality the Spaniards would dominate this council.

From 1571 on, Manila would be the capital of the Spanish government in the region. Legazpi would die suddenly of a stroke the following year. At the time of Legazpi's death in 1572, the Spaniards were ruling the most important parts of the Visayas. The Muslim sultanates of Mindanao were beginning to harass them, however. They also continued to face stiff resistance from many of the tribes of the Luzon group. In our coming chapters, we will learn how the Spaniards slowly grew their colonial empire in the region while pacifying the remaining peoples of the archipelago and introducing Christianity.

Chapter 11

THE SPANISH EAST INDIES

The Spanish conquest and colonization of the Philippines happened in a very slow and piecemeal way. This was due partially to the fact that there are over 7,000 islands in the Philippines and hundreds of cultures. Digesting them all was difficult, even for the powerful Spanish Empire.

But we should also keep in mind that when the Spaniards first arrived in the Philippines, they were not trying to get there. That is to say, they were actually trying to reach the Moluccas, an archipelago known as the Spice Islands in Indonesia. This was where the bulk of the European spice trade occurred. At first, the Spaniards were mainly interested in the Philippines as a stopping off point between America and Indonesia—somewhere to rest at before moving on to somewhere else. The purpose of the Villalobos expedition we mentioned in the previous chapter was to explore the Philippines and find a suitable location for a settlement to serve as a safe haven for Spanish ships going back and forth between the Spice Islands and Mexico. It was only gradually that the Spaniards came to see the value of controlling the Philippine archipelago for its own sake.

To understand the Spaniards' interest in the Philippines and their pattern of colonization, we need to grasp the bigger picture of what the Spaniards were trying to do in East Asia.

Why were the Spaniards so interested in East Asia? The lure of East Asia was its spices. We have mentioned this spice trade before in earlier chapters. The East Indies were home to many exotic spices that were not available to Europeans. European ships regularly came to the East Indies to obtain spices such as pepper, cloves, cinnamon, ginger, nutmeg and more. In exchange, they traded finished products such as sword blades, mirrors, bars of iron, lead, or tin. Often they simply traded in silver coins. The trip from Europe to the Spice Islands and back could take up to three years. It was fraught with dangers—Muslim pirates prowled the seas, and there was always danger from the vessels of other European kingdoms. Storms threatened merchants with shipwreck. And the sheer cost of putting together such an expedition was extremely high. Why did Europeans, such as the Spaniards, want to undertake such a costly voyage for things such as pepper or cinnamon?

We've mentioned that the Europeans did not have access to spices such as pepper and cinnamon, so they were rare in Europe. But why were they so valuable? In a time before refrigeration, spices were used to season meat in order to improve its flavor. Spices were also important ingredients in medicines. In addition to this, spices were a status symbol. Because of their great cost, they were used by the rich as a way of displaying wealth. For all these reasons, Europeans were willing to pay a lot—and undergo many dangers—in order to obtain spices.

As the 16th century wore on, the Spaniards realized that their access to the East Indies depended upon control of the Philippine archipelago. But to whom could the crown of Spain entrust such an important mission?

Chapter 11: The Spanish East Indies

In 1556, the throne of Spain passed to Philip II, son of Holy Roman Emperor Charles V. Philip had a lively interest in exploration and was eager to increase Spain's presence in East Asia. He chose as commander of the Philippine expedition a man named Andrés de Urdaneta. Urdaneta had lived an epic life full of both adventure and misfortune. He had sailed to the Philippines in 1526 as part of a mission to rescue one of Magellan's ships. He had been captured by the Portuguese, however, and held captive in the Portuguese East Indies. After this he spent several years roaming about the Spice Islands, learning about the customs and languages of the peoples there. He was eventually returned to Europe by the Portuguese in 1536 after eight and a half years in the Spice Islands. Upon his return, the Portuguese confiscated all the maps and charts he had made over his many years away. Not daunted, Urdaneta managed to laboriously recreate these materials from memory and presented them to King Charles of Spain, only to have the king give him a cold reception.

This was the sort of man the new king, Philip II, wanted to oversee the Spanish colonization of the Philippines. There was only one problem: after his disappointing reception in Spain, Urdaneta had thrown up his hands, renounced the world and gone to Mexico where he entered a monastery. For some years he had been a professed friar in Mexico City.

However, Philip II was a determined man. As we shall see, nothing would stop his plans, not even Urdaneta's religious profession.

Philip II of Spain.

Brother Andrés walked alone beneath the shaded portico of the Augustinian Monastery of Mexico City. He held in his hands a worn, leather-bound copy of the *Imitation of Christ*. The cover was cracked and weather-beaten from years of use. This copy of *Imitation of Christ* had been with Brother Andrés for a very long time and gone with him on many voyages.

Brother Andrés read the words of the text carefully, mouthing them and pondering their meaning. "When the grace of God comes to a man he can do all things, but when it leaves him he becomes poor and weak.…Yet, in this condition he should not become dejected or despair. On the contrary, he should calmly await the will of God and bear whatever befalls him in praise of Jesus Christ."

As Brother Andrés rounded the corner of the covered walkway, he looked up and noticed two men standing before him in the portico. One was his superior, Father González. The other was a layman Brother Andrés had never seen before, but from his cloak, sword, and feathered hat, Andrés presumed him to be some sort of royal official from the colonial government.

"Ah, Brother Andrés," said Father González warmly. "I want you to meet Don Pablo de Barbero. Don Pablo is here on behalf of his majesty, King Phillip."

Brother Andrés bowed, kissing the hand of his superior and then nodding to Don Pablo. "Long live King Philip," said Brother Andrés. "Before I adopted the religious habit, I served in the fleets of his father, the recently deceased King Charles, God rest his soul."

"That is why I have come to meet you, Brother Andrés," said Don Pablo. "Tell me, is it true you have been to the Spice Islands?"

"Indeed," bowed the friar. "I spent eight years there in the service of the Loaísa expedition and as a prisoner of the Portuguese."

"A most remarkable feat, Brother Andrés. The Loaísa expedition was only the second to circumnavigate the globe after that of Magellan. Your experience must be considerable."

"Ah," said Brother Andrés bashfully. "It was no more than any sailor in similar straits would have accomplished."

Chapter 11: The Spanish East Indies

"Brother Andrés," said Father González, "Don Pablo tells me that your name has come to the attention of the king himself."

"Oh? In what respect?" asked Brother Andrés.

Don Pablo removed a scroll from his cloak and unfurled it. He cleared his throat and began to read. "By order of King Philip II, the most Catholic King of Spain: It is thus decreed that the islands known as the Philippines and discovered in the time of my father, King Charles, shall be colonized and brought under Spanish dominion for the purpose of facilitating Spanish trade in the East Indies. To this end, our Majesty has decided to take the unusual task of appointing as Commander none other than Andrés de Urdaneta, currently under religious profession at the Augustinian abbey in Mexico City."

"You have got to be joking!" Brother Andrés exclaimed, mouth agape.

Don Pablo continued. "Inasmuch as Urdaneta is an excellent navigator, is well versed in the customs of the Indians, and has spent considerable time in the region, we urge Señor Urdaneta to take up the post of command with all haste for the glory of Spain and the exaltation of the Catholic faith. Signed his Majesty, King Philip II, 4th day of June, year of our Lord 1559."

Brother Andrés was flabbergasted. "No, Don Pablo, I am humbled and honored, but it is not possible. I have been professed at this monastery for years now. I am no more a navigator. Please, I beg the king to find somebody else."

"The king wants you," smiled Don Pablo.

Brother Andrés was frantic. "Father González, such a thing is against my religious profession. I am a professed friar of the Augustinian hermits. We are not to engage in worldly matters. Please, tell him, father!"

Father González smiled. "Brother Andrés, Solomon says *The king's heart is in the hand of the Lord, as the rivers of water: he turneth it whithersoever he will.* I have already given my consent for you to go. The duty of every Christian is to spread the faith of Christ.

You, my friend, are being offered a chance to spread the Gospel in far off lands under the banner of the Most Catholic King of Spain. I not only give you my consent, but my blessing."

Brother Andrés thought for a moment, then crossed himself. He bowed deeply to Father González. "I will go as the king wills," said Brother Andrés.

Urdaneta did indeed go. However, he believed having authority over sailors would violate his religious vows of poverty. Therefore, Philip allowed another man to take the office of Commander while Urdaneta was the chief navigator. The Urdaneta expedition took several years to prepare, but it eventually set sail in 1564 and arrived at the Philippine island of Cebu the following year. The Spaniards set up further trading posts and subjected the local Cebuano to their dominion.

Urdaneta would found the first church in the Philippines, Saint Vitales in Cebu. He also founded the Basílica del Santo Niño de Cebú. The story of this church is remarkable. If you recall from Chapter 9, Ferdinand Magellan had once presented King Humabon and Queen Hara Amihan of Cebu with an image of the Child Jesus on the occasion of their baptism. As we saw, the Cebuano had rejected Christianity after the death of Magellan. The chapel constructed for the image had been burned down. In 1565, Urdaneta and his men were scavenging the charred remains of the chapel when a soldier uncovered the image of the Child Jesus, where it had lain for 44 years. Urdaneta immediately founded a monastery on the spot. This would eventually become the Basílica del Santo Niño—the Basilica of the Holy Child. Though never receiving episcopal consecration, Urdaneta would serve as first prelate of the Philippine church during his brief stay.

The most important contribution of Andrés de Urdaneta to the Spanish colonization of the Philippines was not the settlements or

Chapter 11: The Spanish East Indies

the churches, however. Rather, it was the discovery of a safe route back to Spanish territory in America.

Ever since Magellan, men had been reaching the Philippines by sailing west from the Americas using the westward trade winds. However, no reliable return route east had been discovered. This meant that a ship leaving Spanish America for the Philippines had to continue to sail west all the way around India and Africa, stop to resupply in Europe, and then cross the Atlantic back to Mexico. For trade to really develop successfully, the Spanish needed to find a reliable route back and forth across the Pacific between the Philippines and Mexico

Some had tried. In 1529, Álvaro de Saavedra Cerón tried sailing east from the Philippines, but could not find any eastward winds across the Pacific. He made two attempts but eventually had to turn around, returning to Spain by sailing west around Africa. In 1543, Bernardo de la Torre made a similar attempt. De la Torre was an experienced navigator and explorer who had been the first European to sail around the great southern Philippine island of Mindanao. Even so, de la Torre was not able to find an eastern route across the Pacific to return to Mexico. He, too, had to get home by sailing west.

It was Urdaneta, along with fellow navigator Alonso de Arellano, who discovered the return route. Seeking a way back to Mexico in 1565, Urdaneta reasoned that perhaps the winds of the Pacific behaved in a *gyre*, similar to the winds in the Atlantic. A gyre is a very large circular pattern in which ocean winds blow. In the late 15th century, Spanish and Portuguese navigators in the Atlantic had discovered that one could find eastern trade winds by sailing north and catching the eastward circle of the Atlantic gyre.

Urdaneta and Arellano suspected the Pacific had a similar wind pattern. When it was time to return to Mexico in 1565, Urdaneta and Arellano sailed north until they reached the 38th parallel, near the northern coast of Japan. There they discovered the eastern Pacific trade winds and were able to return to Mexico safely.

The discovery of this return route to Mexico was extremely important. It made Spanish shipping to the Philippines much more predictable. From the mid-16th century on, navigators returning east from the Philippines would call the voyage "Urdaneta's Route" in honor of the monk-explorer who discovered it. As for Urdaneta, he returned to Spain to present a report on his expedition to Philip II, then returned to New Spain where he wrote two books about his voyages. He died in 1568 in Mexico City.

The expedition of Urdaneta and those who followed him solidified Spanish influence in the Philippines. The discovery of Urdaneta's route led to the establishment of a global trade route from the Spice Islands to the Philippines, the Philippines to Mexico, and Mexico back to Spain. It would make Spanish trade to East Asia even more profitable.

Other islands outside the Philippines came under Spanish control as well. Álvaro de Saavedra Cerón, whom we mentioned above, would take control of the Caroline Islands on behalf of the King of Spain. In 1565 the navigator Legazpi, whom we met in Chapter 10, seized the island of Guam. Guam is a small island far out in the Pacific, almost 2,500 miles east of the Philippines. The Spanish would fortify Guam and use it as an important stopping over point on the long journey between the Philippines and Mexico along Urdaneta's Route.

Others regional islands were taken throughout the 16th century: Palau by Ruy López de Villalobos in 1543, the Bonin Islands by Bernardo de la Torre in 1543, New Guinea by Yñigo Ortiz de Retez in 1545, the Solomon Islands by Pedro Sarmiento de Gamboa in 1568, the Marquesas Islands by Álvaro de Mendaña de Neira in 1595, the New Hebrides and Vanuatu by Pedro Fernandes de Queirós in 1606.

It is not important to memorize all of these explorers and the corresponding dates. What is important is to note that by the late 1500s, the network of Spanish ports in the Spice Islands, the Philippines, and the other islands under Spanish control were being referred to as the Spanish East Indies and made up a Spanish maritime empire in East Asia.

The Philippines were an essential part of the Spanish East Indies. In 1574 King Philip II decided that the Philippines needed their own governing authority. He thus established the Captaincy General of the Philippines. The Captaincy was created in part to govern the sprawling Spanish settlements, but also to oversee the protection of the Philippines from the Portuguese, who were beginning to creep in upon Spanish trade in the area. The Captaincy was a dependency of the Viceroyalty of New Spain, which meant that technically Mexico and the Philippines were under the same administration. The Captaincy had its capital at Cebu at first, but it would move to Manila in 1595. From 1595 on, Manila would be the capital of the Spanish Philippines and the center of Spanish power in the archipelago. The first governor of the Captaincy was none other than Miguel López de Legazpi. The Governors of the Philippines would continue to administer the islands under the Captaincy General until 1898, the year Spanish rule in the Philippines came to an abrupt end.

But that was still many centuries in the future. For now, let us see how the growing Spanish power in the region brought it into conflict with the powerful Sultanate of Brunei in the latter 16th century.

Chapter 12

THE CASTILIAN WAR

By the late 16th century, the Spanish were ruling over a scattered collection of islands in the Philippine archipelago from their capital at Manila on the island of Luzon. Spanish interests in the Philippines were governed by the Captaincy General of the Philippines, the official representative of the Spanish crown in the islands.

However, Spanish power grew slowly. Muslim Moros from the south continually harassed Spanish shipping and raided their outposts. The various native tribes of the archipelago often resisted Spanish attempts to control the region. There was also the ever-present competition from Dutch and Portuguese ships who were always prowling about the waters of southeast Asia and who seldom missed an opportunity to interfere with Spanish activity.

One of Spain's greatest rivals in the area was the Sultanate of Brunei. We learned all about the Sultans of Brunei in Chapter 8.

Brunei was a powerful Islamic kingdom located on the island of Borneo southwest of the Philippines. In the century before the Spanish arrived, the Bruneians had extended their empire into the Philippines, taken control of the Kingdom of Maynila, and were actively spreading Islam throughout Mindanao and the southern archipelago. As the Spaniards began to come down from Luzon and the northern islands, they came into conflict with the Bruneian Empire, who did not appreciate these European upstarts intruding on the empire they had spent over a century building up.

With Spanish power growing in the north in the Luzon island group and the Islamic power of Brunei dominant in the southern Mindanao island group, there was a question of whether the central island group, the Visayas, would side with Spain, Brunei, or attempt to remain neutral. As we learned in our last chapter, the powerful Visayan kingdom of Cebu had already fallen into Spanish hands and so would support Spain over Brunei. Many other Visayan tribes also threw their lot in with Spain, having a long-standing hatred of the Muslim Moros from the south and their Bruneian overlords.

Thus Spain and Brunei faced off against each other in an uneasy peace, wondering who would make the first move.

It was into this tense situation that the new governor, Francisco de Sande, arrived from Mexico in 1576. After he was installed as governor of the Captaincy General in Manila and briefed on the situation with Brunei, he decided to send an official delegation to Brunei to try to make a peace treaty with the Sultan.

The Sultan at the time was Saiful Rijal. Sultan Saiful received the Spanish delegation from de Sande, but found their demands unacceptable. De Sande wanted the Sultan to call an end to Brunei's support for Islamic proselytism in the Philippines, as well as grant Spanish Catholic missionaries freedom to preach the Catholic faith within the dominion of Brunei itself. Sultan Saiful responded haughtily that he considered the entire Philippine archipelago to be part of the *Dar al-Islam*—that is, under the dominion of Islam.

De Sande was not daunted. Ever since their arrival in the

Chapter 12: The Castilian War

Philippines, the Spanish had detested the presence of the Islamic Moro raiders who were backed by Brunei. De Sande saw the Sultan's rebuttal as an opportunity to make war on Brunei, grow Spanish power in the region, and destroy the Moro threat. He began to prepare an army for war. This conflict would be known as the Castilian War.

De Sande declared war against Saiful and the Sultanate of Brunei in 1578. His force was considerable. He had 400 Spaniards and 1,500 Filipino natives with him, mostly Visayan allies from Cebu who were sick and tired of the Moro raids and were happy to lend their arms against the Sultanate. De Sande also was able to enlist the aid of 300 Borneans who wanted to overthrow the Sultan. These Borneans were led by two Bruneian nobles, Pengiran Seri Lela and Pengiran Seri Ratna. Lela and Ratna offered their allegiance to Spain in exchange for de Sande's help in getting rid of Sultan Saiful. De Sande agreed that if Saiful were defeated, Pengiran Seri Lela would become Sultan and Ratna would become his grand vizier. Both would rule Brunei as a Spanish tributary.

The capital of the Sultanate of Brunei was Kota Batu, an opulent city on Borneo's northwestern coast. Enriched and beautified with the spoils of conquest, Kota Batu's sprawling ports and stately mosques showed forth the power of the Bruneian Empire. The fleet of de Sande quickly overpowered the poorly armed and disorganized navy of the Sultan and attacked Kota Batu. Sultan Saiful was caught completely off guard. Saiful and some of his closest officials fled the capital, abandoning the splendors of Kota Batu to de Sande and the Spaniards. The Spaniards marched triumphantly into the capital of Brunei on April 16, 1578.

The capital of the Bruneian Empire was in Spanish hands. De Sande began making plans to fortify Kota Batu, recruit further fighters from the disgruntled subjects of the Sultan, and begin a conquest of the entire island of Borneo. However, this was not to be, for events soon turned against de Sande. Let us visit Kota Batu in that spring of 1578 to see what transpired amongst the Spaniards.

"Ugh" groaned Pedro, crumpling to his knees on the ground. The soldier's hands were on his stomach. "I have to go again!" he said to his comrade Mateo, dashing off behind some palm bushes.

Governor de Sande came pacing up with his Bruneian allies, Pengiran Seri Lela and Pengiran Seri Ratna. "What was wrong with him?" he asked Mateo.

"Who, Pedro? He's come down with dysentery, Señor." said Mateo. "He's…uh…relieving himself."

"That's the fifth case this morning!" grumbled Seri Lela.

"This is not good," scowled de Sande. He looked out about the marshy lagoons that surrounded the city on the east. "It's all this swamp water you Bruneians have about your city. It fouls the air and it's making the men sick." He grunted and swatted a mosquito that was attempting to drain blood from his neck. "How do you people live here?"

"My Lord," said Pengiran Seri Ratna, "we have word that the forces of Sultan Saiful are regrouping at Jerudong and preparing for a counter assault. Will the Spanish be prepared for such a battle?"

"God willing we shall be!" said de Sande.

"Capitán!" cried a Spanish officer who came running up the street. "Capitán de Sande!"

"Ah," said de Sande, "here comes my trusted attendant Miguel. I sent him to survey the troops to find out our strength. What is the good word, Miguel?" he called to the man.

"Capitán," said Miguel, panting, "Another dozen men have died of sickness. And we have over one hundred more ill with dysentery or cholera, some of them severely."

Lela and Ratna looked at each other with raised eyebrows, saying nothing.

"One hundred!" exploded de Sande in frustration. "That's almost a fifth of our force! What of the Cebuano warriors?"

"They are not happy, Señor," said Miguel. "They complain that the Spaniards have taken all the best plunder. And they are ready to go home."

Chapter 12: The Castilian War

"Some of the Borneans are starting to melt away back into the jungle as well, my Lord," added Pengiran Seri Lela.

De Sande removed his steel helmet and ran his fingers through his matted, sweaty hair. "Mi Señor," he said, making the sign of the cross and looking to the sky. "You deliver Kota Batu into my hands just to strike my men with sickness? What is your will in this?"

Miguel and the two Bruneian nobles looked on in awkward silence as de Sande conversed with God. Somewhere in the distance, soldiers could be heard coughing.

"Well, we'll abandon the city and return to Manila. We simply can't hold it against Saiful's onslaught with so many men ill and the sickness spreading daily. God's will," he said, throwing up his hands. "Miguel, spread the word. We depart at sunset."

Miguel nodded and dashed off, visiting each company and telling them of the news. "We return to Manila! We return to Manila at sunset!" he cried.

Just then Pedro, who had disappeared into the bushes some time ago, emerged, tightening his belt and groaning. "Ugh…what did he say, Mateo?"

"He says we get to go home, amigo," said Mateo, patting Pedro on the shoulder.

But before de Sande abandoned Kota Batu, he ordered his men to burn the grand mosque that was the centerpiece of the downtown district. It was an ornate building, with an elaborate five-tiered roof built in the time of Saiful's grandfather. Spanish soldiers torched the structure, and in a few moments the mosque was engulfed in crackling flames.

De Sande and the Spaniards returned to Manila, too ground down by cholera and dysentery to continue to hold Kota Batu. Many of the men of de Sande's expedition recovered, but some were not so lucky. One of the victims was Pengiran Seri Lela, who took ill on the return voyage and died shortly after de Sande disembarked in Manila. Lela's daughter, however, would marry into a Christian family and the descendants of Pengiran Seri Lela would become eminent Christians in the Christian Tagalog community of Manila.

After de Sande's departure from Brunei, Sultan Saiful, his court, and a thousand Bruneian warriors cautiously returned to Kota Batu. The mosque had been reduced to ashes and the city plundered, but otherwise everything was intact. Saiful and the Bruneians celebrated the withdrawal of the Spaniards. Over time, legends sprung up around the event and later generation of Bruneians made Sultan Saiful and his family into warrior-heroes who valiantly drove the Spanish away from Borneo. This "expulsion" of the Spaniards is still celebrated in Brunei to this day.

Despite his failure to conquer Brunei, de Sande had some other victories in the Castilian War. He raided the Moro bases the Sulu islands and on Mindanao. The Bruneians were never again able to get a foothold in Luzon and were forced to abandon their ambitions in the Philippines. As the Spanish continued to expand their power throughout the Philippines and the neighboring islands, the Sultanate of Brunei gradually lost its island territories, becoming little more than a city-state confined to the island of Borneo.

But that's not to say the Spaniards were always at enmity with the Bruneians. De Sande governed the Philippines until 1580. Many years later, in 1599, another governor named Don Francisco de Tello de Guzmán made peace with the Sultanate of Brunei. Brunei and the Spanish Philippines would go on to become trading partners.

The peace with Brunei allowed the Spaniards to focus on subduing enemies closer to home: the Islamic Moros of Mindanao. In our next chapter we will learn about the Spaniards long, ruthless wars against the Muslims of Mindanao.

Chapter 13

THE MORO FIGHT BACK

By 1600, the Spanish had concluded their wars with the Sultanate of Brunei and enjoyed an uneasy peace with the powerful maritime kingdom. This allowed them to turn their attention to other lands closer to home: the southern island group of Mindanao, which was inhabited by the Moros, a confederation of petty Islamic kingdoms.

If the Spaniards were feeling assertive, they had every right to be. By the early 1600s their capital of Manila was a sprawling fortress-city boasting a population of tens of thousands. The Spanish crown had sent over 1,200 Spanish families to populate Manila and build up the basis of a Spanish aristocracy—to this day, the most prestigious families in the Philippines are those who can trace their lineage back to these original group of 1,200 Spanish families. Meanwhile Cebu City, in the Visayas, also received an influx of settlers, some 2,100 from New Spain (Mexico). More cities were founded, more fortresses established, and Spanish rule solidified.

Many conquistadors—battle-hardened from their long wars with the natives of South and Central America—came to the Spanish Philippines to serve as soldiers. A troupe of Peruvian conquistadors who had fought long and bitter campaigns against the Inca in the Andes Mountains were conscripted specifically to wage war on the Moros.

Spaniards were not the only ones who came to the Philippines. Many colonies of *mestizos* were also settled in the archipelago. A mestizo was one whose ancestry was a mixture of Spaniard and Native American. Several mestizo settlements were established throughout the Visayas and Luzon.

The mixing of Spanish, mestizo, and native Filipino cultures gradually gave rise to a new language called *Chavacano*. Chavacano was a creole language based in Spanish Mexican. A *creole* is a language that arises from the mixing of different languages together. Chavacano contains elements of Spanish, Nahuatl (the language of the Aztecs of Mexico), and Portuguese, as well as the Filipino languages Tagalog and Cebuan. Chavacano was spoken widely throughout the Philippines. It is still spoken to this day, primarily on Mindanao. This all came together to build a unique society that was neither Spaniard nor Tagalog nor Cebuan, but Filipino.

The Moros looked on with anxiety at the growing might and complexity of the Spanish Philippines. These Muslim pirates—often in conjunction with the Chinese, who were trading partners with the Moros—began raiding Spanish settlements throughout the archipelago. In particular danger were Jesuit missions which were spread about the Mindanao island group. Far from Manila and the seat of Spanish power, the Jesuit missions and isolated trading posts of the Moluccas were vulnerable to Moro raids. Tens of thousands of Spanish and Filipinos were taken prisoner by the Moros and sold as slaves across Malaysia and the South Seas.

The Jesuits begged the Spanish government for more protection from the hostile Moros. The Bishop of Cebu took up the Jesuits' cause

Chapter 13: The Moro Fight Back

and convinced the Spanish governor, Juan Cerezo de Salamanca, to approve the construction of improved defenses throughout the south. New bases began going up throughout the Moluccas. The greatest base, however, was Fort Pilar, begun in 1635 as part of Governor de Salamanca's defenses. Fort Pilar was short for Royal Fort of Our Lady of the Pillar of Saragossa, a reference to a particular Spanish devotion to the Blessed Mother at Saragossa in Spain.

For the site of the fort, the Spaniards chose an easily defensible peninsula on the west coast of Mindanao. From here, they could dominate the shipping routes through the Sulu Sea, as well as threaten the island of Mindanao itself. The construction of Fort Pilar was a massive undertaking. Laborers from all over the archipelago had to be imported to work on it, as well as workers from far off Mexico and Peru. A sprawling city called Zamboanga sprung up around the fortress.

Governor de Salamanca was very pleased with the new construction. He began laying plans to launch a general invasion of Mindanao to crush the Moro threat. With Fort Pilar completed, a royal decree was issued in 1636 commanding the conquest and pacification of the Moros of Mindanao. But in the meantime Governor de Salamanca was removed and replaced with a new Governor General. The new Philippine governor was Sebastián Hurtado de Corcuera. Corcuera set out from Fort Pilar at the head of 800 men, mainly conscripts from Peru.

He landed on the neighboring island of Basilan and attacked the local Moro leader, Sultan Qudarat. Sultan Qudarat had been a thorn in the side of the Spaniards for years, responsible for many savage raids on Spanish settlements throughout the Philippines. Governor Corcuera's attack caught the Sultan by surprise. Corcuera scored a stunning victory, capturing the Sultan's cannons and killing many Moro warriors. Sultan Qudarat, wounded gravely, barely escaped with his life. The Spaniards burned the mosque at Qudarat's capital of Lamitan and plundered the city's treasury. Governor Corcuera returned to Manila a hero. To commemorate his victory, the Spaniards instituted a play called the Moro-Moro play, which dramatically told the story of the Moro's defeat at Spanish hands.

But Governor Corcuera was relaxing much too soon, for Sultan Qudarat was certainly not ready to give up. The Sultan took refuge with other Moros near the shores of a great lake called Lanao in the interior of Mindanao. There, Qudarat gathered together many of the Moro tribes who were then debating what to do about the Spanish aggression. Let us join the ranks of the Moros by the shores of Lake Lanao and see how Sultan Qudarat addressed the Moros.

The air was thick and moist. The night was abuzz with the humming of millions of insects, who were ever present in the dense, tropical interior of Mindanao.

But insects were far from the only noise to be heard this night. The air was alive with the excited chatter of Moro fighters who had convened upon the shores of Lake Lanao from all over Mindanao to hear of Sultan Qudarat's harrowing fight with the Spaniards and debate what to do next. The dark waters of the lake were alighted by the reflections of a thousand campfires from Moro encampments hastily thrown up around it. A large mass of fighters were gathered by a cluster of palm trees arguing vigorously around a large campfire.

"Listen to me, men of Lanao!" a tall, bearded Moro in a brightly colored cloak called out. This was Salamat, a Moro chieftain known for his wisdom and diplomacy. "The Spaniards are many, and more come every year. It is inevitable that in time they will subdue all of Mindanao. It is better that we make peace with them now. That way we can at least perhaps retain control of our cities and get off with just paying the Spaniards a tribute. But if we make war on them and they conquer, we will lose everything!"

Some of the Moros nodded, but others complained loudly. "You would just have us surrender to the infidels? Such is not the way of the Prophet!" another cried, a broad shouldered man leaning on a

Chapter 13: The Moro Fight Back

large scimitar. This was Hashim. Hashim was another Moro leader, more known for his prowess in war than his diplomatic skills. "I say we meet the Spaniards in battle and show them what us Moros are truly made of!" This aroused a round of cheers from the many of the younger Moro warriors, who were eager for blood.

"No, no!" insisted Salamat. "To fight the Spaniards is to bring the destruction of Allah upon us. Let us be content to practice our religion in peace here and provoke the Spaniards no more than we already have. The defeat of Qudarat was a warning sign and an omen. We cannot risk such another defeat!"

"Defeat?" came a rich, deep voice from the darkness. "Who said Qudarat was defeated?" A figure stepped into the firelight. It was Sultan Qudarat himself.

"Lord Qudarat!" the men all cried, rushing over to the Sultan to greet him and touch his robes in reverence.

"Your greetings warm my heart," said the Sultan, a slender but muscular man, his face clean shaven but scarred from many battles. "However, the talk of Datu Salamat displeases me greatly," he said brooding.

"Salamat says we should make peace with the Spaniards," said Hashim. "Many of the Lanao tribes agree with him."

"I do so say," said Salamat. " 'Tis better to go on living in peace and pay tribute to the Spaniards, than to court disaster by bringing them here in arms and end up losing our lands and our liberty."

"Liberty!" cried Qudarat. "How can you speak to me of liberty? You men of the Lake! If you would think of liberty, I tell you, you have forgotten your ancient liberty if you submit to the Spaniards. Such submission is sheer stupidity." His eyes were aglow as he spoke by the firelight. Qudarat's voice was elevated, his hands raised in the air. More warriors gathered about to listen.

"You cannot realize to what your surrender binds you. You are selling yourselves into slavery to toil for the benefit of these foreigners. Look at the regions that have already submitted to them! Note how abject is the misery to which their peoples are now reduced. Behold the condition of the Tagalogs and of the Visayans whose chief men are trampled upon by the meanest Spaniard! If you are of no better spirit than these, then you must expect similar treatment. You, like them, will be obliged to row in the galleys. Just as they do, you will have to toil at the shipbuilding and labor without ceasing on other public works. You can see for yourselves that you will experience the harshest treatment while thus employed. Be men. Let me aid you to resist. All the strength of my Sultanate, I promise you, shall be used in your defense!" There were roars of approval.

"But Sultan," called Salamat, "a Spanish invasion will mean the devastation of our island! The loss of our homes, our crops, everything!"

"What does it matter if they are at first are successful?" cried Qudarat, clenching his fists. "That means only the loss of a year's harvest. Do you think that too dear a price to pay for liberty?"

These were the actual words Qudarat spoke that night, as recorded by those who were present. It is no surprise his rousing speech was written down, for his impassioned pleas won the resolve of the Moros, who decided almost unanimously to fight back against the Spaniards with everything they could muster. Qudarat also won over many Moro tribes who had previously decided to make peace with the Spanish.

The following year Qudarat and his followers attacked the Spanish everywhere. Spanish shipping, trading posts, and garrisons were harassed by Moro raiders. Especially feared were the Moro *juramentado* swordsmen. The juramentado were fanatical Moro warriors who trained to kill with swords or other edged weapons. Their attacks were precise and deadly and especially feared because the juramentado cared little for his personal safety. Every juramentado was trained to allow himself to be killed happily if that's what was required to slay their target. As a sign of their discipline,

Chapter 13: The Moro Fight Back

these suicidal assassins went through a ritual of prayer and shaving of the hair to prepare for their bloody task.

Before long, Governor Corcuera was forced to return to Mindanao with a force of 1,500 soldiers in an armada of 80 vessels. Landing on the island of Sulu, Corcuera attacked the city of Jolo, which was heavily defended by thousands of Moro troops. After months of bitter fighting, neither side could gain a decisive victory, so late in 1638 Qudarat and Corcuera agreed to a truce and the Spaniards withdrew, leaving only a small garrison at Fort Pilar.

By 1638 the Moros and Spaniards had been in constant conflict for decades. The Spanish crown had called for an all-out subjugation of Mindanao, which had in turn prompted an equally fierce resistance from the Moros. The conflict with the Moros was far from over, as we shall see. But for now we must turn to other quarters where the Spaniards were dealing with other quarrelsome neighbors.

Chapter 14

THE PHILIPPINES IN CRISIS

We do not usually think of the Chinese and the Dutch together. This is not surprising—there was little that the sprawling east Asian empire and the tiny western European merchant kingdom had in common in the 17th century, save that both had an interest in the Philippines. In this chapter we will learn about Chinese and Dutch opposition to the Spaniards in the archipelago.

By the time Corcuera conducted his truce with Qudarat, the Spaniards had been in the Philippines almost a century. Their presence was certainly not new. But by the 1640s, Spanish power in the Philippines had grown immensely. Thousands of settlers flooded into the Philippines every year from other parts of the Spanish Empire, such as Mexico, Peru, and the Caribbean. Native Tagalog and Cebuan peoples mixed with the Spaniards and mestizos, creating a new Filipino culture, united around the Catholic faith and loyal to Spanish rule. Cities like Manila, Cebu, Butuan, and Zamboanga grew and became sprawling centers of trade and political power.

Moro leaders like Qudarat recognized that Spanish might would only grow if left unchecked, and hence the Moros chose to put aside their own petty squabbles to unite against the Spanish attempts to subdue Mindanao.

For many years the Moros of Mindanao had been in an alliance with the Chinese. The Chinese supplied the Moros with arms and equipment that enabled them to carry on the war against the Spanish. In return, the Moros were given access to lucrative Chinese trading posts throughout the South Sea. The Moro merchants depended upon trade with China. This will be very important, as we shall see.

The truce brokered by Corcuera did not last long. In the 1630s, China was in the midst of a war between two rival dynasties, the Ming and the Qing. Corcuera took advantage of the chaos in China to renew the conquest of Mindanao, believing the Moros would be unable to count on Chinese aid. A new attack on Mindanao was launched in 1639 under Fray Agustin de San Pedro. San Pedro was a Recollect friar who had worked as a missionary and explorer and had dealings with Qudarat in the past.

Fray Agustin de San Pedro was eager for the conquest of Mindanao to succeed because Qudarat had carried off many Christian prisoners from Fray Agustin's missions to work as slaves at Lake Lanao. Fray Agustin, at the head of 560 Spaniards, invaded Mindanao. The Moros put up a stiff resistance, however, and Fray Agustin was unable to capture the Lanao region or regain his captives. Disheartened, he returned to his mission in Luzon to focus on his priestly duties.

Governor Corcuera continued the war against the Moros, throwing all his resources into the conquest of Mindanao. Despite this, he was unable to win any decisive victories. The Moros continued to raid Spanish settlements, enslave Christian Filipinos, and defy Spanish authority, despite the lack of support from the Chinese. When Governor Corcuera left office in 1644, Mindanao

Chapter 14: The Philippines in Crisis

was still unconquered.

During the wars with the Moros, the Spaniards had been driven off of the island of Taiwan by the Dutch. Governor Corcuera was not deeply troubled by this—he himself had recommended to the Spanish crown that the Spaniards evacuate the island off the coast of China because the Spanish could not effectively control it. Now in the hands of the Dutch who were at war with Spain, Taiwan became a haven for Dutch pirate ships preying on Spanish shipping. Meanwhile, the Dutch plotted an invasion of the Philippines.

This was a particularly bad time for the Spaniards in the Philippines. A series of volcanic eruptions from 1637 through 1640 had affected the harvests and resulted in a food shortage in Luzon. The constant wars with the Moros had exhausted the treasury. A rebellion in Manila in 1639 rocked the government there, while several Spanish galleons were wrecked on the way to Mexico, disrupting trade between the far flung corners of the Spanish Empire. The Archbishop of Manila died suddenly in 1645 of fever, leaving the Church in the Philippines without a leader in this time of crisis. From the Spanish point of view, it was the worst possible time for a Dutch invasion—but from the Dutch perspective, this was the best time for an attack.

The Dutch decided to launch a full scale invasion of Manila, sending 18 warships with over 800 soldiers against the Spaniards. The new Spanish governor, Diego Fajardo, could only muster two galleons and 400 men—and the galleons were extremely old, almost rotting. Nevertheless, Fajardo had the men prepare for battle under the command of General Lorenzo Ugalde de Orellana. General Orellana, a pious Catholic, made a public vow to the Blessed Virgin Mary that if victory should be granted against the Dutch, a solemn feast would be made in her honor and all the soldiers would make a pilgrimage barefoot to the Church of St. Domingo in Manila. He then encouraged all Spaniards to pray the Holy Rosary for victory. Governor Fajardo ordered the Blessed Sacrament exposed in Manila's churches for the duration of the campaign.

The Dutch engaged the Spanish in five separate battles. In each of these engagements the Spaniards won a complete victory. The victories were so one-sided as to shock even the Spanish who were praying for them! For example, in the third battle, every single crew member save one on the Dutch ship was killed while the Spaniards did not lose a single soldier. It seemed as if God had heard the prayers of the Spaniards. In the fifth battle, the Dutch were trying desperately to take advantage of a strong wind to escape the Spanish galleons. But the wind suddenly stopped, leaving the Dutch vessels dead in the water. The Spanish blasted the Dutch vessels to pieces. The Dutch were so desperate to escape that many of their soldiers leaped into the ocean rather that stay another moment on their obliterated vessel. It seemed incomprehensible that two rotting old galleons could so thoroughly defeat the superior Dutch forces—but it happened.

The invasion of Manila in 1646 ended in total disaster for the Dutch. Of the 800 men who set out, only 300 returned alive. Meanwhile the Spaniards lost only 15 men in all five battles. These conflicts would become known as the Battles of La Naval de Manila. True to his word, General Orellana and his men walked barefoot to St. Domingo in fulfillment of their vow. In 1652, after lengthy investigations, the Archdiocese of Manila declared the victories of 1646 to be miraculous. To this day, the victory of "Our Lady of La Naval" is commemorated as a feast on the second Sunday of every October.

Though the Dutch threat had passed, the Spaniards were soon threatened again, this time by the Chinese. We mentioned above that the Chinese were in the midst of a long war between two rival dynasties, the Ming and the Qing. By the 1650s, it became clear that the Qing were winning. Generals, soldiers, and officials loyal to Ming fled. In 1662, many of them came to Taiwan, which was then under the control of the Dutch.

One of the Ming loyalists who came to Taiwan was a general named Koxinga. The Dutch were concerned about the arrival of

Chapter 14: The Philippines in Crisis

The Spanish win a miraculous victory at the Battle of La Naval de Manila.

Koxinga and his men. Koxinga told the Dutch, "Hitherto this island had always belonged to China, and the Dutch had doubtless been permitted to live there, seeing that the Chinese did not require it for themselves; but requiring it now, it was only fair that Dutch strangers, who came from far regions, should give way to the masters of the island." He then wrested control of the island from them. Many of the Dutch fled. Those who did not were hunted down and beheaded by the Chinese. Koxinga became the ruler of Taiwan.

After he was established in Taiwan, Koxinga began raiding off the Chinese coast. He soon turned his eyes to the Philippines. Koxinga kept in his retinue an Italian friar named Vittorio Riccio. He sent Brother Riccio to the Spanish governor at Manila. The Governor-General at the time was Sabiniano Manrique de Lara. Brother Riccio told Governor de Lara that Koxinga demanded the Spaniards pay a hefty tribute and recognize Koxinga as lord of the Philippines. Governor de Lara was appalled that a Catholic friar would demand the submission of the Catholic Spaniards to a heathen ruler. Riccio warned the governor that his refusal would mean an imminent attack by Koxinga and his thousands of Chinese warriors.

Koxinga was angered by the Spaniards refusal to pay tribute and began preparations for an attack on Manila. Koxinga was not to be trifled with. He had been a very high ranking and successful army commander under the Ming emperors. He was a seasoned warrior and his professional army numbered in the thousands, all fiercely loyal to him. Governor de Lara was in considerable anxiety from Koxinga's threats.

To add to the trials facing the Spanish, the Moro wars had taken a turn for the worse. Several Moro datus from Mindanao had united and were burning Spanish settlements throughout the Visayas. The governor of Fort Pilar at Zamboanga, a man named Bobadilla, had been waging a fierce war against the Moros with some success. Needing reinforcements, however, Governor de Lara ordered Bobadilla to abandon Zamboanga and bring his men up to Manila. Bobadilla reluctantly obeyed, evacuating Zamboanga in 1663, giving the Moros a much needed rest from Spanish attacks.

Governor de Lara was gravely worried about the presence of large numbers of Chinese in Manila. By 1662, several thousand Chinese immigrants were residing within the city. De Lara was concerned

Chapter 14: The Philippines in Crisis

they would rebel against the Spaniards if Koxinga attacked. As for the Chinese, they mistrusted the Spaniards and rebelled, launching their own attack against Manila. The rebellion was put down with great brutality by the Spaniards and Filipinos, who slaughtered all the Chinese they could get their hands on. Those Chinese who could escape made their way to Taiwan to join the swelling ranks of Koxinga. Meanwhile the Spaniards destroyed many of their own outlying forts, worried that they would fall into the hands of Koxinga.

Koxinga was furious when he heard of the killing of his countrymen in Manila. He resolved that he would not only subdue the Philippines but punish the Spaniards severely. However, Koxinga suddenly died of a fever before the invasion could begin. His son Zheng Jing wished to continue his father's plans for a conquest of the Philippines. Zheng Jing had failed to reckon with the Dutch, however. Angry and seeking revenge for the slaughter of their countrymen by Koxinga, the Dutch had entered into an alliance with the Qing, the powerful enemies of Koxinga's family, who were by that time ruling all of mainland China. The alliance of the Qing and the Dutch prompted Zheng Jing to call off his father's invasion of the Philippines and keep his soldiers in Taiwan in case of a Qing-Dutch attack.

Thus by 1664, both the Dutch and Chinese threats had passed. The preceding three decades had been a time of peril for the Spanish Philippines. The increased aggression from the Moros, the danger posed by the presence of the Dutch, and the failed invasion of Koxinga all pushed the resolve and resources of the Spaniards to the limit. Any one of these enemies could have overthrown Spanish power on their own had things gone differently. The fact that the Spaniards had to deal with all of them almost simultaneously is a testimony to their resilience. Nor must we forget the hand of divine providence in these events—the miraculous defeat of the Dutch at the Battles of La Naval; the sudden death of Koxinga on the eve of his invasion; the manner in which the Dutch and Chinese, both enemies of the Spaniards, turned against each other.

This is not to say that the Spanish came out of this time of trial unscathed. The three decades of unending war with the Moros exhausted their treasury and manpower. That they had to pull back all Spanish soldiers from the entire archipelago simply to defend the city of Manila in 1662–1663 shows how thinly spread they were. The defense of Manila was responsible for perhaps the biggest Spanish setback during this time—the abandonment of the conquest of Mindanao. When Zamboanga and its fortress were evacuated, Qudarat's Moros swept in and demolished the fortifications there. Those Filipinos who chose to stay behind swore allegiance to Qudarat and converted to Islam. Every gain the Spaniards had made in Mindanao since the days of Governor Corcuera was undone. Even the isolated Spanish trading posts in the Moluccas—posts which had been there since the time of Magellan—were lost to the Moros. Spanish power in the southern archipelago had completely evaporated.

The threats posed by the Moros, Dutch, and Chinese demonstrated the remarkable unity of the Filipino culture. Spaniards and native Filipinos worked side-by-side to counter all of these threats. In each crisis, the Filipinos sided unreservedly with the Spanish.

In our next chapter, we will learn more about the emerging Filipino culture and the Christianization of the archipelago.

Chapter 15

CHRISTIANIZING THE PHILIPPINES

Historically, whenever the Catholic faith has been introduced into a culture, the fusion of the Gospel with native society produces a variant of Christianity unique to that culture. If we were to look at Catholicism in, say, Ireland, Mexico, and Vietnam, we would of course see the characteristics that we find amongst Catholics anywhere in the world. But we would also see many things unique to each place, products of the fusion of the Catholic faith with native culture.

The Church now prefers to call this process "inculturation", but it used to be known as *Christianization*—the process whereby the Gospel takes hold of a culture, reforms, and orders the natural gifts of that culture towards Christ. In this chapter we will learn a bit about how the process worked in the Philippines after the arrival of the Spaniards.

The first diocese of the Philippines was that of Manila, established by Pope Gregory XIII in 1579 by the papal bull *Illius Fulti Præsidio*. At first, the diocese encompassed all Spanish territories in Asia and was subordinated to the Archdiocese of Mexico. Although the Spaniards had introduced Christianity in Cebu much earlier than Manila, the abandonment of the Cebuan mission after the Battle of Mactan (1521) had left Cebu deprived of pastors. Missionary focus shifted north to Luzon and the seat of Spanish power at Manila.

The first Bishop of Manila was the Dominican Domingo de Salazar. Salazar had served for years in the missions of Florida and Mexico. He was personally chosen by King Philip II to serve as the first Bishop of Manila. Originally Salazar viewed the bishopric as simply a stepping stone to get to China, his real goal. He later wrote, "One of the reasons which made me accept this bishopric [of Manila] was the fact that these Islands are near China…For a long time I have had the conversion of that kingdom at heart, and with that thought I came to these Islands." His work in the Philippines would be fraught with challenges. Of the twenty Dominicans who accompanied him from Spain, over half died en route, and of the remainder only one was healthy enough to make it all the way to Manila.

Upon taking his see in 1581, Salazar saw that the biggest obstacle to the conversion of the Filipinos was their mistreatment at the hands of the Spanish conquistadors. As they had done in New Spain, the Spanish gentry of the Philippines had gotten accustomed to indenturing natives to labor on their estates in a status that was scarcely different than slavery. Salazar worked tirelessly to improve the lot of the Filipino people, earning for himself the nickname "the Las Casas of the Philippines," after the famous Bartolomé de Las Casas, the episcopal defender of the natives of the New World. The work was laborious. Once, when old, he had to return all the way in person to plead the cause of the Filipino people before the royal court. Salazar was ultimately successful, however. The Spanish court supported Bishop Salazar's work and passed legislation correcting abuses against the Filipinos.

Chapter 15: Christianizing the Philippines

Salazar set an admirable example for future Filipino bishops to follow. He convened a synod of the clergy to regulate clerical discipline. He took the church of St. Potenciana, founded by Legazpi, and elevated it into the Philippines' first cathedral and placed it under the patronage of the Blessed Virgin Mary. The original structure—built of bamboo, wood, and palm branches—burned down in 1583; a stone church was erected a few years later. He established the first college in the Philippines, dedicated to the care of orphans and the education of girls (1589). Later colleges would follow, such as the Jesuit Colegio de Manila (1590) and the University of Santo Tomas, founded in 1611 by one of Salazar's successors Miguel de Benavides. Salazar also established a hospital and worked ceaselessly to provide for the poor, once even selling his pectoral cross to relieve the needs of the impoverished. When he died in 1594, the inscription on his tomb called him, "Father of the Poor, and Himself Truly Poor." He was a model bishop in every respect.

By the early 1600s the Church in the Philippines was organized enough to undertake more systematic missionary work. Three more dioceses were erected (Nueva Cáceres, Nueva Segovia, and Cebu). Christianity had already been spreading throughout Cebu and the Visayas since the time of Legazpi and the baptism of Humabon. From 1600 onward, the spread of the faith would travel southward, from Cebu into the rest of Visayas and Mindanao, which was lumped in with the Diocese of Cebu. The massive size of the Diocese of Cebu proved a daunting task for the missionaries, who were too few and too spread out to make any inroads into the south. To add to their difficulties, the natives often viewed them with suspicion.

It became clear that a different strategy was needed to get the Gospel into the far flung reaches of the south. The Jesuits of Cebu came up with the idea of training young Filipino men to serve as catechists to accompany them on their journeys. Two schools were established, at Cebu City and on the island of Bohol. Here Filipino Christian boys were rigorously trained in virtue, doctrine, and the Jesuit manner of living. Now accompanied by many native

Christians of impeccable character, the Jesuits fanned out across the Visayas and had much more success at winning over the skeptical southern tribes.

Cebu would hold an important place in the heart of Philippine Christianity. Though Manila was the first diocese, it was in Cebu that the first converts were made back when Magellan first landed in 1521. Pope Paul VI in 1965 called Cebu's Basilica del Santo Niño, "the Mother and Head of all Churches in the Philippines" and "a symbol of the birth and growth of Christianity" in the region. Sixteen years later, Pope St. John Paul II called Cebu "the cradle of Christianity" in the Philippines.

The first Bishop of Cebu was the Augustinian Pedro de Agurto. Bishop Agurto followed up on the early missionary successes of the Jesuits by summoning a synod in 1600 to formulate a plan for evangelization. As a result of the synod, a catechism in the Cebuan language was published, which greatly aided the evangelization of the far-flung Visayas.

As was the case in the Americas, the Spanish evangelization of the Philippines was spearheaded by religious communities. We have already mentioned the work of the Dominicans, Jesuits, and Augustinians. In 1621 the Recollects arrived. The Recollects—an offshoot of the Augustinians—had extensive missionary experience in New France amongst the Huron tribes. This experience would be valuable in the wildernesses of the Visayas, where Filipino tribes lived in isolated settlements like the Indians of New France. The Recollects fanned out into the Philippine countryside, forming little mission communities called "reductions" (*reducciónes*). Originally just small stone churches or convents, the reductions attracted converted natives who settled there to live with the Recollects. Many reductions were the nuclei of today's towns and cities. Here, Christian natives were organized into communities on the European model, with homes in town oriented around a central plaza and stone church. Opposite the church always stood the *municipio*, the government building, a tangible sign of Spanish power in every town.

Chapter 15: Christianizing the Philippines

The missionaries continued to spread out across the thousands of islands in the Philippine archipelago, bringing the Gospel of Christ to the region's far-flung tribes. They did not confine themselves to the Philippines, however. Missionaries sometimes left the Philippines altogether to visit many of the other islands of the southwest Pacific. The first Filipino saint, Lorenzo Ruiz, was one of these. St. Lorenzo was a layman affiliated with the Dominicans of Manila. He left Manila for Japan with the Dominicans in 1636. Shortly after arriving in Japan, however, he and his companions were arrested. The Tokugawa Shogunate of Japan was at that time fiercely persecuting Christians. St. Lorenzo was hung upside down over a pit until he died on September 29, 1637. He was canonized in 1987.

Another Filipino missionary saint was Pedro Calungsod, a Filipino lay catechist who came to the Micronesian island of Guam with the Jesuit missionaries in 1669. Guam was inhabited by the Chamorro people, who happily accepted Christianity and were baptized in droves by the Jesuits.

The promising beginning, however, was soon soured by the Chamorro *macanjas*, medicine men. The macanjas were threatened by the growth of the Church. As the Chamorro increasingly turned to the sacraments instead of the magic of the medicine men, the *macanjas* looked for some way to accuse the missionaries and turn the people against them. Their opportunity came with the arrival of a Chinese escaped criminal named Choco. He told the Chamorro that the baptismal water used by the Jesuits was poisonous. This turned the Chamorro chief, Mata'pang, strongly against the Jesuits.

Meanwhile, however, Pedro Calungsod had assisted the Jesuit priests at the baptism of Mata'pang's newborn daughter when the chieftain was away. Mata'pang's wife was a Christian and had asked for the girl to be baptized. When Mata'pang heard that his own daughter had been subjected to the waters of baptism, he was furious. He grabbed a handful of spears and headed off to find the missionaries. Here is what happened next:

The lay catechist Pedro Calungsod and the Jesuit Father Diego Luis de San Vitores were walking up the road from the village of Tumon. After baptizing Mata'pang's daughter, the two men had spent a good part of the day speaking with the Chamorro villagers and teaching the boys of the village to use the Rosary. The prayer beads of the missionaries were particularly popular among the Chamorro. The two exhausted men trudged up the dusty road wearily. They were looking forward to returning to their mission, but Pedro was a bit worried.

"Those medicine men did not look very happy to see us," said Pedro. "Do you suppose they will give us any trouble when Mata'pang returns?"

"It's hard to say," said Father San Vitores. "I know they are threatened by us, but I don't think they mean us any harm. So far the people here have given us a warm welcome."

"True, but have you heard the rumors this Choco fellow is spreading?" said Pedro with a look of concern.

Father San Vitores nodded. "I have indeed. He is trying to make the people doubt the sacraments. Make them afraid of us."

Some distance behind the men, towards the village, there was a great rustling noise.

"What is that sound, Father?" said Pedro, turning back. He squinted, looking back down the road towards the village, sheltering his eyes from the setting sun with his hand. "It sounds like a celebration."

Saint Pedro Calungsod and Blessed Father Diego Luis de San Vitores.

Chapter 15: Christianizing the Philippines

"Not a celebration, my son," said Father San Vitores. "It's an angry mob."

Indeed, moments later a mob of Chamorro from the village came running up the road and overtook the two men. At their head was Mata'pang, their powerful chieftain. He was shirtless, as most of the Chamorro went about. His face was red, the veins on the side of his head bulging. In his hand he clutched several spears. Several *macanjas* flanked Mata'pang, shouting with their faces contorted in anger.

"This looks bad, Father!" exclaimed Pedro.

"Stand steadfast, Pedro," said Father San Vitores. "The peace of Christ will strengthen us."

"You, priest!" Mata'pang shouted as he approached the men.

Father San Vitores stepped forward calmly to try to reason with Mata'pang. He held out a large crucifix in a gesture of blessing. "Mata'pang, peace be with you. Tell me, why have you—" but Mata'pang was in no mood to talk. As soon as he was close enough, he lifted one of the spears and hurled it at the priest. Father San Vitores ducked quickly and the spear passed over him. Mata'pang then threw one at Pedro. A young, athletic man, Pedro was easily able to dodge the cast.

"Run, Pedro!" called out Father San Vitores.

"I will not abandon you, father!" Pedro yelled, stepping forward to protect the priest. At that moment Mata'pang cast another spear. This one struck Pedro squarely in the chest. He fell to the ground, clutching his bleeding breast with the spear still protruding. "Christ, save me!" he called out as he tumbled into the dust.

Immediately one of the Chamorro who was with Mata'pang fell upon Pedro and struck his head with a machete, splitting his skull. Pedro groaned. "My son!" Father San Vitores called out. The priest knelt beside Pedro and absolved him quickly before the young man's eyes rolled up into his head. "May Christ receive your soul!" he murmured, holding the crucifix before the eyes of his dying companion.

Almost as soon as he did, the priest felt a searing pain in his gut. He looked down and saw a bloody spearhead protruding from his belly. *Did that come out of me?* He thought to himself in shock. He reached around behind himself. His fingers touched the solid wooden shaft protruding from his back. The blood ran down the tip of the spearhead and dripped into the dust. *Lord, into thy hands I commend my spirit,* he prayed silently before collapsing.

Mata'pang and his men stripped the bodies of the two men, tied heavy stones to their feet, and sunk them in the ocean. Then Mata'pang took the crucifix of Father San Vitores and smashed it with a rock while blaspheming God. Pedro Calungsod and Father Diego Luis de San Vitores would both be revered as martyrs. Pedro was canonized in 2012 by Pope Benedict XVI and is now honored as a saint. His Feast Day is April 2. Father San Vitores was beatified in 1985 by John Paul II.

Throughout the 17th and 18th centuries, priests both diocesan and religious continued to saturate the Philippine islands with the Gospel of Christ, until gradually paganism faded and a new generation of Filipinos embraced the Catholic faith more wholeheartedly. Catholicism became deeply interwoven with Filipino culture. Further south, however, in Mindanao, the missionaries were fewer and had less success with the Muslim Moros. Here the Spaniards were content to make them into vassals, leaving off the work of conversion until a future time. This initial failure to Christianize the Moros of Mindanao would be the source of much grief in later times.

But for now, let us continue to learn about life in the colonial Philippines under the Spaniards.

Chapter 16

LIFE IN THE SPANISH PHILIPPINES

The Spanish would rule the Philippines for 333 years. During this time, a lot happened—threats from Chinese pirates, the Dutch, the English, the Portuguese, the Moros, and indigenous revolts. It seemed like Spanish rule was always being challenged from somewhere. Nevertheless, the Spanish not only clung to power, but forged a strong system of governance and administration. The Church in the Philippines also flourished. Filipinos adopted the Catholic faith with zeal, spurred on by thousands of devoted clergy over the years. The result of all this was that the Philippines became one of the best administered and most thoroughly Christianized of all Spain's colonies.

Of course, life changed a lot over the 333 years of Spanish rule, too much to cover in a single chapter. Nevertheless, we will try to get a basic understanding of how the Spanish governed the colony and what life must have been like under them.

In the beginning, the Spanish pattern of land use followed what they had done in their American colonies. Called the *encomienda* system, grants of land were awarded to certain individuals—conquerors, wealthy landowners, or officials of the crown. These people were known as *encomenderos*. An encomendero was like a feudal lord. He not only owned vast tracts of land but had a legal right to the labor of the natives who lived upon it. The natives were like serfs who were expected to farm the lands of the encomendero to bring him profit. In exchange, the encomendero was obliged to protect the natives and make sure they had access to the Catholic sacraments and Catholic education. The encomendero also oversaw collecting taxes from the natives on behalf of the Spanish crown.

The encomienda system was rife with abuse, however. Encomenderos often treated native workers more like slaves. The worst also tended to ignore religious instruction and withheld tax revenue from the crown, pocketing it for themselves instead. The problems with the encomienda system led to it being abandoned by the end of the 17th century. Around that time the Spanish Governor-General began appointing his own civil and military governors to rule directly, taking away the authority of the encomenderos. This was not only better for the native Filipinos, but it also meant the collection of taxes was more regular, which was also good for the colonial government.

The Governor-General, appointed by the Viceroy of New Spain (Mexico), was an extremely powerful individual. In many respects he was like a monarch of the Philippines. He did not rule alone, however, but with the help of a court known as the *Real Audiencia de Manila*, or just the Audiencia for short (the Spanish word *real* means "royal"). The Audiencia was a group of officials in Manila who were charged with governing the Philippines. It included several judges, a royal attorney, and many other officials. The Audiencia was a high court with the authority to try cases, but it was also able to make and enforce laws.

The Audiencia was instructed to give special attention to

Chapter 16: Life in the Spanish Philippines

lawsuits involving native Filipinos and to ensure that their rights were respected. It was directed that "the said Indians shall be better treated and instructed in our Holy Catholic Faith, as our free vassals." It also had authority to investigate local officials and even regional governors if they were accused of a crime.

Sometimes the Audiencia and the Governor-General squabbled. For example, in 1590 the Governor-General Santiago de Vera dissolved the Audiencia and sent its judges to Mexico because of their attempts to undermine his authority. Another Governor-General, Francisco Tello de Guzmán, recalled the judges back to the Audiencia in 1596. Usually, however, the Governor-General and the Audiencia worked together to govern the sprawling Philippine archipelago.

Manila was the political and ecclesiastical capital of the Philippines. All power was concentrated in this city, where the Audiencia sat and the Archbishop of Manila maintained his cathedral. The original city of Manila was walled—the walled portion is called *Intramuros*—but during Spain's long rule people flocked to the city and settlement spread outside the old walls in all directions. Various other villages near Manila were eventually swallowed up by the ever-growing city. To this day, the various market squares of Manila are reminders of these ancient villages.

Besides being a center of political power, Manila was a hub of trade. Spanish galleons carrying Mexican silver came to Manila to trade for Chinese silks. Many Spanish merchants came to Manila hoping to get rich quick in the silk trade. The Mexico-China trade also attracted many Chinese to Manila. The Spaniards never quite trusted the Chinese living among them. After all, a fleet of Chinese pirates had once tried to conquer Manila in 1574. And in the 17th century, the Chinese were allies of the Moros of Mindanao, supplying them with weapons in their wars against the Spaniards.

The suspicion of the Chinese sometimes erupted into open violence. In 1603 the Governor-General Luis Pérez Dasmariñas, fearful that the Chinese were plotting to take over the Philippines, attacked the Chinese community of Manila. The Chinese fought back vigorously and Dasmariñas was killed. The Chinese chopped off the heads of Dasmariñas and his men and paraded them around Manila in open rebellion. The Spaniards rushed to put down the revolt, aided by Japanese mercenaries and units of native Filipino soldiers. The revolt was crushed with great brutality—20,000 Chinese were killed. There were additional massacres of Manila's Chinese in 1639 and 1662. Despite these horrific episodes of violence, Chinese continued to settle in Manila and by the late 17th century had been grudgingly accepted as a part of Filipino society.

In our last chapter we mentioned the Catholic mission-towns known as "reductions" (*reducciónes*). Most reductions were built in the lowlands, with the goal of inducing Filipino natives to move from the mountains down into the more arable lands near the reductions. Since the Spanish government encouraged the authorities to take an active hand in conversion, natives were subject to a law called *polos y servicios*. The polos y servicios meant that every native male between the ages of 16 and 60 had to perform occasional free labor for the parish priest or local governor. Many of the churches in the Philippine countryside were constructed this way. Though we may dislike the idea of anybody being compelled to work for free, especially in the service of the Church, we should remember that the Spanish were trying to replicate the feudal system of Europe in their overseas territories. They viewed the Filipino natives like European serfs, who owed service to their feudal lords. Most Christians in Europe were subject to similar laws.

Filipino natives who wanted to be baptized had to memorize the tenets of a book called *Doctrina Cristiana*, which contained basic Catholic prayers, morals, and practices. Before being baptized they had to publicly renounce polygamy, slavery, and promise to make restitution for anything they had stolen. In many native tribes it was considered permissible or even clever to steal something if one could get away with it, so Catholic missionaries made converts expressly renounce stealing and promise to restore anything they had stolen.

CHAPTER 16: LIFE IN THE SPANISH PHILIPPINES

That is not to say Christianization was always without trouble. There were occasional revolts against Spanish rule. In 1621, a native shaman from the Visayan island of Bohol named Tamblot won a following by allegedly performing feats of magic in the villages of Bohol. He told his followers that his powers came from the *diwatas*, local guardian spirits. The diwatas, Tamblot said, were angry with the Spaniards. He promised his followers that the diwatas would make them impervious to Spanish musket balls and that the expulsion of the Spaniards would usher in an age of plenty. Inspired by these promises, the followers of Tamblot began storing supplies and fortifying areas around the island. Tamblot built a shrine for the diwatas deep in the jungled mountains of central Bohol. Many surrounding towns started going over to Tamblot.

By late 1621 the movement had spread beyond Bohol and was winning recruits on the neighboring islands of Leyte and Panay. The local Catholic clergy were the first Spaniards to grasp the severity of what was happening and brought the matter to the attention of Juan de Alcarazo, the Mayor of Cebu. Alcarazo was hesitant to take decisive action, as he did not have the permission of the Governor-General. He tried reasoning with the rebels, but the Boholanos flatly refused to lay down their arms.

Alcarazo finally decided to act before the insurrection spread. With a small contingent of only 50 Spaniards reinforced with Cebuano and Kapampangan warriors, Alcarazo led an expedition to Bohol to put down Tamblot's rebellion. He landed on Bohol on New Years' Day of 1622. Here is what happened next:

Mayor Juan de Alcarazo slapped the mosquito that had been draining blood from his sweaty neck. "Got you!" he muttered. Not that it would matter. Another took its place before its body even hit the ground.

The rest of the expedition was also in a foul mood. Seven days marching in the hellish jungle of Bohol was enough to test any man's mettle. The Spanish soldiery grunted as they dragged their sweat-soaked bodies over yet another forest ridge, their arms stiff from hacking away at the underbrush all morning. The Cebuano and Kapampangan warriors who had lived on these islands were a little more stoic, but far from enjoying themselves. The Cebuano warriors, over 500 of them, carried large wooden shields strapped to their backs.

There was a deep rumbling in the hills. Alcarazo looked up into the overcast sky. "Looks like rain soon, Alcalde," said Francisco, the mayor's attendant.

"I agree," Alcarazo said, wiping his brow with a handkerchief. "Francisco, I think you'd better tell the Cebuanos to ready their shields."

"Aye. You expecting a fight soon, Alcalde?" Francisco asked.

"Yes," replied Alcarazo. "We're getting close to the center of the island. And we had a few skirmishes yesterday. Before long we'll stumble upon Tamblot's camp, and we must be ready."

"I will have the men ready the shields," Francisco said, bowing his head quickly before dashing off to deliver the mayor's orders.

The engagement came quicker than Alcarazo anticipated. The column had scarcely started moving again when shrieking and clashing of arms could be heard from the rear. "Alcalde!" Francisco shouted running up to Alcarazo, "the rear guard has been ambushed!"

Indeed, it was so. Swarms of Boholanos were emerging from the dense foliage, hurling spears and firing arrows at the Spaniards and their allies. A few of the Spaniards had managed to fire some musket volleys at their attackers, but for every one Boholano that fell it seemed another three took his place.

Alcarazo spied a dense bamboo thicket about a hundred yards away. "Fall back, men!" he cried, raising his sword, and guiding his men towards the thicket. The sky again thundered. The first drops of rain could be heard pattering on the forest leaves. "Shields!" he cried loudly. The Cebuano and Spaniard forces hunkered down in the bamboo thicket. The Cebuanos raised their shields over their

Chapter 16: Life in the Spanish Philippines

heads, providing cover for themselves and the Spaniards.

As Alcarazo's men entrenched themselves, the full force of Tamblot's men emerged, almost 1,500 strong and vastly outnumbering the Spaniards. Tamblot himself came forth, clothed in the traditional red tunic of the shamans. He grinned. "Now I have you," he said.

Just then, the sky was rent by thunder and the rain began to fall. The downpour was a torrent. Rivulets of water rushed down the jungle hillsides, turning the ground everywhere to mud. The Boholano warriors hung back, looking at Tamblot for guidance. The shaman laughed. "Why do you hesitate? The diwatas have favored us! Don't you know that the Spanish cannot fire their weapons when the rain wets their powder? Go! The gods have given us victory!" Encouraged by this harangue, the mob of Boholanos swarmed through the trees and charged the bamboo thicket, spears and swords aloft and eyes wild with bloodlust.

But Alcarazo was not shaken. "Hold!" he cried. The Boholanos grew closer. "Hold!" he called again, his Spanish and Cebuano soldiers maintaining iron discipline. The Boholanos were close now. In a moment they would plunge into the bamboo thicket, slaughtering everyone. *Just a few yards closer,* Alcarazo thought…

"NOW!" the mayor cried.

The Cebuano warriors threw down their shields, each revealing a Spanish soldier hidden with a musket—a perfectly dry musket that had been shielded from the rain. The line of muskets exploded in a volley of gunfire. Musketballs tore into the Boholano ranks at close range, to devastating effect. Scores of them fell dead, many more wounded from the flesh-ripping musket shots. A thick cloud of smoke hung in the damp air.

Tamblot was beside himself. He had never seen the Spanish able to fire their weapons in such a downpour. He tore his hair and shrieked at the sight of his grand assault leveled by gunfire.

And it did not stop there. A second volley mowed down even more Boholanos. They began to panic. Tamblot watched in horror as the remnants of his rebel force turned and fled back into the mountains, their faces twisted in fear.

After this victory, Alcarazo made short work of Tamblot and his Boholano rebels. The mountain stronghold was seized, its defenders slaughtered, and its provisions taken. Though history is silent on what happened to Tamblot himself, the other leaders of the rebellion were captured and hanged. But Alcarazo was merciful to the rest of the Boholanos. He told them simply to go home and submit to Spanish rule, which they were more than ready to do. The Governor-General commended Alcarazo for his swift action and rewarded him generously. But Alcarazo could not yet relax. Another revolt broke out later that year, this time on the Visayan island of Leyte. Known as the Bankaw Revolt, it was led by an old datu called Bankaw. Bankaw had known Miguel de Legazpi in his youth and was once a Christian and friend of the Spaniards—King Philip II once even sent him a personal letter of gratitude! But as he got older, Bankaw grew disillusioned with the Spaniards and left the Catholic faith. He built a temple to a diwata and incited people from the surrounding villages to renounce Christianity and rebel against Spanish rule.

Terrified, the local parish priest fled to Cebu and warned Alcarazo. Alcarazo once again assembled a force and went to stomp out the revolt before it could spread. The Spaniards slew Bankaw and burned down his temple. With the memory of Tamblot's uprising still fresh, Alcarazo was in no mood for clemency this time around. He ordered a bamboo stake driven through Bankaw's head and displayed it in public. Bankaw's son—who had joined in the rebellion—was beheaded. Bankaw's associates were shot, and the shamans who had served at the temple of the diwata were rounded up and burned at the stake—over eighty of them. Alcarazo wanted to ensure that no more Filipino tribes would even consider revolting.

Despite occasional bouts of violence such as the uprising of

Chapter 16: Life in the Spanish Philippines

Tamblot and the Bankaw Revolt, Christianization in the Philippines was generally peaceful. Sunday Mass attendance became normal and was even recorded. The bells of churches and monasteries rang out across the mountains and jungles, announcing the canonical hours or calling the faithful to the Angelus at noon. The intercession of the saints gradually replaced the older cults of the diwatas. By the 17th century, Luzon and the Visayas were reliably Catholic. In Mindanao, however, Christianity spread much more slowly due to the strong Islamic character of the island.

Like elsewhere in the lands ruled by Spain, the Spaniards soon developed a racial caste system in the Philippines. A caste system is a social structure where people are ranked based on what group they happened to be born into. Those in higher "ranks" or castes had many more opportunities in society than those in the lower castes.

The caste system in the Philippines was based on how much Spanish blood one had. Because there were so many ethnic groups in the Philippines, the system was quite complex. The most important caste divisions (from highest to lowest) were:

- **Peninsulares:** Person of pure Spanish descent born in Spain (the Iberian Peninsula);
- **Filipino/Insulares:** Person of pure Spanish descent born in the Philippines;
- **Americanos:** This term encompassed three different groups from the Spanish American colonies: **criollos** (a person mostly Spanish but mixed with other European ancestry), **castizos** (1/4 Native American, 3/4 Spanish), and **mestizos** (1/2 Native American, 1/2 Spanish);
- **Tornatrás:** Person of mixed Spanish, Chinese, and indigenous Philippine ancestry;
- **Mestizo de Español:** Mixed Spanish and indigenous Philippine ancestry;
- **Mestizo de Bombay:** Mixed Indian and indigenous Philippine ancestry;

- **Mestizo de Sangley:** Mixed indigenous Philippine and Chinese ancestry;
- **Sangley/Chino:** Person of pure Chinese ancestry;
- **Indio:** Person of pure indigenous Philippine ancestry;
- **Negrito:** Person of pure Malayan ancestry (an ethnic group from southeast Asia, many of whom lived on Mindanao)

The caste system was primarily used for purposes of taxation. The castes who were primarily European (*blancos*) paid the least while sangleys paid the most; mestizos, indios, and negritos paid in between. Note that under the Spanish, the word *Filipino* meant a Spaniard who was born in the Philippines. Centuries later, when the Philippines were declared independent of Spain in 1898, the term *Filipino* was expanded to mean anyone and everyone born in the Philippines, regardless of their ancestry. That is how *Filipino* is used today.

Though the castes were separated for administrative purpose and taxation, they all lived and worked together. This was different from, for example, the United States, where black Americans were segregated in separate communities, schools, and public facilities away from whites. In the Spanish Philippines, all races lived side-by-side. This was encouraged by the Spanish authorities, who wanted all the different castes to get along harmoniously. The Catholic religion, which teaches that all people are children of God and connected all together, was no doubt a source of unity. In the late 19th century, a British official from Hong Kong visited the Philippines and said:

> The lines separating entire classes and races, appeared to me less marked than in [other] colonies. I have seen on the same table, Spaniards, Mestizos, Chinos, and Indios, priests and military. There is no doubt that having one Religion forms great bonding. And more so to the eyes of one that has been observing the repulsion and differences due to race in many parts of Asia. And from one (like myself) who knows that

Chapter 16: Life in the Spanish Philippines

Inhabitants of the Philippines through Spanish eyes as recorded in the Boxer Codex (ca. AD 1590). From top-to-bottom, left-to-right: tattooed Visayans; couple from Zambales with falcon; Visayan couple; Sangley couple in Chinese garb; wealthy Tagalog couple; women of Manila, possibly Muslim; Visayan noble couple; Negrito hunters; woman from northern Luzon.

race is the great divider of society, the admirable contrast and exception to racial discrimination so markedly presented by the people of the Philippines is indeed admirable.

Another English visitor to the Philippines said that the Spanish Philippines had achieved a level of racial harmony unique amongst all the colonies of Europe:

[In the Philippines] Spaniards and natives lived together in great harmony, and I do not know where I could find a colony in which Europeans mix as much socially with the natives. Not in Java, where a native of position must dismount to salute the humblest Dutchman. Not in British India, where the Englishwoman has now made the gulf between British and native into a bottomless pit."

Life in the Spanish Philippines was no worse than other European colonies and was in many ways considerably better. Spanish government was not always efficient, but it was stable and brought a unity to the Philippine archipelago that would have been impossible without their administration. Furthermore, in an age when the British were enslaving Africans and dispossessing native tribes of their lands in their American colonies, the Spanish in the Philippines were living (mostly) in peace side-by-side with Filipinos, marrying, working, and worshiping together.

In our next chapter, we will learn about the great galleon trade that connected the Philippines to the rest of the Spanish empire.

Chapter 17

THE GREAT MANILA GALLEONS

In Chapter 11 we learned about the exceptional life of Andrés de Urdaneta, the Augustinian friar who discovered a favorable sea route between the Philippines and Mexico. For centuries, Spanish ships would follow the course pioneered by the friar, calling it "Urdaneta's Route." In this chapter we will learn about the trade between the Philippines and the Spanish colonies of the Americas.

In the 16th and 17th centuries, Spain was the master of a vast overseas colonial empire that included not only the Philippines, but most of South America, central America, most of the Caribbean, and the southwestern half of North America. These colonies were a great source of wealth for Spain. At that time Spain, like most European colonial powers, operated under a system known as *mercantilism*. Mercantilism was an economic system that governed the relationship between a mother country and its colonies based on the exchange of raw materials for finished goods. For example, silver would be mined from Spanish colonies in Peru. This silver would be shipped to Spain and traded for finished goods, such as weapons, clothing, and tools. These would be shipped back to Peru or the Philippines to be sold there. The exact items being traded could vary, but the point is in the mercantilist system, a colony existed for the purpose of providing raw materials to its mother country, which in exchange supplied it with finished goods for use by its colonists.

Of course, Manila is a long way from Spain—tens of thousands of miles by sea! The mercantilist system could not function without countless merchants who sailed the seas, bringing cargo back and forth between Spanish ports around the world and uniting the far-flung territories of the Spanish Empire. The Spaniards preferred to ship their goods on large ships called *galleons*. The galleons were multi-deck armed vessels made for carrying cargo long distances, but they were slow and vulnerable to attack from pirates or the vessels of rival kingdoms. For this reason, the merchants sailed the galleons in groups called *convoys* for greater protection. If a merchant wanted to participate in the galleon trade, the Spanish government required him to sail with a convoy.

The trade route discovered by Urdaneta connected Manila to Acapulco, Mexico. Let us follow the expedition of a fictional merchant, Luis del Rosario, as he makes the long voyage from Manila to Acapulco and back in 1686.

Luis del Rosario was an *insulare*—that is, he was of pure Spanish blood but was born in the Philippines. He had never set foot in Spain. Luis's father had been a prosperous merchant of Manila, and Luis had entered the trade at a young age working under his father. By 1686 Luis's father had been dead for some time and Luis had been running the Urdaneta route for several years by himself. In fact, this year was the first year Luis would be bringing his own son on the journey—14-year-old Felipe.

Luis and Felipe had been preparing for this journey long before it set sail. They had spent the two months after the Feast

Chapter 17: The Great Manila Galleons

of the Circumcision trading with the Sangley merchants who were regulars at the Del Rosario's trading post in Intramuros. The Sangleys traveled regularly between the Chinese city of Fujian and Manila. They had been visiting Luis's post for as long as Felipe could remember. Felipe was always amazed at the great variety of goods the Sangleys brought from afar: from China, precious spices, exquisite porcelain dishes, jade and ivory statuary, wax, lacquerware, cases of gunpowder, and intricate woven silk garments; from India, beautifully carved amulets of amber, spools of softest cotton, and colorful woven rugs; from Japan, brightly decorated fans, ornately carved wooden chests, decorative folding screens, porcelain, and colorful lacquerware boxes. The Sangleys would lay these items out on the floor of the Del Rosario's storeroom while Luis painstakingly examined them to see which goods he wished to trade.

This sort of thing had been going on for many weeks. The Sangleys knew Luis was making a voyage to Mexico and were eager to sell. "What do you think, Felipe? We are already fairly well stocked on porcelains, ivory, and silks. What else should we bring?" Felipe was intrigued by the Japanese fans, brightly decorated with painting of mountains and sunsets.

"I think the highborn ladies of Mexico would like those fans," he said. Luis nodded in agreement. He gave the Sangleys a handful of silver coins in exchange for a case of the fans.

"Let's hope you're right!" Luis said.

By March, Luis had gathered a storehouse full of goods he planned on taking along to Acapulco. The next month was spent fitting out the galleon and working out the details of the voyage with other merchants. Luis did not own a galleon himself—he was not that wealthy. Rather, he belonged to a merchant's club in Manila that collectively owned a galleon called the *Maria Magdalena*. So long as Luis paid a certain amount to the club out of his gains, he could sail on the *Maria Magdalena*.

But the merchant's club itself had to get permission to trade from another group, the *Casa de Contratación*. The Casa de Contratación was an agency in Seville, Spain that regulated all trade in the Spanish Empire. In theory, no galleon could sail without the permission of the Casa de Contratación. Fortunately, the merchants who owned the *Maria Magdalena* had been on good terms with the Casa for years and could make the Acapulco voyage without hindrance from any authorities.

The ship set sail from Manila on April 5, the Feast of St. Vincent, in the company of six other galleons. It was all so exciting for young Felipe, feeling the salty air of the open sea as he watched first the city of Manila then the green coast of Luzon vanish into the distance with each passing hour.

The first few days on the sea were tense. The Spaniards were vigilant, for Dutch and English pirates infested the waters around the Philippines. The rules of the Casa de Contratación stated that each merchant was obligated to defend the vessel. Luis and Felipe were both required to take turns in the nightly watch rotation to make sure the *Magdalena* was not caught unawares by enemies intent on plunder.

Things settled down after a week or so as the galleons put some distance between themselves and the archipelago, pressing eastward into the open waters of the Pacific Ocean. At first Felipe was excited to break out onto the high seas, but as the days went by he grew restless. The merchants gave him extra tasks around the ship to keep him occupied, but this was not much to Felipe's liking. "The sea just goes on forever! And the days are so uneventful!" the boy complained to his father.

His father removed his hat and whacked the boy upside the head with it. "Pray they stay uneventful! If we are set upon by English pirates or tossed about in a cyclone, you would be on your knees begging the merciful Lord for even one of these 'uneventful days.'"

Fortunately, the days continued uneventful as the *Magdalena* and other galleons pressed steadily onward. On June 26th, the feast of the martyr St. Pelayo, a brownish green ridge appeared on the eastern horizon. "Land, father!" cried Felipe.

Chapter 17: The Great Manila Galleons

"Thank the saints," said Luis crossing himself. "We have made it safely." This was not Mexico, however. This was a wild and rugged northern land devoid of any Spaniards. "It is merely a stopping point for us to relax and replenish our supplies," explained Luis. "The place is called *California*. We put in at a bay called Puerto de Monterrey before moving on southward to New Spain."

The next morning the ship dropped anchor in the smooth waters of the Puerto de Monterrey. Felipe looked ashore in wonder. The lands around the bay were sloping hills covered in scraggly brush and short, hardy trees. "We will forage during the day and sleep on the ships at night," Luis explained. This is precisely what the crew did. The twelve days were spent scouring the lands around the bay for fresh water, trapping animals, and hewing trees for timber. It was tedious work, but necessary, for the galleons still had at least another few weeks on the sea before reaching Acapulco and supplies were low.

One afternoon, while the men were dragging a log down a slope near the seashore, Felipe spotted a strange figure watching them from the crest of a nearby hill. The man wore a skirt of woven grass and was shirtless, his torso covered only in strings of elaborate shell beads. His face was painted, and he wore what seemed to be a crown of feathers upon his head. Felipe stared at the man in wonder and alarm. "Pay him no heed," said Luis. "He is a *costeño*, one of the natives who lives in the hills around the bay. He means us no harm. They are just watching."

When the ships were resupplied and the men rested, the convoy put out to sea again. This time, however, they did not take to the open water, but rather hugged the coast of California, working their way southward towards New Spain. Felipe was mystified by this strange, new land. It looked so wild and untamed. Occasionally, he could see other natives gathered on the shore to watch the passage of the convoy. On one occasion, a group of natives in narrow plank boats made their way out to the *Magdalena* to trade fish and fresh game for beads and trinkets.

About a week after leaving Puerto de Monterrey, the convoy began passing Spanish settlements. The crew cheered when they passed the city of Mazatlán, with its cluster of white buildings and churches nestled on the hills overlooking the sea. Mazatlán was the first major Spanish city the men had sighted and signified that their journey was close to its end.

Not long after, the convey arrived at Acapulco, gliding gently into the city's harbor beneath the shadow of the imposing colonial fortress that stood atop a hillside overlooking the water. The next several days were a flurry of excited work. Luis, Felipe, and the merchants offloaded their goods from the *Magdalena* into storehouses to be cataloged by Spanish customs officials. They met with middlemen to arrange the transport of the goods to the rich markets of Mexico City and Veracruz. Local merchants came in hopes of buying goods cheaply to resell in Peru or elsewhere in Spanish America.

This busywork occupied days, and Felipe soon found himself bored. When he was not needed by his father, he roamed about the streets of Acapulco. It was now early August and desperately hot. Felipe fanned himself with one of the Japanese fans he had brought from home as he wandered through the city plaza one afternoon.

"You there, boy!" a voice called. Felipe turned. It was a beautiful woman, richly adorned and wealthy by the look of it. She was coming out of the noon Mass at the parish church abutting the plaza.

"Yes, Señora?" Felipe answered deferentially. "What do you wish of me?"

"That fan you hold, where did you get it? I've never seen anything like it!" she said, gazing at the Japanese fan in wonder.

"I come from the Philippines, Señora," said Felipe. "My father is a merchant trading here in the city. This fan came from our stores. It was made in Japan."

"Japan!" the woman said, her eyebrows raised in admiration. "Exquisite!" She reached into a pouch and produced a handful of coins. "I'll give you eight *reals* for it."

Eight reals!? Felipe thought to himself. *That's a whole silver dollar.*

Chapter 17: The Great Manila Galleons

We only paid the Sangleys half a real each. He did some quick figuring. *At eight reals, that would be over 175% profit!*

"Of course, Señora," he said courteously. The woman handed him the eight coins and Felipe gave her the brightly decorated fan.

"Gracias!" said the woman, walking off happily with her new fan. "Oh, boy," she called, turning. "Is your father at the storehouse by the harbor?"

"Yes, Señora," said Felipe. "For at least another three weeks."

"Perfect," she said. "I'm sure all the ladies of Acapulco will be eager to have one of these fans after they see me at Mass this Sunday with mine. I'd set aside at least a dozen more."

"Aye, ma'am!" Felipe said excitedly, tipping his hat. The woman nodded and walked off. Felipe burst into a run. He couldn't wait to get back to his father to tell him the good news.

Of course, Luis, Felipe, and everything else in this story is fictional—but it is all based in historical facts about the Manila galleons. Voyages just like that of Luis and Felipe happened every year for centuries, linking the Spanish colonies of the Philippines and New Spain via the galleon route first discovered by Urdaneta.

Chapter 18

THE BRITISH INTERRUPTION

Through the galleon trade, Manila grew to become one of the most important centers of commerce in all of Asia. Year after year Spanish merchants made the long voyage from Manila to Acapulco and back, and year after year wealth flowed into the coffers of Spain. This was good for the Spanish Empire and profitable for the Philippines.

Philippine successes aroused the envy of others, however. The Spanish were not the only traders in east Asia. By the 1700s, the British, too, had built a powerful trading presence in the region. British trade was carried out by the East India Company, whose Asian headquarters was in the Indian city of Calcutta. The East India Company was wealthy and powerful, but it could not compete with the Spanish galleon trade. The officials of the East India Company thus coveted the city of Manila.

They got their chance when Britain went to war against France in a conflict known as the Seven Years War (1756–1763). Though Spain was an ally of France, the Spanish tried to keep out of the conflict. But by 1759 the French had suffered a series of devastating losses and were on the verge of defeat. The Spanish King Charles III began to fear the might of Britain and entered a formal alliance with France in 1761, beginning preparations for war with Great Britain. Britain and Spain declared war against each other in January of 1762.

When war was declared, agents of the East India Company urged the British King George III to attack the Philippines and seize Manila. The British possession of Manila, they argued, would cripple Spain's economy, expand the influence of the East India Company, and bring a great deal of wealth to Britain. King George agreed and approved a plan devised by Colonel William Draper to capture Manila using British forces already stationed in Madras, India.

On September 24, 1762, a fleet of 15 British ships carrying almost 7,000 soldiers entered Manila Bay. They landed two miles south of the city and began an assault. Draper was surprised to see the city's defenses in a state of disarray. The most formidable opposition came from a regiment of 1,000 Pampangos (Filipinos recruits from Pampanga province) who charged the British lines and almost breached them before being driven back. When this failed, native Filipino forces began slipping out of the city, leaving the Spanish to face the British alone.

Given that Manila was such an important city, why was it not better defended? The answer is that the government of the Philippines was itself in disarray. The former Governor-General had recently died. Spain had appointed a new Governor-General named Francisco de la Torre, but he had to travel all the way from Cuba and had been delayed due to the war. By the time Britain attacked, the Philippines had been without a Governor-General for over three years. The Philippines was then under the control of Archbishop of Manila Manuel Rojo del Río y Vieyra, who was temporary Lieutenant-Governor. But Archbishop Rojo was a Franciscan friar

Chapter 18: The British Interruption

who knew little of military matters, and the defense of the city lapsed.

On October 5, the British breached the walls of the San Diego fortress and set fire to some parts of the city. Archbishop Rojo convened a council of war to discuss what to do. Rojo wished to surrender, but the Spanish military officers protested this plan. While the council deliberated, the British breached the final fortifications and surged into Intramuros, the walled center of Manila.

The Spanish officials fled in disorder. Fortunately, an enterprising judge of the Philippine Audiencia named Simón de Anda y Salazar was able to escape with the other royal officials carrying the treasury and many important documents. Anda fled the city through a gate called the Postern of Our Lady of Solitude. From there he took a boat up the Pasig River to Bulacan.

Meanwhile, Archbishop Rojo stayed behind to facilitate the orderly handover of the city to the British. But to the Archbishop's dismay, the British takeover was anything but orderly.

The British army had a reputation for discipline during combat. But what Archbishop Manuel Rojo del Río y Vieyra saw on October 6, 1762 was quite the opposite:

As soon as the British troops marched into Intramuros, they broke ranks and began pillaging. Soldiers kicked in the doors of shops and homes, looting freely. Right across from Rojo's episcopal palace, a troop of British regulars broke down the door of a tailor's shop, threw the linens out into the street, and walked out carrying the tailor's money box. When the tailor attempted to defend his property, a regular hit him in the stomach with the butt of his musket, dropping the man to the ground swiftly.

Rojo ran to the nearest British officer, a lanky man who was standing by stoically while discipline broke down.

"Sir, I beg, in the name of Christ, stop this plunder before it gets out of hand!" the archbishop pleaded in broken English with folded hands.

"Look 'ere, we been on the sea since August and mighty cooped up," said the officer angrily. "The boys need to have a bit of fun! Need to unwind some." In the distance, glass shattered, and a woman screamed. Rojo saw pillars of smoke beginning to billow up from various buildings.

"If you do not stop this, there won't be any city left!" Rojo pleaded. But his pleas fell on deaf ears. The British fanned out across the city, leaving only the churches free from pillage. Nothing else was spared. To make matters worse, the general atmosphere of chaos tempted others to get in on the looting, too. Filipinos, Chinese, and even other Spaniards took to the streets as darkness fell. Moved by covetousness, everybody hoped to take advantage of the disorder to snatch up some plunder. The differences between British, Spaniard, Filipino, Chinaman all melted away with the onset of dark as the situation descended into a tumult of indiscriminate looting.

Rojo retreated to the sacristy of the cathedral. "Bar the doors!" he told Father Martin, the head of the cathedral chapter.

"Yes, excellency!" said Father Martin. The clerics went to work quickly, barricading the massive cathedral portal. The British had promised churches would be spared, but Rojo did not want to take any chances with this anarchy.

Now alone in the sacristy, the archbishop opened an old wooden drawer. Inside was a pistol. He grasped the pistol, loaded it, and tucked it inside his robes. "Lord, forgive me!" he muttered.

The looting continued through the night. Archbishop Rojo led the cathedral canons in prayer before the Blessed Sacrament by candlelight. Outside was screaming, musket fire, and the sound of disorder. "Rescue me from sinking in the mire!" Rojo prayed from Psalm 68. "Let me be delivered from my enemies and from the deep waters. Let not the flood sweep over me, or the deep swallow me up, or the pit close its mouth over me."

The prayers were interrupted by a sudden crash. Rojo jumped. "That crash came from the chancel door!" said Father Martin. "Someone is trying to get into the church!"

Chapter 18: The British Interruption

Rojo jumped to his feet and dashed through the sacristy to the small side door that led out into the street. Indeed, there was a commotion going on the other side of the door—banging, shouting, and the cries of a woman. Rojo's heart was moved with a mixture of pity and rage. He unbarred the door and flung it open, prepared to confront the British and tell them enough was enough.

Upon opening the door, he beheld a pathetic sight: a soldier dragging a woman by the hair and shouting at her. The woman had apparently tried to flee into the cathedral and was being dragged off by the man. The sobbing woman saw Rojo and gave him a desperate, pleading look.

"Have you British no shame?" thundered Rojo at the attacker. "Unhand her this instant or I will report you to your commanding officer for discipline!" he cried out.

"*Vuelve adentro, Excelencia*," came the voice of the soldier. Rojo was startled. This was no Englishman. The archbishop squinted through the darkness to get a better look at the man. He did not wear the red of the British regulars. Rather, this man appeared to be a Spaniard of the Manila garrison!

"I said, go back inside, Excellency," the man told Rojo sternly, turning to glare at the archbishop. His dark, beady eyes were diabolical, possessing an almost demonic quality. A sneering grin crept across his face.

"A Spaniard! The treachery!" growled Rojo.

The man stepped towards the archbishop threateningly, still clutching the trembling woman by the hair, his other hand brandishing a large knife. "This is none of your business, Excellency," he said, now so close that Rojo could smell the man's foul, drunken breath.

Rojo clenched his teeth. Hot tears began to well up in his eyes. His whole body shook with outrage. Swiftly, almost instinctively, Rojo reached into his robes and drew the pistol. He pointed it at the Spaniard's face and pulled the trigger. Blood splattered upon the archbishop, staining his vestment and pectoral cross. The body collapsed at the foot of the woman. She shrieked at the sight of the man whose head had been obliterated by the pistol shot.

"Get out of here!" Rojo cried out, waving the woman away with the pistol. The horrified woman stumbled away into the darkness, sobbing.

Rojo was shaking, filled with so many emotions he could barely think. He turned his back on the crumpled corpse in the street to go back into the cathedral, the pistol still in hand. Father Martin and the canons were standing in the doorway in shocked silence, their mouths agape.

"Excellency! You...you..." Father Martin stammered.

Rojo processed somberly past them, then turning to his clerics said, "I trust any one of you would do the same to me had I been caught in such wickedness."

The looting lasted for almost two days. After the pillaging was over, an official of the East India Company named Dawsonne Drake assumed the title of Governor of Manila on behalf of Britain. He immediately began scouring the capital for gold but found little, as Anda had made off with the treasury. Angry at being deprived of his booty, Drake formed a council known as the Chottry Court. The purpose of the Chottry Court was to arrest Manilans on fabricated charges and extort money from them. Many Manilans were unjustly imprisoned and robbed by Drake through the Chottry Court during his administration.

Drake's financial fortunes soon improved, however, as the British navy captured two galleons along the Acapulco route—the *Filipina* and the *Trinidad*—carrying Chinese porcelain as well as silver from Mexico. The capture of the galleons was a windfall for Drake and the British, netting them around $4.5 million. Entrenched in the capital and now flush with cash, it seemed the British were not going away anytime soon.

Chapter 18: The British Interruption

But meanwhile the remnants of the Royal Audiencia had regrouped and charged Simón de Anda y Salazar with organizing efforts to drive out the British, appointing him Lieutenant-Governor. Anda established his base in the Pampanga province, north of Manila. Anda wrote a letter to Archbishop Rojo, informing him of his appointment and asking Rojo to hand over the royal seal. Rojo, however, refused to recognize Anda's appointment and would not give him the seal. In retaliation, Anda refused to recognize any of the agreements Rojo had signed with the British. He also refused any negotiations with the British until he was addressed by the title of Lieutenant-Governor. He went so far as to send back letters that did not greet him by the proper title.

Before long, Anda had raised an army of 10,000 native Filipinos. The makeshift army closed in on Manila, surrounding the British. The British attempted to drive Anda back in various skirmishes and battles. In one of these battles, the Sangleys defected and joined the British. Anda was furious. He executed 180 Sangleys for aiding the enemy. Other Chinese hanged themselves in fear rather than fall into Anda's hands. Despite the Sangley defection, Anda successfully established a perimeter around Manila. Drake and the British would be unable to extend their rule much beyond the city walls.

A British plot to get native Filipinos to revolt against the Spaniards also ended in failure. The British promised a Filipino revolutionary named Diego Silang military assistance if he would begin a rebellion against Spain in rural Luzon. Silang raised a rebellion, capturing some towns and attacking local Catholic priests in the region of Ilocos. The promised British help never arrived, however, and Silang was soon assassinated. After his death, Silang's wife Gabriela tried to continue the revolt. The Spanish captured and hanged her.

On February 10, 1763, the Seven Years War ended with the signing of the Treaty of Paris. But in those days, it could take months or even years for news to travel across the oceans between Europe and Asia. When the Treaty of Paris was signed, nobody in Europe knew that Manila had been taken by Britain—and the people in the Philippines did not hear that the war had ended until late in 1763. When the news of peace finally arrived, the British were unsure whether to return Manila to Spain. On the one hand, they had no direct orders to hand over the city. On the other hand, the rules of war accepted at the time generally held that lands taken without the knowledge of treaty signatories should be returned. Drake's council was bitterly divided on what to do and hence did nothing. Thus, Drake and the British remained entrenched in the city while 1763 drew to a close.

Things changed in January 1764 when Archbishop Rojo died. With Rojo dead, the rivalry between he and Anda was resolved. The British began addressing Anda as acting governor and negotiations opened between he and Drake for the withdraw of the British. These negotiations proved unnecessary, however, as orders from Britain finally arrived ordering Drake to return Manila to Spain.

Around the same time, the new Spanish governor Francisco de la Torre finally arrived. Anda handed over power to Torre, and the British handed over Manila to the Spaniards. They boarded their ships and left Manila Bay in April 1764. The Spanish were again in control after an interruption of twenty months.

The British rule was only an interruption and not a conquest. This was largely due to the ingenuity and energy of Simón de Anda y Salazar. His quick escape from Manila with the treasury deprived the British of much-needed resources and ensured the Spanish opposition would be well-funded. His spirited organization of the resistance prevented Drake from breaking out of Manila and extending British conquests throughout Luzon. His diplomatic efforts primed the British to hand over Manila even ahead of Britain's formal orders to do so. The Spanish crown also praised Anda's leadership during the crisis and retroactively approved all Anda's actions. He returned to Spain and was made a Councilor of Castille. Anda later returned to the Philippines and became Governor-General in 1770, a post he held until his death in 1776.

Chapter 18: The British Interruption

Dawsonne Drake did not fare so well. When he returned to India, he was criminally charged for extorting the people of Manila through the Chottry Court. He was found guilty and stripped of his rank.

Colonel William Draper, the officer who formulated the strategy for attacking Manila, went on to write the first rules for the game of cricket.

Though the British liked to boast in later years that they had proven their power in East Asia by seizing the Philippines, the truth was more modest. As Francisco Leandro Viana, who was in Manila during the British occupation, explained to the Spanish King Charles III a few years after, "The English conquest of the Philippines was just an imagined one, as the English never owned any land beyond the range of the cannons in Manila."

Chapter 19

THE WORLD MEETS THE PHILIPPINES

The Spanish had beaten back the British and restored Spain's government over the Philippines. Life returned to normal in the archipelago. But back in Europe, things were far from normal. Things were afoot that would drastically change European society. Between 1789 and 1848, a series of revolutionary movements shook the thrones of Europe, signaling the beginning of the democratic era. The coming of the Industrial Revolution during this era also revolutionized the economic life of Europe. Though centered in Europe, these political and economic movements would reach all the way to the Philippines—with tremendous consequences for the future of the region.

In 1789, the French Revolution began in France. Though he at first tried to compromise with the revolutionaries, King Louis XVI of France was eventually condemned to death by the revolution and executed in 1793. In the tumults following his death, the government of France changed hands many times, eventually coming under the power of General Napoleon Bonaparte. The armies of Napoleon fanned out across Europe, conquering most of the continent. Napoleon proclaimed himself Emperor of the French in 1804. All of Europe became embroiled in a massive struggle to free itself from the grasp of Bonaparte.

One of the countries that suffered under Napoleon was Spain. Spain had initially supported Napoleon in an alliance against Britain, but when the British destroyed the combined Spanish-French forces at the Battle of Trafalgar in 1805, the Spaniards began to weary of their alliance with France. The Spanish King, Charles IV, did not have the resources to stand up to Napoleon. Napoleon invaded Spain and forced Charles and his son to abdicate. Napoleon then placed his brother, Joseph, on the throne of Spain in 1808. The Kingdom of Spain became a puppet state of Napoleon.

From 1808 to 1813, the Spaniards waged a bitter war to eject the French from their kingdom. But while the Spanish were occupied at home, their colonies abroad suffered. In many colonies, discontent grew against Spanish rule. Spanish authorities were perceived as lazy, corrupt, and inefficient. There was also resentment against the hierarchy of the Catholic Church in many places, as the Church was viewed as supporting Spanish rule. With Spain distracted by Napoleon, the time was ripe for revolution in the colonies.

The year Spain fell to Bonaparte, Mexico rebelled against Spanish rule. The war in Mexico went back and forth for several years. Napoleon fell from power in 1815 and the son of Charles IV took the throne of Spain. But it was too late. Spain was in disarray and many other colonies had begun to rebel as well. Spain was forced to recognize Mexico's independence in 1821. Between 1808 and 1825, nine other colonies in Latin America were lost to Spain in various revolutions.

The loss of Mexico had a profound impact on the Philippines, as the Philippines had always been subject to the Viceroy of New Spain in Mexico City. With Mexico now independent, Spain had no

Chapter 19: The World Meets the Philippines

Early 19th century lithograph showing an idyllic Philippine scene along the Pasig River.

choice but to govern the Philippines directly. Direct rule began in 1821, the year Mexico was lost to Spain. For the remainder of Spain's sovereignty over the Philippines, the archipelago was administered by the crown authorities in Madrid. In many respects, direct rule was much better for the Philippines than being ruled from Mexico. The monarchs Fernando VII (1813–1833) and Isabella II (1833–1868) were attentive to the needs of the Philippines and sincerely tried to better the standard of living in the colony.

This new attentiveness to the Philippines was due in part to the Industrial Revolution. By 1821 Europe had entered the industrial age. Factories were cropping up everywhere, and new methods of production were transforming life all over Europe. Across Europe there was a tremendous demand for raw materials. The Industrial Revolution reached Spain in the 1830s, and Spain was thirsty for raw materials to feed its own industrial operations. Like other European states, Spain looked to its remaining colonies to provide these raw materials.

This was important for the Philippines. Until the 19th century, the Spanish had viewed the Philippines primarily as a large trading post. The value of the colony was simply as a stop-over point for Spanish galleons to use on their way between Asia and Mexico. But in the 19th century, Spain began to grasp the Philippines' productive value. The archipelago was full of natural resources virtually untapped by the Spaniards. The 19th century would see the development of native Filipino industries that greatly benefitted the quality of life.

This movement had begun a generation before direct rule under Governor-General José Basco y Vargas, who ruled the Philippines from 1778 to 1787. Basco was a naval officer who had conquered the Batanes Islands for Spain, for which he received the title 1st Count of the Conquest of Batanes Islands. But in his administration of the Philippines, the conquering count was very economically minded. Basco did not like that the Philippines were economically dependent on trade from China and Mexico. He wanted the Philippines to become more self-sufficient.

A lithograph showing a view of Manila in the early 19th century.

Chapter 19: The World Meets the Philippines

To this end, Basco created the *Sociedad Económica de los Amigos del País*, or the Economic Society of Friends of the Country. The Sociedad was a collection of professional organizations, akin to a federation of guilds. Their purpose was to stimulate the economic and intellectual development of industry in the Philippines. Basco's Sociedad was successful in this. The production of cotton, spices, sugarcane, and mining all increased under Basco. He also rewarded scientific reforms, hoping thereby to advance the technological skill of the Filipino economy.

The Sociedad's greatest achievement was the development a Philippine tobacco industry. Basco kept strict control over tobacco production. He used the Sociedad to create a monopoly that regulated how much tobacco was produced and then had the Philippine government purchase the entire crop. This scheme was extremely lucrative, making the colony economically self-sustaining for the first time. Within a few years the colony was even profitable.

Under direct rule, the Spanish authorities continued Basco's philosophy of internal improvements to make the colony profitable and improve the standard of living. A railway system was constructed in Luzon. Manila, which was turning into a sprawling metropolis, was equipped with a network of tramcars. Steel suspension bridges were constructed across ravines to facilitate the movement of people and goods.

The economy thrived. Textile manufacturing factories sprung up across Luzon. In other areas farmers cultivated the *abacá*, a species of banana harvested for the strong fiber of its leaf stems. Coconuts were processed for oil, and blue dyes were made from the indigo plant. All throughout the archipelago people were building things, growing things, and making things.

The economy was doing so well that the colonial government established a universal bank for the Philippines in 1851. Called the Banco Español-Filipino de Isabel II, the bank made loans available to Filipino businesses which helped the economy grow even more. But more importantly it was given the authority to print currency.

Early 19th century lithograph showing a typical street scene in Manila.

Beginning in 1851, the Philippines had its own currency, known as the Philippine *peso*.

The Banco Español-Filipino de Isabel II was named after Queen Isabella II of Spain. Queen Isabella cared very much about the Philippines and was zealous to improve the quality of life for all Filipinos, not just those of Spanish ancestry. In 1863 Queen Isabella decreed the establishment of a public school system throughout the Philippines. With the opening of the Suez Canal in Egypt a few years later in 1869, travel time to Spain was cut in half. This made it much cheaper to sail from the Philippines to Spain, and many Filipinos traveled to Europe to study at European universities. These highly educated Filipinos were known as *ilustrados*. Many ilustrados were instrumental in reforming the administration of the Philippines to make society more equitable. The Filipino population increased, growing over 25% between 1877 and 1887.

Other Filipinos traveled abroad to seek adventure in the military as mercenaries. Known as Manilamen, these Filipinos fought in China, Indochina, Mexico, Argentina, and France. Many of these

Chapter 19: The World Meets the Philippines

Manilamen fought in revolutionary movements in Latin America. The exposure of Filipinos to anti-Spaniard revolutionary movements abroad would have profound consequences, as we shall see in our next chapter.

All Filipinos benefitted from the reforms of the direct rule period. Whereas most European nations governed their colonies to benefit only the mother country, Spain sincerely tried to improve the situation for native Filipinos. Other countries were taking notice of the Philippine reforms. John Bowring, the British Governor General of Hong Kong, visited the Philippines in the 1850s. He wrote:

> "Credit is certainly due to Spain for having bettered the condition of [the Filipino] people…The inhabitants of these beautiful Islands, upon the whole, may well be considered to have lived as comfortably during the last hundred years, protected from all external enemies and governed by mild laws, as those from any other tropical country under native or European sway."

Frederick Henry Sawyer was a British civil engineer who worked in Manila as a young man. He later wrote a book about the people of the Philippines. Sawyer observed that, under Spanish direct rule—

> "…the Filipinos were as happy a community as could be found in any colony. The population greatly multiplied; they lived in competence, if not in affluence; cultivation was extended, and the exports steadily increased…Let us be just; what British, French, or Dutch colony, populated by natives can compare with the Philippines as they were until 1895?"

By the late 19th century, the Philippines was considered a model colony. Economically profitable, the archipelago was well on its way to modernization under the stable administration of the Spanish crown. But things were about to change drastically for the Philippines.

Chapter 20

THE PHILIPPINE REVOLUTION

"Grappling hooks!" shouted Spanish Colonel Cayetano Figuera. His soldiers were ready. Upon the colonel's command, they hurled their grappling hooks at the lofty walls of Fort Balanguigui. The hooks lodged themselves into the top of the fort's wooden palisade. The Moro pirates defending Balanguigui desperately attempted to dislodge the grappling hooks, but Colonel Figuera's riflemen peppered the Moros with gunfire, keeping them at bay.

Within moments the Spanish soldiers were scaling the wall, pulling themselves up on the ropes attached to the hooks. "Excellent work, Colonel," said a pale, mustachioed man who slapped Figuera on the back. This was Narciso Clavería y Zaldúa, the Governor-General of the Philippines. "Once we take Fort Balanguigui, the Moro pirates will no longer have a base in Sulu from which to attack our ships!"

"Gracias Señor," said the Colonel saluting. "Our boys will make short work of these pirates once we scale the walls. Then the raids of the Moros will end, and Mindanao will be pacified."

The Moros were not going to go quietly. They threw rocks, spears, and knives at the Spaniards attempting to scale the walls of the fort. Some men were struck and fell. Those who reached the top faced stiff resistance—hand-to-hand combat with sabers and bayonets atop the battlements as the Moros fought wildly to prevent the loss of the fort.

The Spanish force was too much, however. Soon Figuera's men were inside the fort and had unbarred the gates. "Storm the fortress, men!" cried Figuera, sword aloft leading the men. The Moros fired a few volleys before withdrawing—Figuera himself was struck in the leg and collapsed. But the fort was taken. The remaining Moro defenders were either killed, surrendered, or attempted to hide by swimming into the marshes that surrounded Balanguigui.

Governor-General Clavería walked into the fort to the cheers of his men, a look of pride on his gaunt face. He saw Figuera nursing his wounded leg on the ground. "Take heart Colonel, the day is ours."

"*Deo gratias*," replied Figuera stoically, making the sign of the cross.

These events occurred at the 1848 siege of Balanguigui, a Moro held island in the Sulu Sea off the coast of Mindanao. Ever since the Spanish conquest, Muslim-held Mindanao had been a thorn in the side of the Spaniards. Spanish authority here had always been tenuous, and the Moro chieftains constantly challenged Spanish power—sometimes in open insurrection, sometimes by piracy against Spanish shipping. But by the 1840s the Spanish authorities felt sufficiently empowered to stamp out the nuisance of the Moro pirates. Governor-General Clavería determined to make an end of

Chapter 20: The Philippine Revolution

them by capturing their island stronghold of Balanguigui. His 1848 victory saw the capture of three forts and the freeing of hundreds of slaves held by the Moros. This triumph greatly reduced Moro attacks in the area. For his victory Clavería was awarded the title Count of Manila.

Despite this victory, the power of the Spaniards in the late 19th century was only illusory. The truth was that the Spanish empire was in trouble. A liberal revolution in 1854 left Queen Isabella II considerably weakened. She was overthrown entirely by a military coup in 1868 and forced to go into exile. Spain continued to suffer political turmoil through the 1870s. The conflicts within Spain left the Spanish government distracted from affairs abroad, its resources increasingly exhausted by its own civil conflicts, and its colonies ignored and under-garrisoned.

This was unfortunate for Spain, as trouble was brewing in the Philippines. The reforms Queen Isabella had helped the colony significantly, but not all Filipinos were grateful. Among the educated ilustrados, there was a growing sense of indignation against Spanish rule. Though native Filipinos had a higher standard of living than ever before, the most important offices in the government were still reserved to Spaniards, usually peninsulares (Spaniards born in Europe). Promotion to such offices was often given based on ancestry and loyalty alone. As a result, the Philippine colonial government was plagued by cronyism, graft, and incompetence.

Dissatisfaction against the Church hierarchy was brewing as well, as the Church supported the colonial authorities and were viewed by some as complicit in the subjugation of the Filipino people. As in the secular government, important offices in the Church were generally reserved to peninsulares. The missionary friars were especially resented, as the religious orders were zealous supporters of the colonial order. The irony is that some of the fiercest critics of the Philippine hierarchy were themselves members of the clergy—usually parish priests, many of them native born Filipinos who resented the ethnic Spanish domination of the hierarchy.

Nationalist associations began forming in the Philippines throughout the 1870s. Philippine nationalists wanted a more prominent role for native Filipinos in the colonial government. The nationalists were deeply influenced by liberal ideals picked up from Europe. Many were anti-clericalists, socialists, Freemasons, or were affiliated with other ideologies hostile to monarchy, colonialism, and the Catholic Church. They published magazines, wrote essays, and gave speeches promoting Filipino language and culture. These nationalist movements were peaceful at first, but they gradually turned many Filipinos against Spanish rule.

Native Filipino soldiers frequently sympathized with the nationalists. As we discussed in our last chapter, many of them had served abroad and picked up liberal revolutionary ideals from Latin America, France, and elsewhere. Nationalism was rife in the lower ranks of the military. In 1872 a mutiny broke out at the fortress of San Felipe in Cavite, Luzon. The mutineers killed some Spanish officers in hopes that the locals would rise and join them. This did not happen, however, and the rebellion was put down.

The Spanish authorities pinned the blame for the Cavite mutiny on three priests, Fathers Mariano Gomez, José Burgos, and Jacinto Zamora. The evidence upon which the priests were charged was wildly insufficient, but the Spanish were anxious to punish someone for the mutiny. The three men were condemned for sedition and executed by strangling.

The deaths of these three men inspired the formation of the Propaganda Movement. The Propaganda Movement was made up of Filipino intellectuals who wrote books and pamphlets in support of political reform. Some of the reforms they desired were the legal equality of Spaniards and Filipinos, guarantees of basic rights, a more important role for diocesan clergy in the Filipino Church, and opening government service to Filipinos.

One of the most important writers of the Propaganda Movement was José Rizal. Rizal was an eye doctor turned novelist who wrote two books, *Noli Me Tangere* (1887) and *El Filibusterismo* (1891). *Noli*

Chapter 20: The Philippine Revolution

Me Tangere was a novel that portrayed the Catholic friars as brutal oppressors. *El Filibusterismo* was a dark novel about situations when it is necessary to use violence to achieve change. The books were extremely popular in the Philippines. Dr. Rizal was not living in the Philippines when the books were published. Like most of the authors of the Propaganda Movement, Dr. Rizal lived and wrote from Europe to avoid being punished by the Spaniards. His books were banned in the Philippines. The Spaniards feared them because they encouraged Filipinos to think about total independence from Spain.

In 1892, however, Dr. Rizal returned to the Philippines and founded an organization called *La Liga Filipina*, dedicated to the reform. Dr. Rizal hoped that La Liga Filipina would unite all the Filipino nationalists under a single organization to work for change more effectively. The Spanish authorities promptly banned La Liga Filipina, however. Dr. Rizal was arrested and exiled to Dapitan in Cebu. This angered the nationalists. Many began saying that the time for violent struggle was at hand.

A secret society was formed called the *Katipunan*. Led by the merchant Andrés Bonifacio, the Katipunan advocated the violent overthrow of Spanish power. The organization of the Katipunan was modeled on Freemasonry, complete with rites, degrees of membership, and arcane ceremonial. As the Katipunan began to grow, Bonifacio reached out to Dr. Rizal in exile. Rizal was a celebrity among Filipino nationalists. Bonifacio wanted Rizal to support the Katipunan. If Rizal would lend his support to the movement, the Katipunan could wield tremendous influence. Dr. Rizal, however, refused to participate. Frustrated but not deterred, Bonifacio and the Katipunan continued plotting the overthrow of the Spaniards without Rizal's support.

In 1896 the Spanish discovered the existence of the Katipunan. According to popular legend, the Katipunan was discovered when a priest broke the seal of confession and went to the authorities after a member of the secret society confessed his involvement.

Some historians dispute this version of events. Be that as it may, the authorities learned of the Katipunan and began a crackdown on the organization. In response, the Katipunan organized a protest called the 'Cry of Pugad Lawin'. Revolutionaries publicly tore up *cedulas* (residence certificates and identity papers) as symbol of defiance. Violent uprisings broke out in Manila and throughout central Luzon. The armed revolution had begun.

Governor-General Ramón Blanco y Erena was first inclined to seek peace with the Katipunan, but as violence spread across the country, Blanco was replaced with the Camilo García de Polavieja y del Castillo-Negrete. Polavieja was took a more hardline approach to the rebellion. Though Dr. Rizal had sought to distance himself from the revolution, Polaveija ordered him executed anyway. Dr. José Rizal was executed publicly by firing squad on December 30, 1896.

At this critical moment, the Katipunan split into two warring factions in a contest for leadership of the movement. Some favored Bonifacio, others his relative Emilio Aguinaldo. The two factions began killing each other's leaders in a desperate struggle for control. Bonifacio and Aguinaldo formed rival councils, each claiming to represent the revolution. Each condemned the other. Bonifacio was eventually arrested by supporters of Aguinaldo. Aguinaldo made Bonifacio appear before a hastily convened "War Council." The Council condemned Bonifacio of treason and executed him. After a brief sojourn in Hong Kong while tensions cooled, Aguinaldo became sole leader of the revolution.

Meanwhile Spain was unable to mount an effective resistance to the revolution. At the time the fighting started, Spain had a meager 500 soldiers in the entire colony. In the past larger military campaigns were waged using native Filipino conscripts, but many of these had gone over to the revolution. More soldiers arrived from Spain throughout 1897, but they were not used effectively. To make matters worse, Governor-General Polaveija was forced to resign due to bad health. Spain would cycle through three more Governor-

CHAPTER 20: THE PHILIPPINE REVOLUTION

Generals by 1898. Spain seemed to have no clear plan to counter the momentum of what they called the "Tagalog Revolt," since most of the fighting took place in Luzon in the Tagalog speaking regions.

By the end of 1897, the rebellion had overrun the countryside of Luzon. Eight provinces were in open revolt: Manila, Cavite, Bulacan, Pampanga, Tarlac, Batangas, Laguna and Nueva Ecija. The momentum seemed to be with the Aguinaldo and the revolutionaries.

Even so, the Spaniards still possessed the city of Manila and were strongly fortified within the Intramuros. The rebels had considerable numbers and control of the countryside, but they were poorly equipped. Intramuros was heavily defended, and as it provided the Spaniards with access to the sea, they could resupply indefinitely if needed.

Seeing no way to resolve the conflict, Aguinaldo and the Spaniards, now under new Governor-General Fernando Primo de Rivera, agreed to a truce. The result was called the Pact of Biak-na-Bato, signed December 15, 1897. The Pact of Biak-na-Bato preserved Spanish rule but agreed to the creation of a new administrative system for the colony under Filipino self-rule. The revolutionary leaders agreed to lay down their arms and go into exile in exchange for a handsome cash payout from the Spanish authorities and compensation for the families of Filipinos killed in the fighting. Governor-General Rivera hoped this settlement would buy off Aguinaldo. Aguinaldo, however, planned to use the money to buy more weaponry abroad, then return to attack Intramuros later.

Thus the fighting ended, Aguinaldo and his associates went to exile in Hong Kong, and Rivera breathed a sigh of relief. There were some skirmishes here and there, but peace returned to most of Luzon. Spanish authority had been preserved. Rivera left office in April and was replaced by Basilio Augustín.

It was at this moment that an explosion in the Americas changed everything for the Philippines.

Chapter 21

AMERICA VERSUS SPAIN

While Rivera and Aguinaldo were negotiating the Pact of Biak-na-Bato to end the Filipino insurrection, events were unfolding on the other side of the world that would bring the long rule of Spain in the Philippines to an end.

By 1898, most of Spain's overseas empire had been lost. Between 1810 and 1825 the entirety of Spain's holdings in Latin America broke away in a flurry of liberal revolutions. Its largest remaining colony in the western hemisphere was the island of Cuba—the biggest island in the Caribbean just off the coast of the United States. Cuba and the Philippines were Spain's two most important remaining colonies.

At that time, the United States was in the grip of a political philosophy known as *imperialism*. In general, imperialism refers to the aspirations of a country to extend its economic and political power beyond its own borders. In the United States, imperialism was the belief that America should extend its powers beyond the North American continent—specifically, into the Pacific and the Caribbean. For the whole 19th century, the United States had steadily expanded westward until it controlled the center of the continent "from sea to shining sea." Imperialists did not see why U.S. expansion should stop at the oceans. Was not the Caribbean dotted with numberless islands, all ripe for the plucking? And across the vast Pacific were there not more distant lands awaiting American masters to exploit their resources and add them to the American empire? Imperialists believed the natural growth of the United States would propel its interests west and south.

For a long time, American imperialists had set their sights on the Spanish colony of Cuba. Only 90 miles south of Florida, it would be strategically easy to invade. The Spanish Empire was weak and unable to hold the island. Furthermore, Cuba's warm climate made it ideal for growing sugar, bananas, molasses, and other tropical crops. American growers could make a fortune on the island if it were secured for the United States.

The imperialists got their chance in 1895 when the people of Cuba began a war of independence against Spain. The United States watched the revolution unfold with great interest, as there were already many Americans living and working in Cuba. President William McKinley sent the U.S. navy to Cuba to observe and make sure American lives and property were being protected. The battleship *USS Maine* was stationed in Havana harbor with 354 sailors aboard keeping a watchful eye on the situation.

On February 15, 1898, the *Maine* suddenly exploded in Havana harbor, killing 266 sailors. The American press, rabid with anti-Spanish hysteria and fevered with imperialist ambition, immediately blamed Spain for the disaster. A hasty inquiry concluded a Spanish mine was to blame for the tragedy. Spain vehemently denied any responsibility, but it mattered very little. America was eager to go war. "To hell with Spain! Remember the *Maine!*" was the slogan printed on millions of U.S. newspapers. President McKinley asked

Chapter 21: America Versus Spain

for a declaration of war against Spain, which Congress granted on April 25.

It is beyond the scope of this chapter to give a detailed narrative of the American military operations of the Spanish-American War of 1898. Needless to say, Cuba was invaded and captured from Spain. But the U.S. also looked to Spain's Pacific colonies. Americans on the west coast worried about a Spanish attack from the Pacific. Seven ships, the so-called Asiatic Squadron under Commodore George Dewey, were dispatched to the Pacific to pre-emptively attack the Philippines before the Spaniards could move their fleet from Manila.

Once in East Asia, Dewey became acquainted with Emilio Aguinaldo and the revolutionaries who were then in exile in Hong Kong. Dewey surmised that Aguinaldo might be helpful in sweeping away remaining Spanish forces on the mainland. Before this could happen, Dewey needed to clear the Spanish navy from Manila Bay and deprive the Spaniards of access to the sea. On April 30, 1898, the U.S. Asiatic Squadron approached Manila Bay. The Spanish fleet, under the command of Admiral Patricio Montojo, was at a serious disadvantage: its vessels were obsolete and undermanned by inexperienced sailors. Munitions were scarce. To make matters worse, Montojo positioned the fleet out of the range of the coastal artillery, thus depriving himself of land support. This may have been a strategic blunder, but military historians say Montojo knew the battle was hopeless and moved his ships away from the coast to spare Manila a bombardment from Dewey's ships.

Montojo expected Dewey's attack to come at first light, as Dewey was unacquainted with Manila Bay and navigating it at night could be treacherous. Dewey, however, had been given detailed intelligence on the bay and felt confident in a night assault. In the early morning hours of May 1, Dewey moved in and began his attack. Here is what happened next—

The Story of the Philippines

Purple rays of sun began to peek over the hillsides behind Manila, signaling the coming of day. A light mist rolled down from the hills and blew wispily over the still water of Manila Bay. It was just past four in the morning. The *USS Olympia*, the flag ship of the American Asiatic Squadron, was gliding over the still waters into range of the Spanish fleet.

Despite the early hour, the sailors of the *Olympia* did not slumber. They were all wide awake at their stations, preparing for the inevitable engagement with the Spanish fleet. The Spaniards had spread their fleet out across the bay, blocking the mouth of the Pasig River which gave access to Manila. Dewey had moved the *Olympia* in just out of range of the Spanish guns. The *Olympia* moved smoothly, almost gently, across the dark morning waters as it waited for the other ships of the squadron to get into position.

At the guns was a seaman named John Tisdale. Seaman Tisdale was a gun-pointer on one of the *Olympia*'s four 8-inch 35 caliber guns. As a gun-pointer, his job was to keep the *Olympia*'s gun fixed on its target—and fire it when the time came. Tisdale sipped coffee from a tin cup while scanning the bay. His target was the *Reina Cristina*, the flagship of the Spanish fleet. Though he stood calmly sipping his coffee, his heart beat so hard it felt like it would leap from his chest. Waiting for the start of an impending battle was nerve-wracking.

Time passed. The bells tolled five. Word came that the attack was to begin soon. "Don't fire until you hear the bugle sound," Tisdale was told. Tisdale nodded, sipped his coffee again and continued his watchful gaze over the bay and the *Reina Cristina*. By now the sun had emerged, bathing the water in a hue of gold.

BOOM! Went a gun from the walls of the Spanish fortress on the land. An eleven inch shell came roaring like a freight train and sailed over the heads of Tisdale and the crew, missing the *Olympia* by about ten feet.

"Should I fire!? Did the attack start!?" called Tisdale.

"That was just a range finder," a petty officer called. "They're

Chapter 21: America Versus Spain

A contemporary American lithograph showing the action at the Battle of Manila Bay. John Tisdale's ship, *USS Olympia*, leads the American line.

testing their range. Hold your fire until the bugle sounds," he repeated.

"Aye, aye," said Tisdale. He gulped nervously thinking of what would have become of him had the shell been ten feet lower.

Tisdale kept his hand on the spark that would ignite his gun and unleash a torrent of death upon the Spaniards. Shots began firing from the city and the fleet. Explosions could be heard all around. Some shells fell too short and landed harmlessly in the water, while others sailed overhead.

"Hold your fire," came the order again. Tisdale writhed in place. How hard it was to simply sit still and allow oneself to be shot at and not return fire! Everywhere shells were firing. Mines—explosives submerged beneath the waters of the bay—began exploding as the Asiatic squadron moved closer.

"Twenty-three hundred yards," cried the Bos'n. "Hold your fire." The *Olympia* glided effortlessly towards the Spaniards, almost as if she were on parade, shells exploding all around her. Tisdale sat on the gun-seat, his thumb growing numb upon the spark from pressure. Other U.S. ships had begun returning fire. Tisdale could see the Spanish battle flag obliterated on one of the enemy's batteries. A cheer went up from the *Olympia*.

"Twenty-two hundred yards. Hold your fire."

Tisdale kept his eyes fixed upon the *Reina Cristina*. "Any moment now," he said to himself. "Any moment."

"Twenty-one hundred yards." All of the sudden, the bugles sounded. "FIRE!" came shouts up and down the line. Tisdale held his breath, almost choking with nervousness, and depressed his thumb upon the bulb, igniting the spark that would send the 35-caliber roaring. The entire ship quaked as the guns exploded, launching their broadside into the Spanish fleet. The eruption left the *Olympia* swathed in a cloud of white smoke that enveloped the ship like a fog.

Tisdale collapsed in his seat. Meanwhile the great gun slid back on its trunnions into the gun battery. Tisdale listened to the turning of the crank as other seamen opened the breech-block to reload. "Did we hit anything?" some of Tisdale's companions called out.

"Can't see a thing in this smoke," said Tisdale, squinting to make out any shapes through the white mist.

It did not take long, however. A gentle breeze fanned away the veil of smoke, allowing Tisdale and the others to get a view of the damage. The mainmast of the *Reina Christina* was split and tilted, and foremast toppled over entirely. Tisdale and the U.S. seamen shouted with joy at the sight of the damaged ship.

But they had little time for celebration, for the guns of the *Reina Cristina* began pouring a stream of gunfire towards the *Olympia*. Fortunately, the *Reina Cristina* overshot. Tisdale looked through the sight, training the hair-cross on the *Reina Cristina* again.

"FIRE!" came the command. The gun exploded, again enveloping the *Olympia* in a bank of white fog.

Chapter 21: America Versus Spain

And so things went for much of the day. After the *Reina Cristina* was disabled, Dewey led the squadron in a line past the Spanish fleet, raining carnage upon them until they were utterly destroyed. It was a resounding victory for the United States. As for John Tisdale, he went on to write a book about his experiences in the Asiatic Squadron called *Three Years Behind the Guns*. Years later, Dewey—now a celebrated admiral—would read Tisdale's book and say, "The description of the Battle of Manila Bay is one of the best I have ever seen published!"

After the victory at Manila Bay, Dewey contacted Emilio Aguinaldo in Hong Kong. He offered to transport Aguinaldo and his men back to the Philippines so they could continue the revolution. Aguinaldo enthusiastically agreed. He was picked up in Hong Kong by the *USS McCulloch* and dropped off in Cavite on May 16. Aguinaldo quickly marshalled his supporters and prepared to continue the revolution. The truce of Biak-na-Bato was over.

Aguinaldo began a fierce offensive against the Spaniards in Cavite province, south of Manila. Already reeling from the defeat at Manila, the Spaniards had little enthusiasm for battle. On May 28, the revolutionaries under Aguinaldo drove the last Spanish troops from Cavite. On June 12 Aguinaldo read the Philippine Declaration of Independence from his home in Cavite. A Filipino republic was proclaimed, and an interim government established with Aguinaldo as president. All of Luzon was now under revolutionary control save Manila itself.

Governor-General Augustín was in a desperate position. He vainly hoped Spain might send reinforcements and in the meantime tried to buy off Aguinaldo with another bribe, but Aguinaldo refused. When Spain found out he had tried to negotiate a payoff for Aguinaldo, the Spanish government removed him and replaced him with another official, Fermín Jáudenes.

Jáudenes was wise enough to know his position was impossible, but he also knew that simply giving up was not an option. Fearing the wrath of the Filipino revolutionaries if they took Manila, Jáudenes opened secret negotiations with Dewey. Dewey and Jáudenes came up with a plan to deliver Manila to the Americans after a staged mock "battle" that allow Jáudenes to save face by making a show of resistance. After this, the city would be surrendered to the Americans and Aguinaldo would be kept out of Intramuros. The details of the "battle" were worked out in advance to prevent Spanish casualties.

On August 13th Dewey's ships began bombarding an abandoned fort on the southern outskirts of Manila and lobbed a few rounds at the impenetrable walls of Intramuros. American ground troops advanced on the city while Spanish troops withdrew. Shortly thereafter a white flag of surrender was hoisted on the walls of Intramuros, just as planned. The Americans met with Governor-General Jáudenes and received the surrender of the city.

Where were the Filipino revolutionaries at that time? Aguinaldo and the revolutionaries had joined with the Americans to offer support for the attack. As the Americans and Spanish were intentionally plotting to keep the city from falling to Aguinaldo, the Filipinos were not informed that the attack was a mock battle.

During the assault, the Filipino revolutionaries were kept in the rear, away from Intramuros. When word came of the city's surrender, Aguinaldo and his men were overjoyed. They processed joyously to Manila to rejoice with the Americans. To their dismay, however, they found the gates of Intramuros sealed against them. Celebration turned to disbelief as it dawned on the Filipinos that the Americans did not intend to hand Manila over to them. In allying with the United States against Spain, they had merely swapped one colonial master for another.

Chapter 22

THE PHILIPPINE-AMERICAN WAR

The Filipino revolutionaries had been extraordinarily lucky in their war of independence from Spain. The war was relatively quick, Filipino casualties were few, the fighting was geographically restricted to Luzon, and the Spaniards had little energy or resources to put up much resistance. The arrival of Dewey and the destruction of the Spanish fleet seemed miraculously providential.

How quickly the elation of the revolutionaries would change to dejection! How their luck turned to misfortune! No sooner had they thrown off their old colonial master than a new one stepped in to take its place. The swift war against Spain would be followed by a three-year war against the United States that would inflict many more casualties than the original revolution. In Mindanao, the war against America would drag on until 1913. In this chapter we will follow the fortunes of the new Philippine republic as it struggled against the imperialist ambitions of the United States.

Before the struggle with Spain had officially ended, the Filipino revolutionaries had convened a congress called the Tejeros Convention and elected Emilio Aguinaldo president of the new Philippine Republic (1897). Later, when Aguinaldo was in negotiations with the Americans to bring him back from Hong Kong, Commodore Dewey assured Aguinaldo that after the war the United States government would recognize the independence of the Philippines. It was with this assurance that Aguinaldo returned to the Philippines in 1898 to continue the revolution, and that he proclaimed the Philippine Declaration of Independence that summer.

But after the American capture of Manila in the "mock battle," the Americans locked the Filipino insurgents out of Intramuros and negotiated the surrender of the Philippines with Spain directly without any involvement from Aguinaldo or the representatives of the new Philippine republic. It became clear that the Americans were there to stay. The Filipinos were furious, but as nothing official had been decided yet, Aguinaldo decided to bide his time. The revolutionaries devoted the latter part of 1898 to working out a constitution for the new government, the so-called Malolos Constitution.

But on December 10, the revolution's worst fears were realized when the U.S. and Spain ratified the Treaty of Paris, officially ending the Spanish-American War. While Cuba gained its independence, the former Spanish territories of Guam, Puerto Rico, and the Philippines were all ceded to the United States. The take-over of the Philippines was bitterly opposed by many in the U.S. Senate, who opposed U.S. imperialist ambitions. Before the treaty could take effect, it had to be ratified by Congress. President William McKinley framed the Treaty of Paris as a mission to bring democracy and civilization to the Philippines, a policy of "benevolent assimilation, substituting the mild sway of justice and right for arbitrary rule for the greatest good of the governed." Still, the treaty negotiations were fraught with controversy. Congress ratified it by a single vote on February 9, 1899. The United States assumed formal control over the

Chapter 22: The Philippine-American War

Philippines, paying the Spaniards a compensation of $20 million.

Meanwhile, the Aguinaldo government had ratified the constitution of the first Philippine Republic. This was the Malolos Constitution, named after the town of Malolos in Luzon where the work of drafting the document was completed. The constitution was prepared by a committee, but its most important segments were the work of two men: Felipe Calderón y Roca and Felipe Buencamino. Calderón and Buencamino consulted many other constitutions in the preparation process, including those of Belgium, Mexico, Brazil, Nicaragua, Costa Rica, and Guatemala. The French Constitution of 1793 was also considered, demonstrating the liberal-revolutionary sympathies of the committee.

The Malolos Constitution created a representative government with separation of powers, a unicameral legislature (one house, as opposed to two, like the United States Congress), and a president wielding chief executive authority. Certain civil rights were enshrined in law.

The Malolos Constitution was an important step towards Philippine self-government, but the document was stillborn. The Treaty of Paris had granted the Philippines to the United States. No international authority recognized the Malolos Constitution nor the government of Aguinaldo. Even as the committee of Calderón and Buencamino were putting their finishing touches on the document,

Emilio Aguinaldo

the Filipino revolutionaries were preparing for a new insurgency against the United States.

By February 1899 the U.S. and the Filipino revolutionary militias were on edge. Around 19,000 American soldiers were stationed in the vicinity of Manila to keep the Filipinos from capturing it. Commanded by General Elwell Stephen Otis, their orders were to keep the Filipino militias away from American lines. At the time, an estimated 20,000 Filipinos surrounded Manila. All that was necessary to set both sides fighting was a single incident. That incident happened on the evening of February 4, 1899 on Santol Street just within the boundary of Manila.

It was evening in Manila. The sun was sinking behind the city skyline, casting long shadows on the dusty streets. U.S. army Privates William Grayson and Orville Miller walked cautiously up Santol Street. Both men held their 30 caliber Krag rifles at ready. The situation was tense.

"I sure hope the Flips don't come back", said Private Miller. *Flip* was an American slur that was short for Filipino.

"Me too," said Grayson. "They were here earlier today protesting again and Colonel Stotsenburg ran them off. Pushed em' back across the San Juan Bridge."

"Well I hope they stay there, for their own good!" said Miller. "Lieutenant Wheedon's orders are to halt anyone who tries crossing the bridge. If they won't stop, arrest them—"

"And if we can't arrest them, shoot them," said Grayson grimly, finishing Miller's sentence.

The two men continued their patrol. Santol Street was deserted, save for a few stray dogs wandering here and there. Grayson and Miller approached the San Juan Bridge. As they did, they could see a group of four men approaching across the bridge. They wore the distinctive *baliwag* hat with the silver "sun face" cockade that identified them as revolutionary soldiers. The men bore rifles in their hands and the long, deadly bolo knife at their sides.

Chapter 22: The Philippine-American War

"Aw, hell," said Grayson, raising his Krag. "Here come the Flips!"

"Hold off," said Miller, "let's see what they want. They don't look like they're here for a fight." Indeed, it was hard to tell what the men wanted. Their rifles were not raised, and they came walking up casually with no defensive posturing. Armed Filipinos had been prodding about the city outskirts all day, mulling around the checkpoints, talking to American soldiers, and protesting the U.S. presence in the city. So far none of it had been violent.

The men made eye contact with Grayson and Miller. One of them raised his hand and started saying something in Tagalog. Neither Grayson nor Miller could make anything of it. Miller held up his hands, signaling the Filipinos to stop walking, but they continued to advance.

"Whatever they want, orders is orders!" said Grayson. "We are supposed to keep them from advancing up Santol Street and they don't look like they have any intention of stopping!" The Filipino men started talking excitedly, all of them speaking at once.

"Halt!" cried Miller. "Stop!"

BANG! BANG! BANG! The sudden crack of a rifle rent the air. Miller turned and saw Grayson firing at the men. "They were cocking their rifles, Miller!" shouted Grayson. "They mean to attack us!" The Filipino men were scrambling, some turning to flee, some raising their rifles. Miller aimed his Krag and fired a few rounds. With Miller and Grayson both firing, the men darted off back across the bridge.

"Did you hit anyone?" said Miller.

"I don't know!" said Grayson, panting with excitement. "Did you hear them cocking their rifles?"

"I…don't know what I heard," said Miller. "I was just trying to get them to stop, and then the next thing I hear is your Krag going off."

"Well, I'm sure I heard them cocking their rifles," said Grayson. "I mean, I *think* I'm sure."

The exact details of what happened on the evening of February 4, 1899 remain uncertain. Nobody knows the intention of the Filipino men, whether they really were cocking their guns, or whether any of them were hit in the gunfire. It is even debated where the encounter took place. Traditionally it was said to have happened at the San Juan Bridge, but other historians say it happened past the bridge, a few blocks into town. What is certain, however, is that the skirmish ignited the fuse that set the American and Filipino forces against each other.

At the time of the shooting, Aguinaldo was in Malolos working on the constitution. He sent a message to General Otis saying that the skirmish was unintentional and tried to calm things down. Otis, however, responded saying, "Fighting, having begun, must go on to the grim end." Hearing this, Aguinaldo told the Filipinos to consider themselves at war with the United States.

The hostilities outside Manila took the Filipinos by surprise. The Americans launched a full-scale assault on the Filipino lines from the south. The Filipinos under Brigadier General Pio del Pilar fled in disarray. They were forced into the Pasig River, where many of them drowned trying to escape. The fighting continued to the next day. By the end, some 4,000 Filipinos were dead, while the Americans counted only 44 killed in the battle. This was the first conflict of the Philippine-American War.

The week after the Battle of Manila, the American navy bombarded the Visayan city of Iloilo. The city was leveled and then occupied by American forces without the loss of a single American life. Over the spring and summer, American forces swept north from Manila, pushing back the Filipino army as they went. By August, organized Filipino resistance had collapsed in Luzon.

But the Filipinos were not finished. By fall of 1899 they adopted guerilla warfare tactics. Instead of fighting as organized military units under a conventional command structure, they chose to strike the Americans in small, hit-and-run attacks from the wilderness. The Filipinos knew they could not vanquish the U.S. army in the field—rather, they hoped to inflict constant losses over time. These attacks were meant to wear down American morale while preventing the U.S. forces from striking back. By the time American soldiers organized a counterattack, the Filipino insurgents had already fled.

In response, General Otis pursued a harsh policy of suppression. In areas where the Americans faced stiff resistance, civilian Filipinos would be rounded up and confined in internment camps. The conditions in these camps were unsanitary, and many Filipinos died of dysentery. Villages suspected of collaborating with insurgent Filipinos were burned. The American soldiers often made little distinction between civilians and insurgents, shooting any Filipinos they saw on sight. Many around the world became concerned about American treatment of Filipinos. An investigation by the Red Cross determined that Americans were essentially killing Filipinos indiscriminately.

William McKinley's reelection as U.S. president in 1900 demoralized the Filipinos and convinced them the U.S. would not leave quickly. In 1900, the U.S. replaced General Otis with General Arthur MacArthur, Jr. MacArthur had to deal with the problem of Filipino guerilla attacks. Despite Otis's harsh policy of internment, guerilla attacks had continued. Some of these attacks inflicted serious casualties on the Americans, such as the Battle of Paye in December 1899 when a Filipino ambush resulted in the death of General Henry Ware Lawton, the highest ranking American killed in the war.

MacArthur's solution was to place the Philippines under *martial law*. Martial law means ordinary law is suspended and the military rules directly. Filipinos caught fighting for the insurgents out of uniform could be executed, as well as those working to collect taxes or supplies for the Philippine Republic. Those advocating Filipino independence were deported to Guam, another island ruled by the U.S.

During this time, Aguinaldo had been on the run. The conventional forces of the Filipino army had suffered a string of devastating defeats. Though Aguinaldo had continued his attempts to rally Filipino resistance, the American counterinsurgency was slowly depriving him of support. He was forced to change his base of operations many times and by 1901, he was essentially a refugee working to stay one step ahead of U.S. forces. Aguinaldo was finally captured by U.S. forces in March of 1901. He was taken to the Malacañang Palace in Manila—the old residence of the Spanish Governors-General—and there forced to swear an oath accepting the authority of the United States over the Philippines. On April 19, Aguinaldo issued a proclamation of surrender, directing his followers to lay down their weapons and give up the fight.

To the surprise of MacArthur, Aguinaldo's concession did not end the war. The struggle was merely taken up by another, General Miguel Malvar, who launched an offensive against American held positions in Batangas, a region in southern Luzon. The Americans pursued Malvar relentlessly, however, and thousands of Malvar's men deserted him and surrendered. Malvar himself was captured on April 16, 1902, effectively bringing an end to the Philippine-American War.

In July 1902, the United States Congress promulgated the Philippine Organic Act. The Organic Act laid down the structure by which the Philippines would be governed under U.S. rule. It established two legislative houses—a lower house called the Philippine Assembly that was popularly elected, and an upper house called the Philippine Commission, a body of five American officials appointed by the U.S. president. The chairman of the Philippine Commission was known as the Civil Governor, who was the executive head of the Philippine government. The first Civil Governor was William Taft, the future President of the United States, who served as governor from 1901 to 1904.

The Organic Act also extended the U.S. Bill of Rights to Filipinos and abolished the military governor. The new president, Theodore Roosevelt, issued a general amnesty to all who had fought in the conflict on July 4, 1902.

Chapter 22: The Philippine-American War

What of Emilio Aguinaldo? After the war he founded an organization called the Association of Veterans of the Revolution to secure pensions and land grants for Filipino veterans. He would retire from public life for the remainder of American rule. Many years later, after Filipino independence, he would be honored as one of the founding fathers of the Philippine republic.

American rule in the Philippines would last for 48 years. In our next chapter we will learn about how the country changed under American administration.

Chapter 23

MOROS AND MODERNIZATION

The war against the Americans was extremely costly for the Filipinos. While about 20,000 fighting men were killed in battle, it is estimated that somewhere around 250,000 civilians died from famine and disease resulting from the war. For example, cholera outbreaks in the unsanitary internment camps killed thousands of Filipino civilians.

To this must be added the psychological cost. In 1898 the Filipinos were elated by the success of their rebellion against imperial Spain and were in the early stages of creating their own fledgling government. By 1902 they were under the boot of imperial America, their islands had been overrun, their military destroyed, their leaders captured or exiled, and their republic declared illegitimate. The demoralization and sense of national loss were profound.

While the Philippine-American War officially ended in 1902, conflicts throughout the Philippines continued for some time. This was especially true in the southern island group of Mindanao and the Sulu Archipelago. These regions were the home of the Moro peoples, Filipino Muslims who had a long history of resisting foreign rule. The Moro loyalties were to the various sultans and *datus* who governed these regions. The Spaniards never had effective control over Mindanao. Their power was restricted to a series of forts along the coast, from which they would occasionally make raids to punish Moro piracy.

The Moros not only resisted the Spaniards, but they also refused to join the Philippine revolution. The Moros rejected the liberal, secular ideology of the Filipino revolutionaries and the educated *ilustrado* class that led them. Being committed Muslims, they found little common ground with the European educated intellectuals pushing for Filipino independence.

When the Americans came, they wanted to keep the Moros out of the war. U.S. Secretary of State John Hay convinced the Ottoman Sultan Abdul Hamid II to persuade the Moros to stay out of the Philippine-American War. Though the Ottoman Sultan had no formal authority over the Moros, he had considerable moral authority with Muslims worldwide. Abdul Hamid agreed and asked the Moros to stay out of the conflict. The Moros had no interest in aiding liberals like Aguinaldo anyway, and rejected all overtures from the Aguinaldo government

Instead, Sultan Jamalul Kiram II of Sulu signed the Kiram-Bates Treaty with the United States in 1899. The treaty recognized the United States as having sovereignty over the Sulu region. But it also promised the Moros autonomy over their internal affairs and granted Moro leaders hefty cash payouts to fly the American flag. For their part, the Moros promised to remain neutral in the U.S.-Filipino conflict and refrain from attacking U.S. ships or U.S. agents working in the Philippines.

The Kiram-Bates Treaty was fraught with problems from the start. U.S. officials did not understand that Sultan Jamalul Kiram did not speak for all Moros. He was an important ruler, to be sure, but

Chapter 23: Moros and Modernization

political authority in Mindanao and Sulu was a complex patchwork of tribal alliances stretched over hundreds of petty kingdoms. Sultan Jamalul had no authority to compel all Moros to abide by the terms of the treaty. The U.S. was confused and disappointed when Moro piracy continued unabated. From the U.S. perspective, Sultan Jamalul was not honoring the treaty.

Neither was the United States faultless. It seems apparent that the U.S. never intended to honor the treaty in the long term, seeing it only as a temporary measure to keep the Moros out of the war in Luzon. Once the war was over, the Americans immediately began trying to colonize Moro lands in violation of the promises of autonomy guaranteed in the Kiram-Bates Treaty.

Tensions flared in Mindanao and the Moros had several violent encounters with the Americans. American soldiers killed a local datu. Sometime later, Moros murdered some U.S. soldiers to steal their Krag rifles. There were constant arguments about who had control of where. Finally, Colonel Frank Baldwin led an expedition of over 1,000 men to Bayang near the shores of Lake Lanao in spring of 1902. The march was a grueling excursion through thick jungles and bottomless mud pits. Many troops died from malaria, as well as suicidal attacks from the Moro *juramentado* swordsmen.

Eventually Baldwin reached Lake Lanao and his forces attacked and captured two Moro forts. This expedition began an 11-year war against the Moros of Mindanao and Sulu. In 1904 the U.S. abrogated the Kiram-Bates Treaty to pursue its war against the Moros unhindered.

The Americans established a fort on Lake Lanao called Camp Vickers. The many campaigns by which they gradually subdued Mindanao by force and diplomacy are too tedious to chronicle here. It was a piecemeal process involving endless skirmishes, alliances, and negotiations with particular datus. In 1903, the U.S. created the Moro Province in Mindanao, which was in turn divided up into five districts governed by American officers. The districts were subdivided into tribal "wards" under the control of the local datus, who were permitted autonomous rule so long as they promoted larger American objectives in Mindanao.

The American government immediately abolished slavery throughout the Moro lands and tried to introduce other so-called civilizing reforms. Some of these reforms were beneficial, such as the establishment of schools throughout Mindanao, as well as the promotion of trade as an alternative to banditry and piracy. Other reforms had less success, such as getting Moros to accept Filipino law, or introducing private land ownership on the European-American model to break up tribal holdings.

One weakness of the American strategy in Mindanao and Sulu was the choice of personnel. Many of the high-ranking military officials charged with pacifying the Moros were veterans of the Indian Wars. They tended to view the Moro problem through the lens of their own experiences with the Native American tribes of the American frontier. This caused the Americans to misjudge the situation among the Moros and pursue policies not suited to the culture of Moroland.

An example of this is the Massacre of Bud Dajo in 1906. Throughout the Moro conflict, Moros on Jolo Island had fled their villages to escape the violence of the war. Many of them hid in the crater of the extinct volcano Bud Dajo. Bud Dajo had thickly forested slopes, plentiful water, and was difficult for an army to access. By 1906 about a thousand Moros were living in the crater and had begun farming rice and potatoes. The U.S. military, based on its experiences in the Indian Wars, regarded people leaving their homes as an act of aggression. In the American west, any Native American tribe that left its reservation was assumed to be hostile. The military assumed the same about the Moros and ordered them to return to their homes. U.S. officials feared the Bud Dajo community would spawn a Moro uprising.

The Moros of Bud Dajo had no intention of leaving, however. General Leonard Wood commanded Colonel J. W. Duncan of the 6th Infantry Regiment to make an assault on Bud Dajo. Though armed only with spears, swords, and rocks, the Moros fought back fiercely. Americans mounted machine guns along the slopes of Bud Dajo and swept the crater with machine gun fire, cutting down the Moros. This was followed by a bayonet charge. The casualties were appallingly one-sided. Out of 1,000 Moros only 6 survived the slaughter. Many of the dead were women and children. American casualties were only 24. The Massacre of Bud Dajo was a public relations disaster for the U.S. military. The American public was appalled by the violence and questioned what compelling interest the United States had on the distant Philippine island of Jolo.

The Moro war was a constant drain on American personnel and resources. Frustrated with continued Moro resistance, in 1911 Brigadier General John J. Pershing, military governor of the Moro Province, ordered the general disarmament of the entire Moro population. Many Moros did not want to give up their firearms, but by this time many of the datus were supporting an end to the violence and encouraged the Moros to lay down their weapons. Though there was fierce resistance on the island of Jolo, by and large the disarmament was complete. The disarmament was also possible due to the system of roads the United States military constructed through Mindanao, making it easier to navigate the island's dense jungles and move troops from place to place to enforce U.S. policy.

The Moro Province was transitioned to civilian control in 1913, marking the end of the Moro insurgency.

We mentioned the construction of roads throughout Mindanao by the U.S. military. The United States undertook many other modernizing reforms of the Philippines. For example, the Port of Manila was completely renovated, with steel and concrete wharves replacing the old wooden structures that had been built under the Spaniards. The Pasig River was dredged, making navigation much easier—dredging means removing accumulated silt and other material from a river's bottom. Telegraph lines were laid across the country. Large cities were decorated with spacious public parks. A reliable postal service was established, as well as a reliable and relatively corruption-free police force.

Among the most important modern amenities brought to the Philippines by the Americans were the electric tram lines laid down across Manila. By the 20th century Manila was a sprawling metropolis home to a quarter million people. As the Philippine-American War concluded in 1902, the Philippine Commission began seeking bids for someone to construct a tramway for Manila, as well as provide electricity to the growing city. The bid was awarded to Charles Swift, an American businessman from Michigan. Swift founded the Manila Electric Rail and Light Company, known as Meralco. Meralco was responsible for bringing electric light and transportation to Manila, a daunting task! The first electric tram cars began operating in Manila in 1905. Let's take a look at what that must have been like in those early days of the electric tram car:

It was a muggy summer day in 1921. Twenty-eight year old Imme stood on the corner of Luna and San Marcelino in Manila's Paco district, waiting for the tram. Imme was dressed for a day out on Manila's bustling streets: she wore a colorless *camisa* blouse with the characteristic puffy sleeves. About her shoulders and neck was draped a large, folded square cloth called a *pañuelo*. The *pañuelo* was worn partly for modesty—the camisa was low cut with exposed shoulders—and partly to protect her skin from the sun. Around her waist Imme wore the popular *saya*, a double-sheeted skirt that reached to the ground, distinguished by seven folds. She tried in vain to cool herself with her fan while looking up San Marcelino for the tram.

"Mommy, when will the tram arrive?" said her son, seven-year-old Armin. It was his first time on the Manila Electric Company tramline.

"Soon, my little dear. The Meralco tram arrives every morning at 9:00 sharp," said Imme. Armin sat cross legged on the pavement. The fifteen minutes they'd been waiting seemed like forever.

Armin did not have to wait much longer. Presently there came

Chapter 23: Moros and Modernization

a high-pitched metallic squealing sound up Luna street. The people and horses cleared the way for the Meraclo tram car as it rounded the corner. Armin stood up excitedly. "Finally!" he said.

The Meralco tram car was a rectangular carriage, the size of a small bus. It was painted bright red and had large, broad windows. It could carry around twenty people.

The tram car squealed to a halt at the corner of Luna and San Marcelino. "C'mon, Armin!" said Imme. Mother and son climbed aboard the tram and paid the toll. "Sampaloc, Tuazon Street please," she said to the conductor. Imme and Armin took their seats. The tram was about half full—some were day laborers making their way to the city center, others were women like Imme, calling on friends and family.

"Mommy," said Armin, "how long will it take to get to Aunt Mirkit's?"

"Well, your aunt lives in Sampaloc district. We have to cross the Pasig River, and then pass through San Miguel. It will take at least 25 minutes."

The tram squealed and began to move along the double-rail upon which the tram car ran. Imme sat by the window. She sighed with relief. The breeze felt good on her face. She let down her pañuelo a bit. Armin squirmed to get a look out the window. He climbed across Imme's lap and popped his head out the window, looking first at the street, then overhead. The air above the tram car was intersected by many electrical cables running down the street.

"Mama," he said with his head still out the window, "the tram car is not pulled by a horse. How does it move? Does it have something to do with all those cables?"

"Yes, dear. Electricity is provided by those cables overhead," she said, pointing. "The car is attached to the cables by a long rod on the roof that connects to the cable with a roller. So long as the rod is connected to the cable and the wheels of the car are touching the metal railing on the streets, it receives electricity to power the engine and move it along."

"Hmm," Armin said, understanding little. He opened his mouth to catch a bit of the wind. A bug flew into it. "Pleck!" he said, spitting the bug out and ducking back into the tram car.

The tram cruised down San Marcelino, past the city hall and the ancient walls of Intramuros. Hundreds of pedestrians were out going about their business. Despite the heat, the men wore the trendy *Americana* suits that were in style: white pants and suit jacket, bowtie, and boater hats of woven straw rounded with black band. Some of them carried canes—many walked about reading the newspaper.

"*Sajonistas*," Imme said, pointing at the crowd of white-suited men strolling along Taft Avenue—the main thoroughfare of the Ermita District that the Americans had named after the first American Governor-General of the Philippines.

"What's a sajonista?" said Armin.

"A sajonista is a Filipino who dresses like a westerner," said Imme. Armin noticed a hint of resentment in his mother's voice.

The tram car passed on down Taft Avenue and veered to the northeast. The Pasig River came into view. "The Pasig!" said Armin, straining to look out the window. The blue waters of the Pasig were calm today, traversed by many freighters and smaller fishing vessels. The tram car crossed onto the Ayala Bridge and made its way over Manila's great river. To the east Armin could see the famous Isla de Convalecencia, Manila's only island on the Pasig. The island was home to the Hospicio de San José, a hospital run by the Daughters of Charity. To the west, Armin could see the Pasig winding past Intramuros until it joined the sparkling, endless expanse of the ocean.

Coming off the Ayala Bridge, the tram entered the San Miguel District. San Miguel was a more middle-class district. Armin noticed the houses here were in a little better shape than the neighborhoods south of the Pasig. There were a few more stops. Passengers got on and off. Soon the tram veered off to the east and onto Tuazon Street.

Chapter 23: Moros and Modernization

"We have entered Sampaloc," said Imme. "Get ready to get off." The tram squealed to a halt.

"Tuazon and Trabajo!" called the conductor. Imme took Armin by the hand and led him out of the tram and onto the street. Armin stood on the street corner, a little amazed. He had been to Sampaloc in a horse-drawn carriage, but it always took much longer before.

"What did you think of your first ride on the Meralco?" Imme asked.

"Can we go to Aunt Mirkit's every week?" he said with wide eyes.

———◆———

By 1906, around 39 miles of track had been laid around Manila. By 1924, that had expanded to 62 miles with around 170 tram cars carrying Filipino and American passengers all across the city and its outskirts.

It is undeniable that the rule of the United States raised the standard of living of many Filipinos. American technology, infrastructure, and administration were far superior to those of the Spaniards. The Americans modernized the Philippines, and in doing so, improved the material circumstances of the archipelago considerably. Even wild Mindanao benefitted from the modern road system constructed by the U.S. military.

That being said, many Filipinos considered these benefits as negligible so long as they were still under foreign domination. The U.S. could be very heavy-handed, as we saw in their treatment of the Moros during the Moro Rebellion. The Americans did not tolerate dissent, and while the intellectual ilustrado elites continued to advocate independence, they had to be careful their ambitions did not cross the thin line from advocacy to insurrection.

As the Americans were transitioning the Philippines to civil control around 1913, events half a world a way were in motion that would plunge Europe into World War I. In our next chapter, we will learn about the Philippines in World War I, as well as the decades leading up to World War II.

Chapter 24

BETWEEN THE WARS

Six months after the end of the Moro Rebellion, World War I broke out in Europe in June of 1914. This devastating conflict would last for four years and cause 20 million deaths. Though it began in eastern Europe, this war would eventually draw in 30 nations and be fought on four continents. At the time it was called "the war to end all wars."

The United States stayed out of World War I for the first several years, although America's sympathies were clearly with the Allied Powers, represented by France, Great Britain, Russia, Italy, and Japan. Since the United States controlled the foreign policy of the Philippines, obviously the Philippines, too, were aligned with the Allies.

The U.S. finally joined the war on the side of the Allies in 1917. As part of the American war effort, the Philippine Assembly created a Philippine National Guard. At 25,000 strong, the National Guard was supposed to be joined to the larger American Expeditionary Force in Europe. The war ended before these units ever saw action, however. The Philippines also funded the construction of two naval warships.

One of the priorities of the United States during this period was the disestablishment of the Catholic Church, which had been called for in the Philippine Organic Act. Like in Spain, Catholicism had been established as the official religion of the Philippines. Under Spanish rule, the Church enjoyed government patronage and the protection of the law. The friars—Franciscans, Dominicans, Augustinians, and Recollects—owned hundreds of thousands of acres of property, mostly in the greater Manila area of Luzon. And they wielded tremendous social influence. Mostly made up of the elite peninsulare class, they had been the most ardent supporters of the Spanish government during the wars of independence.

The U.S. authorities believed that it was necessary for their objectives in the Philippines to break the influence of the friars. Part of the disestablishment of the Church called for in the Philippine Organic Act authorized the U.S. to break up the large estates of the friars and sell them to Filipino farmers. This obviously was very jarring for the friars, who had enjoyed a privileged place in Filipino society for centuries. Let's see how this might have played out in a fictional monastery outside Manila, the Dominican friary of Santa María de las Colinas:

"Padre, there is an American here to see you," said Brother Diego. Padre Domenico looked up from his writing at the anxious brother standing before him. "Oh? Who is he? What does he want?"

"It is a Mr. Jameson, from the Bureau of Insular Affairs," said Diego. Padre Domenico shifted uneasily in his chair. The Bureau of Insular Affairs was the American agency that handled all the sticky legal questions that had arisen after the end of Spanish rule. A visit from the Bureau was not a happy occasion.

Chapter 24: Between the Wars

"They probably want our land," said Padre Domenico. He stood up from behind his writing desk, brushed off his habit, and said, "Have this Mr. Jameson wait for me in the reception hall. I will be there in a few minutes." Brother Diego nodded and withdrew. Padre Domenico walked over to the old crucifix which adorned the wall of his office. The image of Christ was agonized and excessively bloody, as Spanish crucifixes of the late Baroque period were. He made the sign of the cross and bowed his head. "Lord Jesus, defend us." He prayed silently for a few moments.

When he left his office, another friar, Brother Gil, entered. "Padre, there is an American here from the Bureau!" Gil said excitedly.

"I know, Brother Gil. Diego has already told me. I am on my way to see him."

"Padre, you have heard how they are trying to take the lands away from the friaries all over the country? Do you think that's what they want with us?" asked Gil, pacing alongside Padre Domenico down the hall that led to the receptory.

"If that's what this Mr. Jameson wants, he's going to be disappointed. This monastery has been here since 1695. These 200 hectares were given to us in a grant by Governor Fausto Cruzat himself, signed with the royal seal of King Carlo II. For six generations the Friars of Santa María de las Colinas have lived, prayed, worked, and died in this monastery. I'm not going to be the Superior who yields it all up to some upstart American."

"And I can't believe Papa Pio X would permit it!" added Brother Gil.

Padre Domenico and Brother Gil entered the reception hall. Mr. Jameson was standing about, looking at the old paintings on the wall. He was a lanky man, mid-thirties with a thin, dark mustache. He wore the white suit and hat characteristic of the *Americana* style. He carried a leather attaché case. Brother Diego was there as well, setting up two chairs for the Superior and the American.

"Mr. Jameson, I presume," said Padre Domenico. "Won't you sit down?"

Mr. Jameson smiled but remained standing. He opened the attaché case and handed Padre Domenico some documents. "Good afternoon, Padre. I am representing the U.S. Bureau of Insular Affairs. As you know, the Organic Act of 1902 ordered the disestablishment of the Catholic Church in the Philippines."

Padre Domenico perused the papers. They seemed to be a bunch of legal and diplomatic documents. "I am well aware of the law," he said, looking over the papers. "As I understand it, the particulars have been tied up in negotiations with the Vatican for years."

"Until now," said Mr. Jameson. "The Vatican has finally agreed to the terms proposed by the United States. The property of Santa María de las Colinas will be assumed by the U.S. government."

"Blasphemy!" exclaimed Brother Diego. "The pope would never agree to such a thing!"

"Actually, if you will look at the end of the packet, Padre, you will see I have included the communique from the Vatican."

Padre Domenico flipped to the end of the packet. There was a document in Latin bearing the seal of the Vatican Secretary of State. Padre Domenico read the document silently. "He's right, brothers. Signed by Cardinal Secretary Rafael Merry del Val. The Vatican has agreed to sell off our lands to the U.S. government." Brothers Diego and Gil gasped. Padre Domenico looked at Mr. Jameson, crestfallen.

"Santa María de las Colinas sits on 200 hectares. The Bureau is dispossessing you of 190 of them. I am authorized by the United States government to offer you payment of $3,000 in compensation." He produced a check from the attaché case and held it out. Padre Domenico was too shocked to take the check. Instead, he collapsed into the chair. Brother Gil took the check.

"When will this take effect?" said Domenico weakly.

"The land transfer will take effect in 90 days," said Mr. Jameson. "If you have any questions, come see me at the Bureau's office in Manila. Good day," he said, tipping his hat and walking out.

Chapter 24: Between the Wars

During the first decade of American rule, 390,000 acres of church lands were gobbled up by U.S. government, which paid the Church $7.5 million for the land. The lost property was not the only consequence faced by friaries such as Santa María de las Colinas. Spanish born friars and clergy were to be gradually removed in favor of Filipino or other non-Spaniards. In our story, Padre Domenico and the others would have all most likely been peninsulares, men born in Spain. They would have gradually been sent back to Spain while the monastery was taken over by native Filipinos. Sometimes the confiscations deprived the monasteries of so much property that they were unable to maintain themselves and were forced to close.

The United States intended to sell the land to small farmers to improve the economic standing of average Filipinos. The U.S. passed the Public Lands Act which established a system like the United States Homestead Act, allowing Filipinos to claim lands in exchange for five-year tenancy and a promise to improve the property. But the Public Lands Act was a failure—the average Filipino was unable to navigate the complex bureaucratic requirements of the act, and most claims were given to landowners who already possessed large estates. Only one-tenth of the claims were approved. In the end the monastic lands were sold off to private investors, many of whom were already wealthy.

The Church not only suffered attacks from without, but schism from within as well. During the revolt against Spain, there were some Filipino clergy who advocated creating a national Filipino church independent of Rome. Since the higher ranks of the Catholic clergy in the Philippines was dominated by Spaniards, these reformist clergy viewed the Catholic hierarchy as another tool of colonial oppression. Around the time Aguinaldo was declared president, a priest from Ilocos Norte named Gregorio Aglipay began advocating for an independent church. After the Philippine-American War ended in 1902, Aglipay renounced the authority of the Pope and formed the Philippine Independent Church, known as the Aglipayan Schism amongst Catholics. He was excommunicated for these actions.

Aglipay's church was radically different from Catholicism. He immediately did away with the requirement of celibacy, allowing priests to marry. Latin was replaced with vernacular in worship, and the liturgy was modeled on the Anglican Book of Common Prayer. Aglipay looked to the Freemasons for his theology—he officially joined the Masonic Lodge in 1918. Under Masonic influence, Aglipay came to reject the divinity of Jesus and the Trinity.

The Aglipayans drew significant support from Filipinos in their early years because they were viewed as a nationalist church that supported the Filipino cause against colonialism. Over time, however, they split into factions. By the 1940s their influence was minimal.

From 1902 to 1913, American policy in the Philippines was unapologetically imperialist. But the American outlook began to change in the second decade of the 20th century. The U.S. president from 1913 to 1921 was Democrat Woodrow Wilson. Wilson was not an imperialist like his Republican predecessors Taft, Roosevelt, and McKinley. During his first presidential campaign in 1912, Wilson said, "The Philippines are at present our frontier, but I hope we presently are to deprive ourselves of that frontier." As president, Wilson instituted policies that were meant to prepare the Philippines for full independence.

The most notable change under Wilson was the Jones Law of 1916. Authored by Democratic Congressman William Jones of Virginia, the Jones Law replaced the Philippine Organic Act and became the guiding document for U.S. policy in the Philippines. It explicitly called for the full independence of the Philippines, though it did not say when. It also abolished the Philippine Commission, replacing it with a new elected body, the Philippine Senate. The Philippine Assembly was renamed the House of Representatives. For the first time, the entire Philippine legislative branch was entirely in Filipino hands. The executive branch was still headed by a Governor-General appointed by the United States.

Among Filipinos, the dominant political movement became the

Chapter 24: Between the Wars

Nacionalista Party. Founded in 1907, the Nacionalista Party called for full independence for the Philippines, but peacefully and within the framework of the American system. The most notable leader of the Nacionalistas was Manuel L. Quezon. Quezon had a long history in the Philippine independence movement: he had served as an aide-de-camp to Emilio Aguinaldo, then as a member of the Philippine Assembly in 1907. In 1909 he became one of two Filipino "resident commissioners" to the U.S. House of Representatives, where he pushed the U.S. Congress to commit to Philippine independence. After the passage of the Jones Law, Quezon was elected to the new Philippine Senate and soon became Senate President, the highest ranking Filipino elected official and the voice of the independence movement.

Since the Jones Law did not say when or under what conditions the Philippines would be given independence, the Nacionalistas sent "independence missions" to the United States to lobby the U.S. government for independence. Manuel Quezon headed the first independence mission to the United States in 1919. Meeting with Secretary of War Newton Baker, Quezon argued persuasively that the Philippine government was stable and ready for full independence. President Wilson agreed and said the U.S. had a duty to grant Philippine independence. Wilson, however, was leaving office by that time and had little influence. The Republicans who controlled Congress decided against Wilson's recommendation.

Further independence missions were sent in 1922, 1923, 1930, 1931, 1932, and two in 1933. Meanwhile, Quezon continued to work for independence through other means. He became the formal head of the Nacionalistas in 1922 and used his position to pressure the U.S. to commit to a specific timeline for independence. An example of this was Quezon's role in the passage of the Tydings-McDuffie Act.

The story of the Tydings-McDuffie Act is long and complex. As momentum for independence grew throughout the 1920s, various bills were submitted to Congress for Philippine independence.

In 1932, Congress passed the Hare-Hawes-Cutting Bill, which promised Philippine independence after 10 years, but reserved several military and naval bases for the United States, as well as imposing tariffs and quotas on Philippine exports. The bill required the approval of the Philippine Senate. As Senate President, Quezon urged the Senate to reject the bill. The Philippine Senate followed Quezon's advice, rejecting the Hare-Hawes-Cutting Bill and instead sending another independence mission to Washington to secure a better arrangement.

Quezon personally led the mission, and the result was a new bill: the Tydings-McDuffie Act, passed by Congress in 1934 and ratified by the Philippine Senate. The Tydings-McDuffie Act also called for independence after 10 years. But the 10 years were to be used as a "transitional period" when various aspects of Philippine independence were to be worked out. This government during this time was known as the "Commonwealth of the Philippines." The Tydings-McDuffie Act stipulated that independence would be granted on the July 4th after the tenth year of the Commonwealth. As the Commonwealth was officially inaugurated on November 15th, 1935, independence was scheduled on July 4th, 1946.

The ten years between 1935 and 1946 were full of activity. A Constitution similar to the American Constitution was established. The Commonwealth government featured a strong executive headed by a presidency, an unicameral legislature (one house), and a Filipino Supreme Court. Manuel Quezon was elected to the presidency in the first election in May of 1935, becoming the country's second president (Filipinos regard Emilio Aguinaldo of the Philippine Republic as their first president).

Quezon's government worked tirelessly to prepare the Philippines for independence. Tagalog was made the national language. There was a flurry of reforms in the areas of economy, defense, transportation, and education. Women's suffrage was introduced. Extensive work was put into modernizing Mindanao. In 1939–1940, the Constitution was amended to restore the old

Chapter 24: Between the Wars

bicameral legislature. The economy grew steadily, and the quality of life improved for many Filipinos.

Not all was peaceful, however. The Quezon government abandoned the pursuit of land reform, meaning agricultural land remained concentrated in the hands of a small class of large owners. This caused periodic unrest in the countryside. It also allowed an opening for Communist ideology to start making inroads into parts of the archipelago, for the Communists were zealous proponents of land reform. There were also concerns over how much influence the U.S. would hold over the new Philippine state, and how the Philippines would fit into the larger diplomatic puzzle of southeast Asia.

By 1940, the Philippines seemed to be in an excellent position for independence. The Commonwealth government was stable under the responsible presidency of Quezon, relations with the United States were good, and the economy of the Philippines was growing. Filipinos needed only to wait six more years for the clock to run down to independence on July 4, 1946.

Given how well things were going, nobody could have imagined the catastrophe that was about to overtake the archipelago.

Chapter 25

THE JAPANESE INVADE

It had been exceptionally bad timing for the Filipinos that their war of independence against Spain happened simultaneously with the Spanish-American War. A similar misfortune befell them as they again anticipated independence in 1946 only to have their plans thrown into chaos by the outbreak of World War II.

Throughout the 1930s, the Empire of Japan was undertaking an aggressive campaign of military expansion throughout East Asia. They had invaded Manchuria in 1931 and launched a full-scale war against China in 1937. In 1940 they invaded French Indochina (Vietnam). Militarily, Japan sought to build an East Asian empire. Diplomatically, they wanted to isolate China and end European influence in the Pacific.

Tensions with the United States increased throughout the thirties. In 1937, the Japanese attacked the *USS Panay*, an American gunboat on the Yangtze River in China. In 1938, when the Japanese took the Chinese city of Nanking, the American consul John More Allison was struck in the face by a Japanese soldier. Though the Japanese government apologized for the incidents, Japanese soldiers were allowed to pillage American property in China without restraint. President Franklin Roosevelt asked U.S. companies to stop selling implements of war to Japan and halted trade of gasoline and certain mechanical parts with the Japanese. The Japanese regarded these actions as hostile, and the situation grew worse.

By 1940, U.S. officials were sufficiently worried about the situation that President Roosevelt moved the U.S. Pacific fleet from San Diego to Hawaii. He also began a troop buildup in the Philippines to deter a Japanese attack. The American military in the Philippines was commanded by General Douglas MacArthur, son of the famous General Arthur MacArthur whom we met in Chapter 22. Even with the troop buildup, MacArthur believed U.S. forces were insufficient to defend the Philippines from a Japanese attack. He estimated he would need a force ten times the size of the 40,000 men Roosevelt provided to sufficiently defend the islands. Such a massive troop commitment was impossible, however. By 1941 military strategists advised that the best response to a Japanese attack would be to abandon the archipelago.

American preparations were not unfounded. The conquest of the Philippines was an important military objective of imperial Japan. For the Japanese, the Philippines were strategically important for several reasons. Conquering the Philippines would deprive the U.S. of an advance base in East Asia. The Japanese could also use the Philippines as a base for attacks on the Dutch East Indies (Indonesia). Possession of the Philippine archipelago would also secure Japanese lines of supply and communication between the home islands and their conquered territories.

On December 7, 1941, the Japanese attacked the American naval fleet at Pearl Harbor, Hawaii. The very next day the invasion of the Philippines began when the Japanese landed on the northern island of Batan, in the Luzon island group. Meanwhile Japanese air attacks

Chapter 25: The Japanese Invade

throughout Luzon destroyed many American planes on the ground, preventing the Americans from mounting any resistance by air. U.S. naval forces withdrew, hoping to elude Japanese air strikes against them.

The main invasion began on the morning of December 22. The Japanese landed in Luzon at three different points and advanced towards the center, hoping to hem American forces in. The Americans engaged the Japanese at Rosario in central Luzon and were pushed back. General MacArthur began to execute the American contingency plan, which called for a withdrawal into the Bataan Peninsula, identified as the most defensible position on Luzon.

The withdrawal was very orderly. American and Filipino forces held roads until all troops had passed and then blew up bridges to prevent the Japanese from following. The Japanese desperately tried to cut off the Americans before they became entrenched in the Bataan Peninsula. The U.S. 194th Tank Battalion engaged the Japanese to buy the rest of the army time to escape. The 194th Tank Battalion was successful in holding off the Japanese, but at the staggering cost of 50% casualties. By January 6, 1942 the American and Filipino forces had completed their withdrawal into the peninsula.

What ensued was the three-month long Battle of Bataan as the Japanese attempted to take the peninsula. American victories in the north prevented the Japanese from overrunning Bataan, while a Japanese amphibious landing from the south was disrupted. Despite these initial successes, the Americans were gradually worn down from lack of supplies, illness, and the weariness of constant fighting. Headquartered on Corregidor Island in Manila Bay, General MacArthur awaited instructions from Washington.

By February, the situation had become hopeless. President Franklin Roosevelt ordered MacArthur to evacuate Corregidor and relocate to Australia. On March 12th, MacArthur and a small circle of his family and associates were taken from Corregidor Island by ship to Mindanao, where he then was taken by plane to Australia.

Philippine President Manuel Quezon was evacuated as well.

By April the American and Filipino forces were overwhelmed. The Japanese swarmed the Bataan Peninsula, taking 60,000 prisoners. A few Americans managed to escape to Corregidor Island—these would hold out for another month before surrendering as well.

The Japanese under their General Masaharu Homma were now faced with transporting 60,000 sick and wounded prisoners out of Bataan and relocating them to prisoner camps in central Luzon—a distance of around 69 miles. Lacking enough mechanical transport to easily move so many people, Homma made the prisoners walk. This event is remembered as the Bataan Death March, a horrific instance of Japanese cruelty.

Private O'Murphy and Lieutenant Lay stood in ankle deep water in the boggy rice field, hands above their heads in the universal sign of surrender. O'Murphy and Lay were only two of the thousands of American and Filipino prisoners who were being processed by the Japanese.

"What will they do with us, Lieutenant?" asked O'Murphy nervously.

"I imagine they will march us north to their encampments in Tarlac Province," said Lay. "We'll be sitting out the war there, unless Uncle Sam bails us out in the meantime."

Three Japanese soldiers approached O'Murphy and Lay, weapons drawn. Through their gestures, they communicated that O'Murphy and Lay should turn all their pockets inside out so the soldiers could see if they were hiding anything. The Americans did as commanded. Lay had nothing but a worn New Testament he always kept on him. The Japanese tossed this carelessly into the muddy water.

O'Murphy, however, had a few Japanese coins he had picked up in Manila some months earlier. Upon seeing the coins, one of the soldiers slapped O'Murphy across the face and seized the coins from his hand. While O'Murphy was still in shock from being slapped, another Japanese soldier put his pistol to O'Murphy's forehead and

Chapter 25: The Japanese Invade

shot him. O'Murphy fell backward, his lifeless body sloshing into the mud.

Lieutenant Lay choked but tried not to act fazed. If he showed fear it would only embolden his captors. The soldiers continued down the line. Word passed through the American ranks that they were executing any Americans who held Japanese souvenirs or money, as these were presumed to have been scavenged from the bodies of dead Japanese soldiers.

Lay was grouped in with about a hundred other American and Filipino prisoners and forced to march up to the city of San Fernando, a trek of nearly 50-miles. The conditions were brutal. Lieutenant Lay was given only a small cup of water per day. In the sweltering heat, this was not enough. After a few days, the men were in poor shape. Many struggled to move. Japanese soldiers yelled at them and prodded them with bayonets to keep them walking.

The man in front of Lieutenant Lay kept tripping and mumbling to himself. Lay saw from his insignia that the man bore the rank of Sergeant. He seemed to be losing his wits.

"Sergeant, what's your name?" asked Lay.

"Kuntz," said the man groggily. "Leo Kuntz, Madison, Wisconsin."

"Well Sergeant Kuntz, I'm Lieutenant Lay. Pleased to meet you. Why don't you tell me a bit about Wisconsin?" Lay hoped that by keeping Kuntz talking, he could focus the man's mind and keep him alive. It seemed to work. Kuntz started talking about his parents' farm, his job as a mechanic before the war, his fiancé, and many other reminders of home. Kuntz began to walk with a bit more energy and regularity.

Lucky for him! A few hundred yards ahead there was a certain American prisoner who was fatigued and shuffling a bit. Lay saw a Japanese soldier approach the man without warning and bayonetted him through the back. The man howled and fell to the ground. A small crowd of soldiers circled around him like vultures and bayonetted him repeatedly until he stopped moving. The man had not stumbled or fallen behind at all—his only offense was walking irregularly.

The Filipino soldiers fared even worse. The Japanese seemed to bear a special hatred for the Filipino people. One day a Japanese officer, Colonel Masanobu Tsuji, ordered all the Filipino non-commissioned officers separated out from the main bulk of prisoners, around 400 men in all. Lay and Kuntz watched as the line of Filipinos was marched off to the banks of the Pantingan River by the road to Pilar-Bagac. "This doesn't look good," said Lieutenant Lay.

"No sir, that it does not," said Kuntz, squinting to see what would become of the men as they descended to the riverbank.

"Eyes to front!" shouted a Japanese officer in broken English. Lay and Kuntz faced forward and continued their march. A minute later they heard shouting and an eruption of machine gun fire from the riverside. None of those Filipino men were ever heard from again.

The prisoners were in bad shape by the time they reached San Fernando. A large railway passed through this town, and the Japanese intended to herd their captives into rail cars and ship them the remainder of the journey to the prison camp at Tarlac. Lay was a strong man in the prime of life, but the march from Bataan had worn him down considerably. He coughed a harsh, rasping cough and trembled a bit. He had been shaking for the better part of a day. Even if the Japanese did not kill him, he began to wonder if his health would hold out.

The men all milled about the trainyard as the Japanese loaded them onto railcars. Some could not make their legs hold them up anymore and many collapsed onto the dirt road beside the yard, desperate to rest their aching limbs. A trio of privates not far from Lay had done so and had just closed their eyes when a Japanese army truck came roaring up the road. The driver saw the three men and swerved, intentionally running them over and crushing their bodies beneath the tires. The men shrieked as they disappeared beneath the treads.

Chapter 25: The Japanese Invade

"Move!" a soldier shouted to Lieutenant Lay before he could process what was happening. At bayonet point he and dozens of other men were corralled into boxcars.

"Finally we will get to rest our legs!" said Kuntz. But it was not to be. The Japanese ordered the men to stand and packed them so tightly that there was not enough room to sit even if one wanted to. Lieutenant Lay was already drenched in sweat when the Japanese closed the boxcar and locked it. The men were in total darkness. The car had no ventilation or light source. By the time Lay and Kuntz heard the chugging of the wheels and felt the car begin to move, the temperature inside had already risen to a sweltering 110 degrees. The rhythmic creaking of the boxcar was punctuated only by the groans of sick and suffering men wafting through the hot darkness.

Lieutenant Lay licked his cracked lips, but it did no good. His mouth was devoid of saliva—he had not tasted water in over 24 hours. What fluid he had left in his body was rapidly being sweated away. He coughed and convulsed. "Lord, help us," he wheezed into the darkness.

Of the 60,000 prisoners marched out of Bataan, around 18,000 died on the way—most of them Filipino. Of those who reached the Japanese prisoner camp, many more would die of illness from the unsanitary conditions. Years later, after the war, Japanese General Masaharu Homma was captured by the Americans and sentenced to death for what happened on the Bataan Death March. He would be executed by firing squad in 1946—with MacArthur's blessing.

But that was still some time off. In spring of 1942 Homma's grip on the Philippines was complete. He was installed as Governor-General and began consolidating Japanese power over the archipelago. Meanwhile, Douglas MacArthur arrived in Australia. In Melbourne, he gave a speech to reporters who wanted to know about the situation in the Philippines. MacArthur famously said,

"I came through, and I shall return." American authorities in Washington asked MacArthur to amend his statement, saying instead, "*We* shall return." MacArthur refused.

Chapter 26

ISLAND HOPPING TO FREEDOM

In our last chapter we mentioned that Philippine President Manuel Quezon had been evacuated at the time of the Japanese invasion. What became of him during the Japanese occupation, and what of the Commonwealth of the Philippines?

President Quezon had been elected to a second presidential term in 1941 but fled the Philippines before his inauguration. Along with other Filipino officials, Quezon made his way to Washington, D.C. where he established the Commonwealth government in exile. He served as a member of the Pacific War Council and carried on governmental duties from his exile, complete with a full cabinet.

In June of 1942, Quezon addressed the U.S. House of Representatives. He stressed the strategic importance of the Philippines in the Pacific War effort and urged the Americans to adopt the slogan "Remember Bataan!" He hoped the government would prioritize liberating the Philippines. Quezon's health was beginning to fail, but he used what strength he had to advocate tirelessly for the recapture of the Philippines.

Doing so immediately was impossible, however. The Japanese defensive perimeter was vast, stretching from Alaska to the Solomon Islands. The Philippines was deep within Japanese territory; U.S. planes could not reach the Philippines from U.S. territory even if they wanted to. Before the Philippines could be attacked, the U.S. needed to push back the Japanese perimeter and secure airfields in the Pacific from which to press further into Japanese territory.

The U.S. did this with a strategy of amphibious landings and "island hopping." The plan was to stage amphibious landings on certain strategic islands. Once conquered, these islands would be used for airfields from which the U.S. would launch attacks to further push back the Japanese. As the Japanese were pushed back, another amphibious landing would be staged deeper into Japanese territory, another airfield established, and the process repeated until Japan itself was within range of U.S. fighter planes.

The first amphibious landing was staged at Guadalcanal in the Solomon Islands in August 1942. The U.S. seized a strategic airfield, halting Japan's efforts to threaten New Zealand and Australia. While U.S. naval forces under Admiral William "Bull" Halsey pushed north into the Solomon Islands, General Douglas MacArthur pushed the Japanese back across the northern coast of Papua New Guinea, securing the island by summer of 1943.

The Japanese had many well-fortified positions scattered throughout the Pacific, such as the fortress of Rabaul on the New Guinean island of New Britain. Rather than sacrifice thousands of troops and ships taking them, the American military preferred to isolate these islands by sea, causing the cut-off Japanese garrisons to weaken from starvation and disease. Meanwhile, less fortified islands were seized, adding to American gains. This practice of hopping from one less defended island to another was an essential component of U.S. strategy in the Pacific.

By 1944, enough islands had been secured that a strike on

Chapter 26: Island Hopping to Freedom

Japan itself was possible. By mid-1944, U.S. forces were only 300 miles southeast of Mindanao. Aircraft carrier-based warplanes were already carrying out strikes against Japanese airfields in the Philippines. While the U.S. began preparations to attack Japan, General MacArthur and Admiral Chester Nimitz argued for an invasion of the Philippines. Preparations were made for MacArthur to return to the archipelago.

The Japanese occupation of the Philippines was harsh. They committed many atrocities against the Filipinos. Thousands of Filipinos were pressed into slave labor to serve the Japanese war effort. The Filipinos were eager for an American invasion to end the hated Japanese occupation. Furthermore, the Philippines was still scheduled to become independent in 1946, according to the Tydings-McDuffie Act. Securing the promised freedom in 1946 was contingent upon driving the Japanese out.

Filipinos were not content to simply wait for America to do the job for them, however. Filipino guerilla fighters resisted the Japanese across the archipelago, making it impossible for the Japanese to secure the jungles or mountainous areas. The result was that the Japanese controlled only about half of the country.

Meanwhile the Americans had settled on October 20, 1944, as date of the invasion. The Visayan island of Leyte was chosen as the landing site. On that day, the U.S. Sixth Army, supported by significant naval and aerial forces, landed on the eastern shore of Leyte. The Japanese underestimated the size of the American invasion force and overcommitted themselves, getting drawn into the massive three-day Battle of Leyte Gulf. The Japanese lost four of its aircraft carriers, as well as numerous battleships, cruisers, and other ships. The Imperial Japanese Navy was never again able to fight a major battle after its crushing defeat at Leyte Gulf.

As the American invasion unfolded, Filipino guerilla units merged with the American army to aid the U.S. battle efforts. They kept roads and bridges clear of congestion for American forces. They carried out scouting and intelligence operations.

General Douglas MacArthur and Philippine President Sergio Osmeña return to the Philippines during the American liberation, October 1944.

They dynamited bridges in Japanese controlled areas to prevent Japanese troop movements. And they fought along side U.S. forces in battle, sometimes as regular units incorporated into the U.S. army, sometimes staging guerilla attacks on Japanese supply bases. Throughout the war, it is estimated that 200,000 Filipinos fought alongside U.S. forces.

By December of 1944, the U.S. army had moved north to the island of Samar and was preparing for the seizure of Mindoro. Mindoro is a large island south of Luzon and Manila Bay. As Japanese power was strongest in Luzon, MacArthur wanted to use Mindoro to construct airfields from which he could bomb Japanese positions in Luzon at will. Fortunately for MacArthur, Mindoro was only lightly defended by the Japanese and already overrun with Filipino guerillas. Mindoro was quickly occupied, and U.S. army engineers spent the rest of December constructing airfields at San José. By January 1945, the Americans were ready to begin the main siege of Luzon.

Chapter 26: Island Hopping to Freedom

The invasion came on January 9, 1945 at Lingayen Gulf on Luzon's southern shore. General Walter Krueger's Sixth Army with over 175,000 troops established a twenty-mile beach head at Lingayen. With new P-51 Mustang fighter planes providing air support, the army pushed inland and seized the strategic Clark Airfields, only 40 miles from Manila. More landings followed, and by February the city of Manila was cut off in a pincer movement.

MacArthur wanted to seize the island of Corregidor, from which he had been driven in 1941. Possessing this island was important, as it allowed control of Manila Bay. It took most of February to secure Corregidor. This was followed swiftly by the invasion of Manila itself. The Battle of Manila was brutal. Japanese Marines refused to surrender or withdraw—sometimes they fought to the last man, as at Fort Drum, a fortified island in Manila Bay. When it became clear the Japanese would not surrender, U.S. forces resorted to a drastic plan to capture the position:

While American soldiers were already overrunning Manila, the concrete fortress of Fort Drum defied all U.S. attempts at taking it. U.S. army Lieutenant Miles Schafer and Captain Benny Biancho of the 38th Infantry Regiment scratched their heads.

"It's like a concrete battleship," said Lieutenant Schafer.

"Correction, it *is* a concrete battleship—with four massive 14-inch guns in two turrets," responded Captain Biancho.

"Poor fellas don't realize the battle is already lost for them," said Schafer, shaking his head. "If only they'd just surrender."

Rata-tat. Rata-tata!

Machine-gun fire erupted from Fort Drum. Schafer and Biancho took cover. The bullets sailed harmlessly overhead and plinked into the water. "The Japs won't surrender. For them, it's a matter of honor. They would rather die," said Biancho. "We're going to have to force them out somehow. It's gonna be tough because that entire island is one concrete block.

"We've come up with a solution for that," chimed in a third

man. It was Major General William Chase, commander of the 38th Infantry Division. Schafer and Biancho stood at attention. "At ease men," said the Major General. "The top brass has a plan for breaking the Japs out of Fort Drum. We tried it at Fort Hughes back in March and it worked like a charm. It's a doozey, but it sure does the trick."

"We're all ears, sir," said Biancho.

Rata-tata! Another volley of machine-gun fire exploded from Fort Drum. The three men huddled and listened to General Chase's plan, struggling to hear over the mortar rounds that also flew out of the embattled fort.

The next day everything was in position to carry out the plan. A landing ship medium—a type of troop transport ship used for amphibious landings—moved into position near Fort Drum. It had been modified with a large bridge structure. On board were Captain Biancho, Lieutenant Schafer, and a hundred men of the 38th. When the ship got close enough, Biancho called out, "Lower bridge!"

"Lower bridge!" Schafer echoed. A team of men scrambled into action, working pulleys and cranks to lower the bridge. It landed on the concrete deck of Fort Drum with a heavy thud. Another team of several dozen men stormed across the bridge and on to the deck. The huge 14-inch cannons of Fort Drum had been spiked and rendered useless by the Americans when they surrendered in 1942, but the men were wary of a suicidal ambush by the Japanese defenders using small arms and grenades. However, the Japanese had retreated into the assumed security of the fort's lower decks, waiting to attack the Americans when they attempted to enter.

"The deck is secure, sir!" called Lieutenant Schafer.

"Excellent!" cried Biancho from the landing ship. Then, turning to his crew: "Fuel team, move!" Another team of soldiers came running from the ship to the bridge, dragging a large, long hose. The hose was connected to a tank on board the landing ship that was filled with 2,500 gallons of diesel fuel mixed with gasoline.

"Find the air vents!" ordered Schafer. The first team had already located the air vents, the small two square-foot openings atop the

Chapter 26: Island Hopping to Freedom

deck that provided access to the interior of the fort. The soldiers broke the vent coverings off the opening while the fuel team shoved the hose into the duct. The hose being in place, the team leader gave a thumbs up. Schafer saw the thumbs up and gave a thumbs up to Biancho. Biancho nodded, and turning to one of his officers on the Landing Ship, gave him the signal to turn on the pump. The man cranked a large wheel, opening the valves of the tank and sending gallons of the diesel fuel through the hose.

The hose began belching out hundreds of gallons of fuel down into the darkness of the ventilation duct. Within a few moments the fuel team could hear the panicked cries of the Japanese soldiers within echoing up the duct. They must have realized what was about to happen when they saw their command station being flooded with fuel. The U.S. soldiers did not waver though—they stood stoically atop the deck, holding the hose firm until all 2,500 gallons had been evacuated into the vent.

"Clear deck!" shouted Lieutenant Schafer. In an instant, all the soldiers upon the deck of Fort Drum retreated back across the bridge onto the landing ship. Lieutenant Schafer was the last man to leave the deck. In his hands he dragged a massive wooden spool threaded with copper wire. As he retreated, he unwound the spool. The wire was connected to a timed detonator that had been lowered down the ventilation shaft. He hopped back into the landing ship.

"How much wire do you have left?" said Biancho.

"I'd say 400 yards," replied Schafer.

Captain Biancho nodded. "Move us out about 400 yards!" he called to the ship pilot. When the ship had moved off 400 yards, the spool was almost completely unwound. A pair of soldiers took the wire from the spool and fused it into a detonator, a metallic black box with an ominous red button. It only took a moment to splice the wire into the detonator.

Schafer handed Captain Biancho the box. "Care to do the honors?" he said to the captain.

Biancho took the box. "Here's a present from Uncle Sam!" he

yelled towards Fort Drum. Then he pressed the red button with his thumb.

Fort Drum rumbled and exploded in a blast of destruction that shocked even Biancho and Schafer. The concrete deck of the fortress fragmented into thousands of pieces and was flung hundreds of feet into the air by the force of the explosion. Smoke and flame engulfed the entire concrete island.

"Cover!" shouted Schafer. The men on the landing ship covered their heads. Moments later a shower of dirt and pebbles rained down upon them. Fortunately, the heavier pieces of concrete had not fallen so far out, or the landing ship could have been severely damaged.

The men uncovered their heads and looked at the hell they had made of Fort Drum: wreathed in flame, smoke pouring from every opening, the 14-inch gun turrets charred and useless, metal glowing orange, crumbling pieces of concrete deck falling into the orange inferno that had once been the command station.

Captain Biancho grinned. "Schafer, send a message to Major General Chase. Tell him Fort Drum has fallen. Manila is ours."

The destruction of Fort Drum was total. Every single one of the sixty-eight Japanese soldiers inside was killed, obliterated in the explosion.

The capture of Fort Drum marked the end of major U.S. operations in Manila, although the city was not completely cleared of Japanese troops until early March. The invasion of Luzon was the largest American operation in the Pacific War, involving more U.S. troops than had fought in North Africa, France, or Italy.

Once Manila fell, the rest of the Philippine campaign was a mopping up operation. Mindanao was invaded in April, followed by Cebu and the Sulu Archipelago. The Sulu islands would become bases from which Americans would launch other attacks throughout the South China Sea. By June, all Japanese forces in the Philippines

Chapter 26: Island Hopping to Freedom

had been defeated, save isolated pockets who continued guerilla resistance until the formal surrender of Japan on August 15, 1945.

The American re-conquest of the Philippines had been an overwhelming victory for the U.S. While the United States lost 14,000 men, the Japanese suffered a staggering 336,000 killed, in addition to the final destruction of the Imperial Japanese Navy at the Battle of Leyte Gulf.

The Philippines, however, was in a bad state. Many roads and bridges had been destroyed in the fighting. Local economies were disrupted—and around half a million Filipinos had died in the war between 1941 and 1944. At the time of Japan's surrender, the promised Philippine independence under the Tydings-McDuffie Act was little more than ten months away. Would the U.S. honor the provisions of the Act? After so much carnage, would Philippine independence really be recognized in a few months? We will learn about this in our next chapter.

One final word about World War II in the Philippines. Because it is such an extraordinary tale, we must mention the amazing story of Hiroo Onoda. Hiroo Onoda was a Japanese intelligence officer serving on Lubang Island at the time of the U.S. invasion in 1944. Onoda's entire unit either surrendered or was killed by February 1945, save three soldiers. Onoda ordered his men to take to the hills of Lubang to hide.

Onoda and his men did not know that Japan surrendered in August 1945. Leaflets were dropped by plane telling them the war had ended and urging their surrender, but they did not believe them. Over the years they were engaged in shoot outs with local police, surviving by stealing the crops of nearby farmers. The men remained in the mountains for decades. By 1972 all the men except Onoda had been killed or surrendered. In 1974 a Japanese explorer found Onoda and told him the war had ended long ago, but Onoda refused to surrender unless commanded to by a superior officer. The Japanese government tracked down Onoda's former commander, Major

Yoshimi Taniguchi. Taniguchi personally made a trip to Lubang and ordered Onoda to surrender. With much fanfare, Hiroo Onoda surrendered to Filipino President Ferdinand Marcos on March 11, 1974, turning over his officer's sword. Onoda returned home to Japan a celebrity.

Chapter 27

THE THIRD REPUBLIC

While the Philippines was under Japanese occupation, the Japanese had set up a puppet government under a Filipino judge named José Laurel, who became president from 1943 to 1945. Called the "Philippine Republic", this government was *collaborationist*. Collaborationist means cooperation with the enemy against one's own citizens during war time. The Philippine Republic of José Laurel was extremely unpopular, especially given the destructiveness of the Japanese occupation. Laurel spent most of his presidency trying to ensure Filipinos did not starve due to the shortages brought on by the war.

The Philippine government in exile was also in trouble. President Manuel Quezon's second presidential term was set to expire on December 30, 1943. According to the Filipino Constitution, he was supposed to be succeeded by his Vice-President, Sergio Osmeña. Quezon, however, suggested that it was unwise for power to change hands in the middle of the war and was reluctant to hand over his office to Osmeña. Osmeña disagreed and requested the input of the U.S. Attorney General's office. The Attorney General agreed with Osmeña and requested Quezon let go of power. Quezon in turn appealed to President Franklin D. Roosevelt, but FDR did not want to get involved. He preferred to let the Filipinos solve the matter themselves. A meeting was convened between Quezon, Osmeña, and other members of the Philippine Cabinet. Osmeña agreed to suspend the provisions for presidential succession until the liberation of the Philippines. Osmeña did not have to wait long to take power. Manuel Quezon died of tuberculosis that August. Sergio Osmeña became President of the Philippines.

Osmeña returned with MacArthur when the Philippines was invaded in 1944 and was present at the Battle of Leyte Gulf. José Laurel was soon deposed, but Osmeña's power was not unchallenged. He faced a stalwart opponent in Manuel Roxas. Roxas has been a secretary to the collaborationist President José Laurel. Elections were held in April of 1946, only a few months ahead of the scheduled date of Philippine independence. The April elections brought Manuel Roxas to the presidency. Roxas campaigned on a platform of participation in the new United Nations, fostering close ties with the United States, transparency in government, and national reconstruction.

The United States ceded its sovereignty over the Philippines on July 4, 1946 according to the provisions of the Tydings-McDuffie Act. Manuel Roxas became the first president of an independent Republic of the Philippines. The ties with the United States were not cut entirely, however—the U.S. was to retain control of its military bases for 99 years. A treaty called the Philippine Trade Act was also signed, which gave the United States special economic privileges in the Philippines and tied the economies of the two countries together. Many Filipinos would resent this special status granted to the United States. The U.S. also contributed $2 billion for rebuilding the Philippine infrastructure.

Chapter 27: The Third Republic

The period from 1946 to 1965 in the Philippines is known as the Third Republic, the first being that of Aguinaldo, the second the puppet state under Laurel. The leaders of the Third Republic faced significant challenges—rebuilding after the devastation of World War II, moving the Philippine economy away from dependence on the United States, and establishing efficient, honest government that benefitted Filipinos first.

Roxas tried to bring about national healing by issuing a general pardon for all Filipinos who may have collaborated with the Japanese during the occupation—this included former President José Laurel, whom MacArthur considered a traitor. He had him arrested and charged with 132 counts of treason, but fortunately for Laurel, President Roxas was more forgiving than MacArthur.

In other respects, Roxas's government struggled. His administration was notably corrupt and functioned by bribery. He died after only two years in office, stricken by a heart attack during a public speech in 1948. Roxas was succeeded by Elpidio Quirino, his Vice President.

Quirino signed a bill moving the capital from Manila to Quezon City, a suburb of Manila named for the late President Manuel Quezon. Quirino wanted to distance the government of the new republic from Manila, the old colonial seat of power.

The post-war years also saw the rise of the *Hukbalahap* as a threat to the republic. Hukbalahap is short for Hukbong Bayan Laban sa mga Hapon, which means "The nation's army against the Japanese soldiers." Members of the Hukbalahap were known as Huks. The Hukbalahap was founded by Luis Taruc during World War II as a Communist insurgency group against the Japanese. After the conclusion of the war, Taruc and the Huks agitated for land reforms to benefit Filipino peasants. Many Filipino peasants sympathized with their platform: better relations between landlords and tenants, low interest loans from landowners, government banks, and laws protecting small landowners from big landowners. Supporters of the Hukbalahap believed the government—whether Spaniard,

American, or Filipino—was governed by elites who cared little for the needs of Filipino peasants. They had significant support in central Luzon and a private army of 30,000.

President Quirino initially sympathized with the Huks and was inclined to enact some of their reforms if they agreed to lay down their weapons and participate in the political process. But Quirino failed to enact the reforms and negotiations broke down. Taruc called for the overthrow of the government and began a violent insurgency.

The rebellion of the Hukbalahap consisted mainly of ambush attacks along country roads. Armed soldiers hiding in the trees would fire on government vehicles, then disappear into the mountains and woods. One such attack in 1949 ended up turning popular opinion against the Huks.

A cigarette hung loosely from Hilario's lips as he looked through his binoculars at the winding Baler-Bongabon Road. He sat cross legged on the hillside behind his Type 92, a heavy machine gun mounted on a tripod. Like most weaponry of the Huks, the Type 92 was a Japanese gun that had been taken from the enemy in the closing days of World War II. Now it was being used to wage an insurrection against the government of President Elpidio Quirino.

The handheld radio receiver clipped to Hilario's belt crackled. "See anything, Hilario? Over," came a static voice from the speaker.

Hilario put down his binoculars, unclipped the receiver, pressed the button, and spoke into it. "Nothing yet. Over." He clipped the radio back to his belt and continued monitoring the road.

Hilario was not alone. Almost two hundred members of the Hukbalahap were spread out along the hillside overlooking the road. A few were armed with mounted heavy machine guns, like Hilario. Most carried small arms. They were all waiting for a very special car to drive by.

They did not have to wait too much longer. A black Buick sedan came into view on the far side of the valley. Hilario spied it through

Chapter 27: The Third Republic

his binoculars. Tinted windows with two Filipino flags attached to the front.

Hilario dropped his cigarette and excitedly got on the radio. "This is Hilario. Target sighted. Repeat, target sighted, over!"

"Understood," came the crackling voice from the other end. "Wait for the strike team then fire at will." Hilario knelt behind the Type 92, checked his sights, and put his finger on the trigger. He was nervous, but excited.

A minute later the Buick Sedan was rumbling up the road immediately in front of Hilario's position, about 300 yards down the hillside. Suddenly, a group of armed men in green army fatigues appeared on the road. These men were his comrades, part of the so-called "strike team." The Buick slowed to a stop.

Hilario could not hear too well from his position on the hillside, but the leader of the strike team shouted something at the car. The windows of the car rolled down, revealing a military man. "Very high ranking. A general, by the looks of it," said Hilario to himself.

"Step aside!" shouted the general from the window. Hilario could hear his booming voice clearly. "Don't you know this car is carrying Mrs. Aurora Quezon?"

Aurora Quezon! That was the target. Quezon was the widow of former President Manuel Quezon, as well as the Chairwoman of the Philippine Red Cross. She was a powerful symbol of Philippine democracy.

The leader of the strike team held his hand aloft and made a fist. *The sign!* Hilario stared down the sights of his Type 92 and pulled the trigger. An explosion of gunfire erupted from the hillside—and not from Hilario alone. Many other gunners had seen the sign as well. Bullets riddled the car from all directions.

PANG! PANG! PANG! PANG! rattled the bullets as they tore apart the body of the Buick.

A moment later other vehicles came speeding up the road, including two military jeeps full of soldiers of the Filipino army. Hilario stopped firing. His Type 92 was smoking. A pile of empty shells lay on the ground beside him, at least thirty empty rounds.

"Move out!" came the voice from the radio. "Mission accomplished."

By the time the Philippine military who were behind Mrs. Quezon arrived, it was too late. Aurora Quezon had been killed, along with her daughter and the Mayor of Quezon City, both of whom were riding in the Buick. It is estimated that around 200 Huk gunmen fired on the vehicle.

People all over the world were horrified at the cold-blooded murder of Mrs. Quezon. Even the Hukbalahap tried to distance themselves from the murder by saying they did not approve of the attack. Nobody wanted to claim responsibility. Support for the Huks took a significant hit.

The following year Quirino appointed Ramon Magsaysay Secretary of National Defense and commanded him to stomp out the Communist insurgency. Magsaysay's counter-insurgency was successful, not only at defeating the Huks in the field, but in improving the reputation of the Philippine army. By 1951 Taruc was forced into hiding in the mountains. He surrendered to the government in 1954 and was sentenced to twelve years in prison.

Though Quirino succeeded in rebuilding the country and improving the Philippine economy, the problems amongst the Filipino peasantry went unaddressed. He was defeated in the 1953 election by Ramon Magsaysay, the popular Secretary of National Defense. Magsaysay—with support from the American government—wanted to focus on helping improve the lives of the peasants so they would not be susceptible to the doctrines of Communism. Magsaysay was an outspoken opponent of Communism. He believed the growth of Communism was the biggest threat facing southeast Asia and tried to unite the governments of the region against Communism. The Manila Pact of 1954 was an agreement between the Philippines, the

U.S., and several other southeastern nations aimed at containing the spread of Communism in the region. Magsaysay was popular with the common people, with a reputation for strength and honesty. Unfortunately, he was killed in a plane crash in Cebu in 1957. His funeral was attended by over two million people.

Magsaysay's Vice President Carlos Garcia took over as president. Garcia was concerned that so much of the Filipino economy seemed dependent on the United States. He wanted the Philippines to be more economically independent. Garcia pushed a program called the "Filipino First" policy. The Filipino First policy gave preference to Filipinos over foreigners in business and government. Businesspeople from China, Japan, and the U.S. complained that Garcia's policies discriminated against them. Garcia argued that his policy was not anti-foreign. Rather, it was meant to give Filipinos priority in the control over the country's basic industries and their development.

After serving two terms, Garcia was defeated by his Vice President Diosdado Macapagal, who was from the opposition Liberal Party. Macapagal finally enacted some needed land reforms. One of the most important was the Agricultural Land Reform Code of 1963. The Land Reform Code benefitted small farmers in many ways. For example, it limited the amount of interest farmers could be charged on loans and established a Land Bank to serve the financial needs of Filipino farmers. Its most important provision, however, was that it ordered that peasants' pay their landowners in the form of fixed rents rather than a percentage of the harvest. This transformed the Filipino farmers from peasants into something more like renters and made them much less dependent on wealthy landowners.

Macapagal's Liberal Party was opposed by the Nacionalistas. By the mid-1960s, the voice of the Nacionalistas was Senate President Ferdinand Marcos. Marcos had once been an ally of Macapagal and the Liberal Party but had switched sides and gone over to the Nacionalistas. Marcos stood against Macapagal in the 1965 election and defeated him. It seemed like a routine change of power, but the advent of Marcos was anything but routine.

The Third Republic was characterized by competent presidents who helped build up the social and economic strength of the Philippines. Quezon, Roxas, Quirino, Magsaysay, Garcia, and Macapagal were all capable men who faced down various challenges in their efforts to strengthen the new republic. Even so, corruption, agricultural problems, and economic instability continued to trouble the country into the 1960s. In our next chapter, we shall see how the long presidency of Ferdinand Marcos fundamentally altered the framework of the Philippine state.

Chapter 28

THE DICTATORSHIP OF MARCOS

The new president Ferdinand Marcos had a distinguished career in the Philippine government. After the Second World War he had served in the Philippine House of Representatives and was a member of the Senate since 1959. At the time he defeated Macapagal, he had been elevated to President of the Senate. Marcos had risen to power with the Liberal Party, but by 1965 had switched to favoring the Nacionalistas.

The major issue facing the Philippines in 1965 was whether to get involved in the Vietnam War. After its crackdown on the Hukbalahap, the Third Republic became decisively anti-Communist, and as such was a global ally of the U.S. in the Cold War. The Filipinos did not like the prospect of Vietnam being united under a Communist regime, but nor did they relish the idea of getting involved in an undeclared war in which they had no direct stake.

As President of the Senate, Marcos had opposed military

intervention in Vietnam. After his election to the presidency, however, he bewildered his supporters by suddenly arguing in favor of sending Filipino forces to aid the American war effort. When asked about his unexpected change of heart, Marcos replied that his reasons were something he "cannot reveal in a public manner." The proposal caused an uproar in the Philippine government and representatives and senators furiously debated the situation in Vietnam.

It soon became apparent that Marcos's support was based on American pressure. The U.S. government was seeking to get other nations involved in Vietnam and had promised the Marcos government significant financial aid if the Philippines would get into the fight. Some Filipinos found this exchange scandalous. One Filipino congressman, Pablo Ocampo, argued vehemently against Marcos's plans, saying it amounted to an exchange of Filipino blood for American cash:

> "It is obvious that the main factor behind the administration's drive to send troops to South Vietnam, which President Marcos says he 'cannot reveal in a public manner,' is the promise of the United States to send economic aid to this country in exchange for our sending troops to South Vietnam. No President could reveal the brutal truth that in order to get the wherewithal for a program of development with which to achieve a successful administration, this country must send Filipinos to die in South Vietnam. No matter how the spokesmen of Mr. Marcos try to cover it up, the truth remains that the overriding factor which motivates the Marcos administration is the promise of American aid."

It is understandable why Marcos wanted this aid. While the Philippine government was certainly not bankrupt, it was running at a considerable deficit—as much as 2 million pesos a day. The aid promised by America would fill government coffers considerably.

Chapter 28: The Dictatorship of Marcos

In the end, Marcos agreed to outfit a Filipino brigade called the Philippine Civic Action Group-Vietnam (PHILCAG). Comprised of around 2,000 men, PHILCAG fought alongside the United States in Vietnam from 1966 to 1969.

Since independence, no Philippine president had ever been elected to a second term. Marcos wanted to change that. He planned massive infrastructure projects to modernize Philippine schools, roads, and agriculture. The problem, however, was that his government did not have the money to pay for these projects. To fund them, Marcos took out $50 million in foreign loans which he had neither the plans nor the ability to pay back. Before long, the Philippines was sunk in crippling debt. Some of Marcos' debt is still being paid off to this day. The projects were popular with the public, however, and going into 1969 Marcos's reelection seemed assured.

The years 1968 and 1969 would be full of crises that would challenge Marcos's reelection. In 1968, it came to light that President Marcos had been planning a mission to secretly infiltrate and destabilize the Malaysian island of Sabah in preparation for a Philippine invasion. To accomplish this, the Philippine army was training Muslim troops from Mindanao. It was believed that the Moro troops would more easily blend into the Muslim culture of Sabah. The Moro recruits were taken to Corregidor Island for training. When they found out their mission was to invade another Muslim country, however, they refused to carry it out. Not wanting the details of the secret mission to get out to the public, the military rounded up the Moro recruits and shot them. Only one—a man named Jibin Arula—survived. He was found by two fishermen floating in Manila Bay, shot and barely clinging to life. When Arula recovered, he related the entire story.

The killings became known as the Jabidah Massacre. The massacre resulted in a congressional investigation and outrage from Muslims around the world. But especially furious were the Moros of Mindanao, who believed they were second-class citizens under the Marcos government. They called for the impeachment of Marcos.

Some went farther—the former governor of Cotabato, Datu Udtog Matalam, formed the Muslim Independence Movement (MIM), a Muslim-dominated organization working for the secession of Mindanao from the Philippine Republic. The MIM was immediately rent by discord over the use of violence to achieve secession, and in 1972 a splinter group calling itself the Moro National Liberation Front (MNLF) was founded. The MNLF employed violence against the Philippine authorities, initiating a second Moro insurgency. Violence between Moros and Philippine authorities would continue well past the Marcos presidency. It still endures to this day.

The Jabidah Massacre cast Marcos in a villainous light. The debt-spending of Marcos also came to a head in 1969 as the economy grappled with out-of-control inflation, leading to protests and social unrest. Marcos's assured reelection was beginning to look a lot less certain. Marcos utilized all the power at his disposal to ensure a victory.

What followed was the most corrupt election in the young republic's history. Marcos mobilized the Philippine armed forces to spread pro-Marcos propaganda. Armed thugs, paid by the government, beat up opposition leaders and terrorized voters in regions hostile to Marcos. Leftists took to the streets to protest the violence of Marcos, who was increasingly behaving as a dictator.

As a result of the violence and fraud, Marcos won reelection in 1969. His second term was marked by violence and corruption. Protests against Marcos spread throughout the Philippines in 1970. First Lady Imelda Marcos was caught attempting to bribe delegates to a constitutional convention in 1971 to alter the constitution in ways that would grant Marcos more power. Other opposition leaders were arrested on charges of being Communists, the term Marcos applied to all his opponents. In August of 1971, Marcos announced Proclamation No. 889, which suspended the writ of *habeas corpus*. The writ of habeas corpus requires a person under arrest to be brought before a judge or into court, especially to secure the person's release unless lawful grounds are shown for their detention. By suspending

Chapter 28: The Dictatorship of Marcos

habeas corpus, Marcos obtained the power to arrest people without cause and imprison them without trial.

In 1972, Manila was rocked by a series of bombings. Marcos blamed the newly formed Philippine Communist Party, but the attackers were never found. Opposition was intensifying. On September 23, 1972, Ferdinand Marcos declared the entire Philippines to be under martial law. Martial law means rule by the military. Marcos was now dictator of the Philippines.

Opposition to Marcos came from two camps, referred to as "Moderates" and "Radicals." The "moderates" included church organizations, civil libertarians, and nationalist politicians who wanted to create change through political reforms. The "radicals", including a number of labor and student groups, wanted broader, more systematic reforms. Many radicals were communists or sympathetic to communism and were not opposed to using violence. Marcos tended to label all his opponents as radicals and treated them with maximum harshness. Over time, the severity of Marcos pushed many otherwise moderate opponents into the radical camp.

Philippine Communists formed the New Peoples Army (NPA) to oppose Marcos. The NPA raided a military armory, capturing guns, grenade launchers, bazookas, and thousands of rounds of ammunition. The Communist authorities in China supported the NPA, shipping them 1,200 M-14 and AK-47 assault rifles. Thus by 1972, Marcos was facing armed insurgencies from the Islamic MNLF in Mindanao and the Communist NPA.

Marcos cracked down on civil liberties, curtailing freedom of the press, shutting down media establishments, and dissolving the Philippine Congress. Prosperous Philippine businesses were seized by the government and handed over to friends of the Marcoses. Often it was Marcos's wife, Imelda, who was charged with handing over these confiscated businesses to family friends. Anyone who voiced opposition to the Marcos regime was imprisoned.

Marcos announced that he planned to form something called the *Bagong Lipunan*, "New Society." He said that society needed

President Ferdinand Marcos and his wife, Imelda Marcos.

to be reformed under the guidance of a "benevolent dictator" who could guide the masses through the chaotic transition to the Bagong Lipunan. What exactly was the Bagong Lipunan? Marcos was a little vague on the details. He envisioned it as a kind of constitutional authoritarianism that would reconcile the poor with the privileged and enable them to work together for the common good. The Bagong Lipunan was promoted with a vast propaganda campaign, including speeches, books, pamphlets, slogans, and even songs.

In 1973, Marcos held a national referendum on his martial law declaration, effectively asking the public's blessing on his assumption of power. The elections were carefully managed to obtain the outcome Marcos wanted, with voting taking place in "citizens' assemblies" who voted by show of hands under the supervision of government moderators. The referendum asked Filipinos "Do you want President

Chapter 28: The Dictatorship of Marcos

Marcos to continue beyond 1973 and finish the reforms he has initiated under the martial law?" The referendum yielded a result of 90.67% in favor, 9.33% opposed. The results are hardly credible, as observers noted that many of the "citizens assemblies" were never even convened. Either way, Marcos had his way. From 1973 on, his dictatorial rule carried the veneer of legitimacy.

Marcos ruled with the help of a group of associates known as the Rolex 12—the name stemming from the legend that each had received the gift of a Rolex watch from President Marcos. The members of the Rolex 12 were high ranking officials in the military and Philippine police forces. Together with Marcos, they enriched themselves while using their positions to solidify Marcos's authoritarian control over all aspects of the Philippine government. The Rolex 12 were responsible for many human rights abuses: arbitrary arrest, murder, torture, seizure of property, and displacement of people from their homes. To ensure his regime stayed in power, Marcos quadrupled the size of the Filipino army, from 65,000 in 1972 to 275,000 by 1976. By 1977, over 60,000 Filipinos had been arrested by the army for political reasons.

One might wonder how the United States viewed the Marcos dictatorship. Because of Marcos's strong anti-Communist stance, the United States government was content to overlook the abusive nature of his regime. For example, in 1981, Vice President George H.W. Bush praised President Marcos for his "adherence to democratic principles and to the democratic processes." The U.S. government also gave Marcos money to keep him in power. Between 1972 and 1981, the United States gave the Marcos regime $2.5 billion directly and another $5.5 billion through other organizations such as the World Bank. The U.S. even turned a blind eye to Marcos harassing Filipino dissidents on U.S. soil. In 1981, two anti-Marcos labor activists were assassinated in Seattle, Washington by agents of Marcos. The CIA knew about the presence of Marcos's agents in the country and prevented the FBI from investigating the killings. This caused great resentment towards the American government on the part of Filipinos.

By 1977, reports of human rights abuses had grown so numerous that there was international pressure on Marcos to restore democratic rule. U.S. President Jimmy Carter urged Marcos to release Benigno "Ninoy" Aquino, a prominent liberal politician who had been jailed by Marcos. Marcos refused to release Aquino, but he did concede to hold free parliamentary elections in 1978. The 1978 elections were notoriously corrupt, featuring pre-stuffed ballot boxes, phony registrations, buying votes, and manipulated election returns. Of the new parliament, Ferdinand Marcos controlled 91% and took the title of Prime Minister in the new government. With Marcos enshrined as the leader of the new government and 91% of the parliament in his control, he issued Proclamation 2045 lifting martial law in January, 1981.

Some believe this was done ahead of Pope St. John Paul II's historic visit to the country in February. The pope spent a week in the Philippines from February 17–22, 1981. The pope celebrated Mass in Manila and elevated Manila's cathedral to a basilica. In Baclaran he presided over a gathering of Philippine and Asian bishops. In Quezon City the pope addressed Filipino students at the University of Santo Tomas, reminding them to use their energy and talents for good. On February 18, John Paul II beatified the Filipino martyr Lorenzo Ruiz in Rizal Park, Manila. Ruiz was martyred in Japan in 1637. His beatification was the first ever held outside of Rome. The pope continued his progress south, visiting a seminary in Cebu then Davao City in Mindanao. In Mindanao he met with representatives of local Islamic communities, as well as refugees from Laos, Cambodia, and Vietnam. His trip concluded with a Mass for indigenous tribes in Baguio City in Luzon and a meeting with members of the Philippine media.

Shortly after John Paul's visit, things began to fall apart for Marcos. With the lifting of martial law, attacks by the Communist NPA intensified. The government became increasingly vulnerable, and violence got worse. In 1985 alone, 2,644 military personnel and

Chapter 28: The Dictatorship of Marcos

civilians were killed in attacks by the NPA. The economy began to collapse as well. The Marcos government could not keep up with all the debt it had incurred. Things got worse after 1981 when the U.S. went into a recession. Since the economies of the U.S. and Philippines were closely tied, the recession in the U.S. hurt the Philippine economy. By 1984–1985, the Philippine economy was in the worst state it had ever been.

In 1983, opposition leader Ninoy Aquino was assassinated. Aquino had been imprisoned since the 1970s. He had been permitted to travel to the United States for heart surgery and was returning home when he was shot dead while getting off his plane at the Manila airport. The killers were Philippine military personnel who were cronies of Marcos.

In 1985 the Philippine legislature tried to impeach Marcos, specifically on the crime of diverting American financial aid for personal use. Marcos had stolen millions of dollars in foreign aid and used it to make real estate investments in the U.S. Though the impeachment failed, a movement called "People Power" began. Supported by opposition politicians, members of the Catholic hierarchy, and average Filipinos sick of Marcos, the People Power movement advocated for new elections and the removal of Marcos.

Marcos called for an election in 1985. The People Power movement united behind Corazon Aquino, the widow of the murdered Ninoy Aquino. The Catholic Church threw its support behind Aquino as well, united behind Jaime Cardinal Sin, Archbishop of Manila. Nevertheless, Marcos was declared the winner, but poll watchers said cheating and violence was rampant on both sides. Supporters of Aquino and the People Power movement took to the streets in protest and overran parts of Manila. With his election in doubt and his health failing—Marcos was suffering from kidney problems and an autoimmune disease—Marcos and his wife Imelda fled the Philippines, along with 90 of their closest associates. They arrived in Hawaii on February 26, 1986.

Ferdinand and Imelda Marcos did not leave the Philippines

empty handed, however. Let's see what they brought with them when they arrived in Hawaii:

Officers Wilson and Akana of the United States Custom Services stood about the airplane hangar with members of the Immigration Naturalization Service, FBI, U.S. Air Force, CIA, and many other agencies. This hangar at Hawaii's Hickam Airforce Base had been set aside to hold the cargo President Ferdinand Marcos had brought with him from the Philippines. And what a massive cargo it was!

"We've got a final count, sir," said a man with a clipboard, reporting to Officer Wilson. "Looks like 359 crates, boxes, and containers."

"Marcos doesn't know the meaning of traveling light," said Officer Akana. "I'd hate to go on vacation with him."

Officer Wilson smirked. "Well, gentlemen, shall we see what sort of goods Marcos packed for his little 'vacation'?"

A host of officials with crowbars fanned out across the hangar and began prying open the wooden crates to catalog the belongings of Marcos. It was the jurisdiction of the Customs Service to index everything brought into the United States, and given the high profile of Marcos, the U.S. government had a great interest in his cargo.

The hangar was filled with the sounds of creaking wood as the men opened the crates.

"Look at this!" a man yelled.

Officer Wilson walked over to the freshly opened crate. His eyes widened at the sight of U.S. $100 bills that filled the crate to the top.

"There's about twenty-four cubic feet of space in that crate," said Officer Akana. "I'd guesstimate there must be two million dollars in there.

"Here's another one!" somebody shouted.

"And another!" came another cry. Crates all over the hangar were found to be filled with cash.

Chapter 28: The Dictatorship of Marcos

"This is astonishing!" said Officer Wilson, dashing to and fro about the hangar inspecting each find.

"Sir, what do you make of this?" said one official, puzzled at what he found in his crate. Wilson and Akana peered into the large crate and saw only boxes of diapers.

"I knew Marcos was getting on in years, but I didn't think he was to this point yet," said Akana.

"Very funny!" said Wilson stoically, but I bet there is more here than meets the eye. Wilson took out a pocket-knife, sliced open one of the diaper boxes, and shined a flashlight inside. The flashlight beam revealed a host of sparkling colors. "Gems!" he cried. "Hundreds of them!" Each diaper box was opened, and everyone was filled with a fortune in gems.

"Here's pearls!" someone else called.

"And gold bars!" came another astonished cry.

Officer Wilson could barely keep track of everything—each find was more astonishing than the last. "This is unbelievable!" he exclaimed to Akana. "Can this guy get any more over the top?"

"Sir!" someone called. "You'd better have a look at this!" Wilson turned to see several men lifting a statue out of a crate. It was a three-foot-tall solid gold Buddha encrusted with diamonds. Wilson's mouth dropped open.

"Looks like you spoke too soon," said Akana.

The loot Marcos took from the Philippines was immense: $717 million in U.S. cash, 300 crates full of gold and silver jewelry, $4 million worth of gems (all found in diaper boxes), 65 luxury watches, a 12 x 4-foot box crammed with precious pearls, $200,000 in gold bars and coins, $1 million in Philippine pesos, $124 million in deposit slips for banks in the U.S., Switzerland, and the Cayman Islands, and the three-foot-tall statue encrusted in diamonds. All this wealth had been amassed during his long reign, pilfered from the people of the Philippines, or embezzled from U.S. foreign aid.

Within two weeks of his arrival in Hawaii, a host of legal cases were being filed against Marcos. Even so, it would take some time before the immensity of Marcos's crimes and theft were fully comprehended. In the meantime, the Philippines began the arduous task of recovering from twenty years of dictatorship.

Chapter 29

RETURN TO THE REPUBLIC

As chaos engulfed the Philippines and Marcos was preparing to flee, Corazon Aquino was sworn in as president. President Aquino would face the formidable task of restoring Philippine democracy while dismantling the corrupt power structure created by Marcos.

Aquino had been pushed to the presidency by the People Power revolution. The People Power revolution—also known as the Yellow Revolution due to the yellow ribbons worn by protestors—worked for the restoration of democracy after decades of dictatorship. Once in power, Aquino's first act was to suspend the Constitution of 1973, which Marcos had used to cement his dictatorial powers. Instead, she promulgated a new constitution, the so-called "Freedom Constitution" of 1986. The Freedom Constitution gave her significant authority to govern while a new, more permanent constitution was drafted.

Corazon Aquino, wife of slain opposition leader Benigno Aquino, rode the People Power movement to the presidency in 1986.

Filipinos were outraged when they discovered the extent of Marcos's embezzlement. President Aquino formed a Presidential Commission on Good Government to go after Marcos in hopes of recovering the millions in plundered loot. The Commission was unsuccessful, however, as it came to light that Commission members themselves were trying to loot and amass wealth just as Marcos had. This episode with the Commission on Good Government highlights one of the core problems the Philippines faced in the post-Marcos era: despite the desire for reform, corruption had become so entrenched in government that it was a way of life. Bringing good government to the Philippines would take much more than changing institutions or swapping out leaders. It would require an entirely new mindset.

Aquino did what she could. She abolished the repressive laws

Chapter 29: Return to the Republic

enacted by Marcos. The Marcos-era parliament known as the Batasang Pambansa was dissolved. In 1987 a new constitution was adopted that restored a bi-cameral legislature (Senate and House of Representatives) and featured three branches of government with separation of powers, similar to the United States. Safeguards were also put in place to ensure that no future president could declare martial law indefinitely. A declaration of martial law expired in 60 days and could only be extended by the legislature. In addition to this, presidents were limited to a single term. Marcos's cronies were purged from the government. Monopolies established by Marcos were dismantled.

Still, the government was debt-ridden and the economy nearly bankrupt. In many places, there were continuous power outages as the country's decades-old power grid struggled to keep up with demand. But Aquino's biggest challenge was civil unrest from insurgent groups. The Communist NPA was still staging attacks against the government. Marcos loyalists were also still lurking around making trouble. Between 1986 and 1990, there were nine attempts to overthrow Aquino.

The most severe insurgency, however, came from the military. Within the military was a cabal of army officers known as RAM— the Reform of the Armed Forces Movement. It is hard to classify the aims of RAM. On the one hand, these were all officers who had risen to prominence during the years of martial law under Marcos, but they were not Marcos supporters. Indeed, many had worked to destabilize the Marcos government during his latter years. But they also resented what they thought was the lax condition of the military under Aquino. They wanted a greater role for the military in the new government, as well as a general reform of military discipline and morals.

Led by Colonel Gregorio Honasan, the RAM wanted to dislodge Aquino and take over. They launched their attack in metro Manila on December 1st, 1989. Let us visit Malacañang Palace, the seat of Philippine executive power, on the morning of the coup.

People ran in confusion at the loud roar of military aircraft darting across the skies over Manila. "Why is the Philippine air force attacking the capital?" they asked each other in confusion. "What's going on?"

Indeed, it seemed to be true. A trio of propeller-driven T-28 fighter planes turned and swooped towards Malacañang Palace, the executive seat of the Philippine presidency. Tourists scrambled away from the palatial lawn as the T-28s' machine guns rattled. A spray of bullets strafed the mansion, shattering windows and blasting off the historic plaster façade as the planes swooped by.

Fleeing from the palace lawn that day were 14-year-old Lucia and her father Andre. Andre and Lucia lived in Quezon City. They took the train to Manila today to see some of the historic sites. Lucia was especially excited to see Malacañang Palace, the old center of Spanish colonial power and the current residence of President Corazon Aquino. Now father and daughter were fleeing for cover as the aircraft under RAM control fired on the building.

Lucia covered her ears with her hands as she crouched behind a bench. The roar of the planes' engines and gunfire was deafening. "Dad, what's happening?" she cried.

"The military must be staging a coup," said her father. "That's the only reason they'd be attacking Malacañang. They're trying to get rid of President Aquino!"

There was a momentary lull in the noise as the planes swooped around for another pass. Andre grabbed his daughter's arm. "Let's get out of here!" The two joined the throngs of fleeing tourists trying to exit the area. They dashed through the scenic Malacañang gardens as Manila's San Miguel district erupted in the sound of sirens and emergency alarms.

Andre hoped to get out of the area through the gardens, but as they approached the looming government administration building at the gardens' northeast end, he saw the place was swarming with soldiers. The soldiers were looking into the sky in confusion.

Chapter 29: Return to the Republic

"Whose side are they on?" said Lucia.

"I don't know, but we'd better not go near them. We'll try another way." The two turned onto José Laurel Street, a tree-lined lane that ran adjacent to the palace. The street was full of stopped cars and people milling about. "Maybe we can take José Laurel to get to the Nagtahan Bridge and cross the Pasig. We need to get out of the San Miguel district."

A crackling voice came blaring over a loud speaker somewhere. "CLEAR THE STREETS. TAKE COVER. THIS IS NOT A DRILL. CLEAR THE STREETS. TAKE COVER. THIS IS NOT A DRILL." The voice was drowned out by the sound of the T-28s returning for another attack on Malacañang. The people in the street again began screaming and running.

It took some time, but Andre and Lucia finally made it to the Nagtahan Bridge. The bridge was crammed full of cars and people, and traffic was at a standstill. It was impossible even to get near it due to the crowds. But Andre did get a better sense of what was going on—across the Pasig he could see the roofs of certain high-rise buildings had been occupied by military personnel. He had heard from others on the street that these were members of the RAM, the elite military cabal that was attempting to wrest control of the government from Aquino.

"They're attacking the palace and have all the biggest buildings in Manila," said Lucia as she clasped her father's hand and watched the planes scurrying across the Manila skyline. "Is the government going to fight back?"

"I hope so," said Andre. "It isn't looking good for Aquino right now."

Fortunately for President Aquino, the tide did turn against the rebels. Aquino asked the United States for help. The United States initiated Operation Classic Resolve, scrambling F-4 Phantom fighters from Clark Air Force Base. The U.S. planes harassed the RAM planes, prevented them from taking off, and shot at those in flight. The RAM fighters could not compete with the U.S. Air Force and gave up the air attacks.

Meanwhile, Aquino went on television to announce that the mutineers had two choices, "Surrender or die." Gradually the government forces took back all the positions overrun by the RAM insurgents and the coup was over by December 9th.

Though Aquino put down the coup, it was a disaster for her. She looked weak and vulnerable. Tourism came to a halt, and investments in the Philippines dried up, bringing further economic distress.

The country had scarcely recovered from the chaos of the coup when it was rocked by another devastating challenge—this time from Mother Nature. In June 1991, the volcanic Mount Pinatubo in central Luzon erupted. The eruption was cataclysmic, one of the largest eruptions in the 20th century. The peak of the mountain was obliterated in an explosion that spewed millions of cubic tons of gas into the air. The smoke from the eruption rose 22 miles into the atmosphere. Volcanic ash was spread all over Asia—ash from Pinatubo was found as far away as the Indian Ocean.

Almost 1,000 Filipinos were killed in the blast, mainly from the weight of volcanic ash collapsing the roofs of houses. Thankfully most had been evacuated before the blast, but the effects on agriculture were devastating—800,000 head of livestock killed and 200,000 square acres of farmland ruined. The livelihood of thousands of farmers was also ruined. Mudslides after the eruption caused further evacuations, displacing thousands more. The damages exceeded $175 million. Countries around the world contributed money and humanitarian aid to help the Philippines deal with the crisis. The economic and environmental effects of the Mount Pinatubo eruption would continue to be felt for years after.

One other notable event of the Aquino years was the final removal of U.S. forces from the Philippines. Following independence in 1946, the United States retained several military bases in the

Chapter 29: Return to the Republic

Philippines by treaty. By 1991, only two remained—Clark Air Force Base and the naval base at Subic Bay. The treaty allowing America to use these bases was set to expire at the end of 1992. The United States wanted to renew their use of these bases, but the Philippine Senate rejected the U.S. proposal. This was upsetting to President Aquino, who was very pro-American and was initially hoping for a continued U.S. presence. The U.S., however, refused to state clearly whether they were keeping nuclear weapons on the bases, something that was unsettling to Filipinos. President Aquino grew tired of the evasiveness of American officials and told the U.S. military they had to leave by the end of 1992. Clark Air Force base was subsequently closed. Subic Bay was evacuated on November 24, 1992. This date marked the first time no foreign military forces were present in the Philippines since the arrival of the Spaniards in the 16th century.

When Aquino's term ended, Filipinos elected Fidel Ramos as president in 1992. Ramos was a distinguished military man who had served as Secretary of Defense under Aquino. Filipinos considered him a national hero because during the Marcos years he had broken from Marcos to support the People Power movement. Ramos was concerned with the political divisions in the country: Communist insurgents, military cabals such as the RAM, and Muslim separatists in Mindanao. Ramos believed the best way to address these groups was through reconciliation. He granted a general amnesty to all insurgents, as well as Philippine police and military who had committed crimes while fighting the insurgents. The amnesty meant that nobody would be prosecuted for crimes they may have committed during periods of insurgency or crisis. In the interest of reconciliation, the government agreed to just move on. Among those pardoned by Ramos was Gregorio Honasan, the mastermind of the 1989 RAM insurgency. Honasan would go on to become Secretary of Information and Communications Technology under President Rodrigo Duterte.

Ramos's reconciliation policy was successful to some degree. A peace agreement was reached with the Moro National Liberation

Front (MNLF), bringing an end to the decades' old insurgency. The Communist Party of the Philippines was also granted legal recognition, bringing Communists into the political process.

Ramos also continued the work of Aquino in dismantling the autocratic policies from the Marcos years. For example, he did away with Marcos-era regulations on the oil industry. This brought more freedom to the Philippine economy, although sometimes with negative consequences—his deregulation of the gas industry caused the price of gas to go up dramatically, angering Filipinos.

The years from 1986 to the end of the 20th century were a time of great challenge and promise for the Philippines. While the political freedom made it possible to move beyond the dictatorial past of the Marcos regime, persistent corruption, economic problems, and political instability plagued the governments of Corazon Aquino and Fidel Ramos. Even as the Philippines continued to grow economically and find its place on the world stage, the country still struggled with fundamental questions forty plus years after independence—what sort of government should we have? How do we bring these thousands of disparate islands and cultures into a single political unity? Where does the Philippines fit into the broader global community? And what does it even mean to be Filipino?

In our next chapter we will study how the Philippines has dealt with these issues in the first two decades of the 21st century.

Chapter 30

INTO THE 21st CENTURY

The coming of the 21st century brought more of the same—corruption, economic problems, violent insurgency, and continued political squabbling over the structure of the Philippine government. Even so, the Philippines made significant strides in other areas: infrastructure development, economic growth, and technological advances.

The 20th century ended with an economic crisis, the so-called Asian Financial Crisis. The crisis did not originate in the Philippines. Rather, it was a result of currency devaluations in Thailand that rippled throughout the Asian economies. Lasting throughout the summer of 1997, the Asian Financial Crisis caused the Philippine *peso* to lose almost half of its value and exports fell. Though the Philippines did not suffer as much as some Asian countries, it was a difficult time for the Philippine economy. The Philippine people were looking for stability and certainty during the economic troubles.

Into the midst of this crisis came a new president, Joseph Estrada. Estrada was a famous movie celebrity who had gone into politics. He rose to become vice president during the Ramos administration and had a background in combatting organized crime. When he became president, Estrada promised economic recovery and put together a strong team of economic advisers. Despite this, debt increased and the president's economic policies faltered. The president became associated with incompetence and corruption. The economy would eventually recover from the crisis, largely in spite of Estrada rather than because of him.

Hoping to improve his reputation, Estrada turned his attention to the Moro insurgency which had flared up again in Mindanao. As we saw in our last chapter, President Ramos secured a peace treaty with the Moro National Liberation Front (MNLF), ending the decades long insurgency. The peace was short lived. A splinter group called the Moro Islamic Liberation Front (MILF) refused to accept the peace and continued its campaign of bombings, kidnappings, and murder. Estrada proclaimed an "all out war" against MILF, attacking their camps aggressively.

The Catholic bishops of the Philippines thought Estrada's approach would lead to more trouble. They petitioned Estrada to negotiate a cease-fire with MILF. Estrada refused, arguing that to do so would only embolden them more. Throughout the spring of 2000, Estrada's offensive paid off. Fifty-six MILF camps were seized by government forces, including the MILF headquarters known as Camp Abubakar. The MILF declared a jihad, or holy war, against the Estrada government, but to little effect. The MILF commander, Hasim Salamat, was forced to flee the country. Estrada raised the Philippine flag in Mindanao on July 10, proclaimed victory, and ordered a general arrest of all MILF leaders. MILF forces began surrendering in droves as Estrada attempted to formulate a plan for integrating Mindanao into the rest of the Philippine economy. MILF, however, was far from vanquished as we shall see.

This ambitious plan would falter, however, as Estrada ran into

Chapter 30: Into the 21st Century

his own problems later that year. In October of 2000 it came to light that Estrada had stolen tens of millions of dollars of public money. Filipinos were outraged. An impeachment commission was formed to investigate the alleged crimes of Estrada. The impeachment trial fell apart when certain Senators refused to examine evidence of Estrada's guilt. The prosecution panel walked out of the trial in protest.

Meanwhile, protests were forming at the Shrine of Mary Queen of Peace in Manila, the same site where the People Power protests led to the downfall of Marcos in 1986. Seeing the potential for civil unrest, the Armed Forces Chief of Staff Angelo Reyes decided to withdraw his support from Estrada. Instead, he sought out Vice President Gloria Macapagal Arroyo and pledged allegiance to her. The following day—January 20, 2001—Estrada resigned and the Philippine Supreme Court recognized Arroyo as president.

The new Arroyo government formed a special commission to charge Estrada with the crime of "plunder." Estrada's supporters took to the streets to protest, and Estrada began denying he had ever resigned. A state of rebellion was declared, and the military was called out to restore order. Eventually Arroyo gained the upper hand and peace was restored by May. Estrada was arrested and brought to trial. He was found guilty of plunder in 2007 and sentenced to perpetual imprisonment. President Arroyo, however, gave him a full a pardon scarcely a month into his imprisonment. Estrada would later serve two terms as the Mayor of Manila.

Arroyo served as president from 2001 to 2010, difficult years as the world grappled with the aftermath of the 9/11 terrorist attacks and the United States's "Global War on Terror." The Philippines, too, would suffer from Islamic terror during this time. On March 4, 2003, a bomb exploded at the Francisco Bangoy International Airport in Davao City in Mindanao. The bomb killed 21 people and wounded over a hundred others. The perpetrators were MILF, who were resurfacing in Mindanao and eager to show their power against the U.S.-aligned Philippine government.

The country had scarcely begun to process the Davao bombing when the stability of the government was again threatened by a military coup. Called the Oakwood Mutiny, a cabal of army officers calling themselves the Bagong Katipuneros ("New Katipunan") seized an apartment tower in Manila on July 27. Motivated by a fear that Arroyo was about to declare martial law and become a dictator like Marcos, the Bagong Katipuneros hoped to use the coup as an opportunity to expose corruption in Arroyo's government and get rid of her. They also wanted to call attention to the poor state of the Philippine armed forces.

The public failed to offer substantial support to the Bagong Katipuneros, however, and the rebellion ended bloodlessly after only 18 hours. The rebels personally apologized to Arroyo for the coup. Nevertheless, the rebels were put on trial and sentenced to various prison terms. However, like many political rebels in the Philippines, most were later pardoned.

The fears about Arroyo seizing power were not entirely unfounded. The Philippine constitution said that a president could only serve one term. Arroyo, however, had not been elected, but assumed office upon the resignation of Estrada. She argued that the law allowed her a second term since she had never actually been elected president. Arroyo ran for an unprecedented second term in 2004 and appeared to have won easily. However, it soon became apparent that the election was dishonest. Audio recordings surfaced of Arroyo talking to an official of the national elections commission about rigging the election to produce one million extra votes for her. Arroyo admitted having an improper conversation with the official but denied rigging the election. With scandal brewing, members of her cabinet began to resign in protest. Articles of impeachment were prepared against her.

In the middle of the 2006 impeachment, the military staged another coup against Arroyo, this time led by an army official named General Danilo Lim. The plot was uncovered before the military had a chance to act, but Arroyo used the occasion to declare a state of emergency. During the state of emergency, she arrested opponents without warrant, seized property, and imposed limits on the press. The state of emergency was lifted after one week. Though the Supreme Court upheld Arroyo's emergency declaration, they ruled that her warrantless arrests and seizure of property were illegal. Danilo Lim spent four years in prison for the coup. After his release, he ran unsuccessfully for Senator but was eventually appointed as Chairman of the Metro Manila Development Authority, another example of the Philippine tendency for former rebels to be awarded government positions.

Despite the illegality of Arroyo's arbitrary arrests during the emergency, her impeachment failed in the Philippine Congress. She left office in 2010 at the expiration of her second term. However, after she left office, she was arrested in 2011 on charges of sabotaging the 2004 election and embezzling $8.8 million. She remained in government custody from 2012 to 2016, though not in prison due to illness. In 2016 the charges against her were dismissed and Arroyo was freed. It should be noted that Arroyo still managed to successfully get elected to the House of Representatives in 2013 while under government detention.

The impeachment of Estrada and arrest of Arroyo—along with the coups of 2001, 2003, and 2006—demonstrate the political instability that still characterized Philippine government into the 21st century. Mindanao, too, continued to be a cause of trouble. Back in 1989, the government of President Corazon Aquino signed the Organic Act of 1989 which established self-government for Muslims in Mindanao. This region was made up of five provinces and was known as the Autonomous Region in Muslim Mindanao (ARMM) and was essentially a state within a state. ARMM had its own capital, legislature, laws, and infrastructure. While certain governmental functions were reserved to the Philippine central government, day-to-day administration was handled locally. It was hoped that granting Muslims self-government in Mindanao would help put an end to the constant violence there.

As we have seen, this did not stop the emergence of new groups like MILF from continuing their insurgencies. Local rivalries could also turn violent, as in the case of the 2009 Maguindanao Massacre. Control of the province of Maguindanao was contested between two clans, the Ampatuans and the Mangudadatus. The Ampatuans had held power in Maguindanao since 2001 and used their extensive clan to quash challenges to their rule. In 2009, the Vice Mayor of Buluan, Esmael Mangudadatu, launched a political campaign against the Ampatuans with the aim of displacing Governor Andal Ampatuan. The Ampatuans threatened Mangudadatu if he filed to run against Governor Andal. Undaunted, Mangudadatu assembled a convoy of lawyers, journalists, and family members to meet him in the city of Shariff Aguak and watch him file his campaign paperwork. Mangudadatu hoped the presence of so many reporters and lawyers would dissuade the Ampatuans from violence.

Esmael Mangudadatu underestimated the viciousness of his opponents. On the morning of November 23, 2009, the Mangudadatu convoy was stopped on the road by 100 armed men loyal to Governor Andal Ampatuan. The 58 members of the convoy were taken from their vehicles and executed—several of the women were raped first. Among the dead were Mangudadatu's wife, two sisters, aunt, 34 reporters, and aides. The bodies were hastily buried in a mass grave that had been prepared for them. With 34 reporters killed, the Maguindanao Massacre was the single deadliest event involving the killing of journalists in history.

News of the slaughter shocked the Philippines. President Arroyo declared martial law in Maguindanao. Authorities raided property belonging to Governor Andal Ampatuan and confiscated 330,000 rounds of ammunition and other military equipment—enough to arm a battalion of soldiers. Scores of militiamen were arrested. In the end, 200 members of the Ampatuan clan were arrested and put on trial, including the governor. The trials dragged on for almost a decade as the Ampatuans attempted to bribe officials to drop the charges or hold up proceedings with bureaucratic wrangling.

Andal Ampatuan died before the trial's conclusion. In the end, 45 defendants were convicted, but most of the suspects went free. Esmael Mangudadatu went on to win the election and serve as Governor of Maguindanao for ten years.

The development of the Philippine republic in the 21st century can best be described as rocky. The Philippine economy recovered from the shock of the Asian Financial Crisis and grew considerably during the early 2000s. The Philippines became one of the most promising economies of East Asia. The standard of living improved, and the government became more transparent and reliable. Even so, corruption and graft continued to plague the government, even at its highest offices. In Mindanao, religious separatism and clan rivalries strained the ability of the government in Manila to maintain stability there. And the ranks of the police and military were ever present sources of dissent, as expressed in the various failed coup attempts of the Arroyo years.

In our final three chapters, we take a look at the challenges facing the Philippines today, examine the role of the Catholic faith in Philippine culture, and consider briefly the impact Filipinos are making as they settle in other countries across the world.

Chapter 31

Facing the Future

The Philippines has gone through an immense transformation since the day Ferdinand Magellan first set foot on Homonhon Island in 1521. From a collection of distinct tribal territories to a Spanish colony, from a Spanish colony to an American colony, from an American colony to an independent republic, from an independent republic to a dictatorship, and from a dictatorship back to a democratic republic. Most of these developments have happened just since 1898. As an independent country, the Philippines is still in its infancy with many issues still unresolved. It is a nation in the process of formation, a continued subject of experimentation as Filipinos search for the right balance. In this chapter, we will explore some of the issues that the Philippines is still grappling with today.

One of the most profound challenges facing Filipinos today is a cultural one—the question of identity. Living in a country of multiple religions, hundreds of languages, and thousands of islands, what does it mean to be Filipino? More specifically, how does the Spanish cultural heritage factor into Filipino identity?

So much about the Philippines comes from Spain, which ruled the islands for four centuries. Countless cities were founded and named by Spaniards, with thousands of old city-centers throughout the archipelago still standing that were built by the Conquistadors. Though Spanish is no longer the dominant language, Tagalog and Cebuano languages borrow heavily from Spanish. It is to the Spanish friars, of course, that the Filipinos owe the practice of the Catholic religion. The very notion of a Philippine country at all comes from the Spaniards, as it was the Spanish who first united the islands of the archipelago together under a single government. Before the Spaniards, there was no cultural or political unity within the archipelago whatsoever. The Filipino identity was forged over centuries of Spanish rule, impressed with Spanish customs and mores. The very words *Filipino* and *Filipina* are Hispanic words. To deny the heritage of Spain is to completely gut the historic identity of the Philippines as a nation.

On the other hand, the Spaniards were not always kind. Regardless of how benign their motives, they were still conquerors. The Spanish religious orders worked together with the Spanish government to maintain colonial power. At times Spanish rule could be oppressive, as we saw during the period from the 1870s through 1890s where the Spanish authorities brutally suppressed expressions of Filipino national identity that they considered too subversive. Progressive Filipinos advocate for a rejection of their Spanish heritage, proposing clumsy terms like *"Filipinx"* to replace the Hispanic terms *Filipino* and *Filipina*. Such initiatives seem doomed to failure, akin to trying to purge oneself of one's own blood because of resentment against a parent. And Spain is, indeed, a parent of Filipino culture.

One evident challenge to the Philippines today is the problem posed by Mindanao. With its own distinct religion, cultural traditions, and political history, Mindanao has always resisted

Chapter 31: Facing the Future

Manila's efforts to impose uniformity upon it. We have seen how the creation of the Autonomous Region of Muslim Mindanao in 1989 was an attempt to solve this dilemma by granting the Moros regional autonomy. The creation of ARMM did not stop the violence, as separatist groups like MILF continued to fight for secession of Mindanao from the Philippines.

Sometimes the situation has escalated into open battle, as in the 2015 at Mamasapano in Maguindanao. U.S. special forces and members of the Philippine military and police forces staged an attack on a militant stronghold garrisoned by MILF and other Islamic insurgents. The encounter turned into a full-scale battle in which 44 Philippine government forces were killed.

Under the administration of President Benigno Aquino, III (2010–2016), the government entered talks with MILF and other separatist groups about granting even further autonomy to the region and enlarging the autonomous area. The result was the creation of the Bangsamoro Autonomous Region in Muslim Mindanao (BARMM), established in 2019. BARMM is essentially a reconstitution of ARMM, with some major differences: the government of BARMM is parliamentary, more powers are devolved to the Bangsamoro government, and a few other territories have been added.

The creation of Bangsamoro and the question of Mindanao is part of a larger discussion about Philippine federalism. Federalism is a mixed form of government where a national government co-exists with regional and local governments in a single system. The best example of a federal system is the United States, where government is shared between federal, state, and local authorities. The Philippines is not a federal state. Rather, it is a *unitary* state—that is, the only government is the national government. Provinces, cities, and *barangays* (villages) are simply administrative districts of the national government. There is no government authority apart from the national government.

During the Philippine revolution, both José Rizal and Emilio

Aguinaldo wanted a federalist system for the Philippines. Aguinaldo had proposed dividing the Philippines into three states of Luzon, Cebu, and Mindanao. The Philippine constitutions of 1935, 1973, and 1986–1987, however, have all maintained a unitary system. Calls for federalism in the Philippines have increased since the year 2000. One of the most vocal proponents of Philippine federalism is President Rodrigo Duterte (2016–2022). Duterte and the supporters of federalism cite many arguments in its favor: federalism will deliver better services to the people; it would help solve the ethno-religious conflicts in Mindanao; a diversity of regional and local governments would better suit a country so ethnically diverse; and it will stop the concentration of wealth and power in Manila. Filipinos are undecided on federalism. As of today, Bangsamoro remains the only Philippine experiment in federalism.

President Rodrigo Duterte was notable as being the first president from Mindanao, having formerly served as the Mayor of Davao City. Duterte's complaint about the concentration of wealth and power in Manila is not mistaken. For most of its history, the Philippines has been characterized by a disparity of power between metro Manila and everywhere else. President Elpidio Quirino tried to address this problem by moving the capital to Quezon City in 1948. But with all the wealth and power of the country concentrated in Manila, Ferdinand Marcos moved the capital back by decree in 1976. Since then, other cities have grown in importance—such as Davao, the largest city in Mindanao and the third most populous city after Manila and Quezon City. Still, the disparity between metro Manila and other regions of the country has led to a disproportionate distribution of resources that several Philippine presidents have tried to address.

Modernity has brought blessings and curses to the Philippines. One of the curses is the rise in illegal drug use. No country in the world is completely free from drug use. But the real danger in the Philippines is from drug trafficking. Due to its location as a stop-over point between mainland Asia and the Malay-Indonesian

Chapter 31: Facing the Future

islands, drug traffickers use the Philippines as a hub for drug trade. Its thousands of remote islands also afford infinite places to carry out illegal activity unobserved. Multiple Chinese drug cartels are active in the Philippines. Mexican drug cartels have been found there as well. Sometimes drug traffickers are aided by the military, police, and other government officials.

President Rodrigo Duterte made cracking down on drug trafficking one of the major platforms of his 2016 campaign. Duterte's heavy handed methods have drawn criticism from all over the world. Thousands of persons were killed between 2016 and 2022. Exact numbers are uncertain—the official death toll of Duterte's "war on drugs" is about 5,000, but his opponents say the real number is much higher, around 20,000. Of the thousands dead, how many were truly drug traffickers? The following scene has played out thousands of times across the Philippines:

Members of Ignacio's family and friends stood on one of the many side streets of Zamboanga crying in sadness and confusion. Ignacio, a boy of fifteen, lay dead in a pool of blood in the middle of the road. He had gone missing a few days earlier. His brother had found his body earlier that morning.

Several police officers stood about taking notes and photos of the body.

"Single bullet to the head," said one of the officers.

"Mhmm," said the other, taking notes. "Classic drug killing."

A woman, her face streaked with tears, shouted angrily. "Drug killing!? I am his mother. Ignacio never touched drugs in his life!"

"That's right!" cried Ignacio's brother, David. "Ignacio was a good kid. He studied hard and was responsible. He had *nothing* to do with drugs or drug trafficking!"

"Calm down, folks!" one of the officers said, holding up his hand. "We're looking into it."

"Calm down!?" cried Ignacio's mother. "My son is laying in a pool of blood and you want me to calm down!"

"We will investigate this fully!" said the other officer.

"No you won't!" cried David. "It will be just like every other killing. You say you'll investigate, but you don't. You do nothing. You're probably working with them!" The crowd gathering in the street began to murmur, nodding with David and grumbling against the police.

The two officers shifted uncomfortably. They put their hands on their pistols. The two men got into David's face, looking at him sternly. "Look young man," said one of the men, "we know you are sad about your brother's death. To us, this looks like a drug killing. We're not sure. But we know something terrible happened here, and we'll look into it."

"And if you're not careful," added the other officer, "something might happen again."

A week later, David and his mother received a call from the police department. Ignacio's killing was classified as a drug related homicide, no leads, no suspects. The case was declared closed.

This type of "justice" is called *extrajudicial killing*—the execution of perceived criminals outside of the judicial system, with no trial, no conviction, and no public record. As we can see from the story, it can have terrible consequences when innocent people are killed. Even if victims are guilty, the deprivation of a right to trial is unjust. Though extrajudicial killing is considered an abuse of human rights, Duterte seemed undeterred. He publicly bragged of extrajudicial killings carried out under his government. Even so, Duterte enjoyed broad support from the Filipino people, who were happy that someone was doing something about the drug problem.

Politics in the Philippines is deeply enmeshed with family loyalty, and political power in the country is often dynastic. President Benigno Aquino was the son of President Corazon Aquino. President Gloria Macapagal Arroyo was the daughter of

Chapter 31: Facing the Future

President Diosdado Macapagal. Even the children of Ferdinand Marcos wield political power—Ferdinand Marcos, Jr., known as "Bongbong" and Imee Marcos both became Senators from Ilocos Norte, a region still fiercely loyal to Marcoses. In 2022, Bongbong Marcos was elected president of the Philippines. Clan-based political loyalty is even more deeply entrenched in Mindanao, where dynastic politics stretches back to the days of the sultanates. The fight between the Ampatuans and the Mangudadatus we discussed in Chapter 30 that led to the Maguindanao Massacre was ultimately a feud between rival clans. The dynastic nature of power in the Philippines becomes even more evident when one goes down the ladder to smaller towns and *barangays*, where official appointments are little more than confirmations of entrenched dynastic power.

Ever since independence in 1946, every Philippine president has tried to grow the Philippine economy. Since the dawn of modern times there has always been a gnawing sense that the Philippines was not reaching its full economic potential. The Spaniards were the first to realize this during the 19th century period of direct rule when they began an aggressive campaign of modernization during the reign of Queen Isabella II. Later, the Americans improved the economy with the creation of roads and infrastructure throughout the country. After independence in 1946, the first presidential administrations were eager to build up a native Filipino economy that did not depend so heavily on America.

The waste and debt of the Marcos years set the Philippine economy back considerably. Every presidential administration since the fall of Marcos has grappled with this problem. But there have been some successes. Today the Philippines is one of the most dynamic economies in East Asia. As its cities grow and the standard of living improves, the economy continues to swell. Real estate, tourism, insurance, and financial services are particularly strong areas of the Philippine economy. Poverty has decreased. The economy has grown steadily since 2010, moving the Philippines from a lower middle-income country to an upper middle-income country.

One of the greatest examples of the Philippines' emergence as a sophisticated, modern economy is the launch of Diwata-1. Diwata-1 is a satellite that was put into orbit from the international space station in 2016. Diwata-1 represented many firsts for the Philippines: the first satellite launched by the Philippines, and the first satellite entirely designed and built by Filipinos. Diwata-1 was followed by another satellite, Diwata-2, in 2018.

As we can see, the Philippines will have many challenges to face in the 21st century. In our next chapter we will look at one of the most formative aspects of Filipino culture: the Catholic religion.

Chapter 32

CATHOLICISM IN THE PHILIPPINES

We have come a long way! From the arrival of the first humans in the Philippine archipelago on rafts, through the long years of Spanish dominion, into the 20th century, the World Wars, and the modern Philippine republics. It has been quite a journey, and we have seen and discussed many developments along the way. In this chapter, we will look at one of the great constants of Philippine society: the Catholic religion.

The Philippines is unique as the only Catholic country in Asia. At the time of the writing of this book, the population of the Philippines is about 110 million. Of that 110 million, an overwhelming 86% are Catholics. Of the remainder, 4% are Muslim, 2% Protestant, and 2% observe non-western or indigenous/pagan practices. Another 6% belong to what are known as "cults," religious movements sometimes loosely based on Christianity but incorporating an eclectic range of ideas and centered around a charismatic, cultic leader. Such cults include the Iglesia ni Kristo, the Philippine Benevolent Missionaries Association, and Rizalists—groups who worship José Rizal, the father of the Philippine revolution.

The Philippine Church is divided up into 72 dioceses in 16 Ecclesiastical Provinces, as well as 7 Apostolic Vicariates and a Military Ordinariate. The Catholic Bishops' Conference of the Philippines (CBCP) is the organizational assembly of the country's Catholic bishops. The primatial see of the country is the Archbishopric of Manila. In recent years, some members of the Philippine hierarchy have attained prominence in the universal Church, most notably Luis Cardinal Tagle, Archbishop of Manila who was made Prefect of the Congregation for the Evangelization of Peoples by Pope Francis in 2019.

The historic heart of Catholicism in the Philippines is Cebu, the landing place of the original Spanish conquistadors. Catholicism spread out from Cebu throughout the 16th century, spreading north and west, but not making much headway into Muslim dominated Mindanao. The religious orders played a major role in Christianizing the region: Redemptorists, Augustinians, Recollects, Jesuits, Dominicans, Benedictines, Franciscans, Carmelites, Divine Word Missionaries, De La Salle Christian Brothers, Salesians, and the indigenous Religious of the Virgin Mary were all active in this evangelical work. Under four centuries of Spanish rule, the Filipinos became perhaps the most thoroughly Christianized of any people colonized during the age of exploration.

During the long centuries of Spanish rule, the clergy and religious orders wielded considerable political influence. Under American rule and after independence, this transformed into more of a moral force. But the Church could still muster considerable weight if it wished. For example, in 1986 Archbishop of Cebu Ricardo Cardinal Vidal, who was also President of the Catholic Bishops Conference of the Philippines, called upon all bishops and Filipinos to resist the President Marcos's attempts to tamper with the presidential election. This was followed by Archbishop of Manila, Jaime Cardinal Sin,

Chapter 32: Catholicism in the Philippines

who went on the radio and urged Catholics to support anti-regime rebels. The support of Cardinals Vidal and Sin was instrumental in galvanizing the People Power Movement that ousted Marcos. To this day, politicians still court the clergy for support.

Since the Second Vatican Council (1962–1965), what Catholicism looks like in the Philippines varies tremendously. Contemporary Catholicism, folk Catholicism, and the charismatic renewal all exist side-by-side under the Catholic umbrella. The charismatic renewal is particularly vibrant. Known as the El Shaddai movement, the renewal boasts 8 million members across the country.

Catholic education is widespread throughout the Philippines. The Church operates hundreds of primary and secondary schools and dozens of colleges, including the renowned University of Santo Tomas in Manila, which has consistently been praised as one of the best colleges in the world. Catholic education remains vibrant and relevant in the Philippines, unlike many places in the West where Catholic education has been declining for many decades.

Three popes have visited the Philippines four times between 1970 and 2015 to minister to the millions of Catholics there. Their visits have been greeted enthusiastically by the faithful. John Paul II held World Youth Day in Manila in 1995. Even so, the papal visits have not been without drama. In 1970, a crazed Bolivian artist disguised as a priest tried to stab Pope Paul VI with a *kris* dagger at the Manila airport. Paul VI escaped with only light wounds and continued his scheduled tour of the Philippines. The man later said he tried to kill the pope just to get attention.

The visit of John Paul II for World Youth Day in 1995 was the occasion of another attempted assassination, this much more complex than that of 1970. Known as the Bojinka Plot, it was part of a vast conspiracy of Islamic extremists linked to the terrorist group Al-Qaeda. Fortunately, a random accident revealed the plot before it could be carried out. Let us visit the quaint Doña Josefa apartments in Manila on the afternoon of January 6, 1995 to see how the plot was uncovered.

Smoke billowed from a sixth-floor window of the Doña Josefa apartment complex in Manila. Panicked residents made their way down the stairs of the building, filing out into the street as the police and fire brigade pulled up.

Police Major Francisco Bautista and one of his officers, Aida Fariscal, looked up at the smoke pouring out of the window. "Probably a kitchen fire," said Bautista

"Looks like we're not going home early today," sighed Fariscal. She was right. This was going to take awhile. Bautista and Fariscal followed the fire brigade up the stairwell to the sixth story. When they entered the hallway of the sixth floor, however, something was amiss. Access to the burning room was being blocked by two men standing in the hallways shouting hysterically.

"No! No! No come in!" cried the men, holding their arms up to prevent the fire brigade from passing. They did not appear to be Filipino, but Middle Easterners.

"We're just here to help! Don't worry!" explained one of the fire fighters. "We need to put out the fire." He spoke slowly and loudly, thinking perhaps the men did not understand his language clearly or what the fire brigade was there for.

"What's with these guys?" said Fariscal, exasperated.

Major Bautista lost his patience. He shoved his way to the front, grabbed one of the men by the shirt collar and hurled him out of the way. "The building is on fire. Get out of the way!" he growled. The two men began jabbering in Arabic and fled down the hallway, disappearing into the stairwell. Bautista, Fariscal and the fire brigade entered the apartment. As Bautista predicted, the kitchen sink was on fire.

"All this trouble for a grease fire!" he exclaimed while the fire brigade worked quickly to extinguish the flames. After the fire was out, however, Bautista noticed something strange. Four portable electric stovetops were packed together in a box near the sink. On the countertop were buckets filled with what appeared to be rolls of cotton soaking in a milky liquid. Fariscal sniffed one of the buckets.

Chapter 32: Catholicism in the Philippines

"Phew...stinks like chemicals," she said.

Meanwhile Bautista and the fire brigade were looking at the sink where the fire had started. The area was soaked with water from the firemen's hoses and much of the countertop and walls were scorched from the flames, but Bautista noticed there were no pans. "This was no grease fire," he said. "Nobody appears to have been cooking. At least not with pans."

The kitchen table was curious as well. It was strewn with rolls of green, red, yellow, and blue electrical wiring. A bag with an unknown, powdery substance sat on the chair beside the table.

"Gentlemen," said Major Bautista gravely, "I think we are dealing with a bomb plot gone awry."

"No wonder those guys didn't want us to come in here!" said Fariscal. The two officers paused and looked at each other in sudden alarm.

"Those were the bombers!" cried Bautista. "We let them get away!" The police officers immediately turned and dashed out of the apartment, hoping to catch up with the suspects in the street.

The suspects were eventually arrested. When interrogated, they revealed the complex plot that stunned officers in its breadth and complexity. The men in the apartment were Abdul Hakim Murad and Ramzi Yousef. Murad and Yousef were part of a vast conspiracy to kill Pope John Paul II, blow up 11 U.S. bound airliners with bombs over the Pacific, and crash a hijacked airliner into the headquarters of the CIA in Virginia. Murad had been prepping the bomb that was supposed to kill John Paul II, but he mixed some chemicals incorrectly and started a fire in the kitchen. Had the plot been successful, 4,000 people could have been killed.

Fortunately, the Bojinka Plot was foiled before John Paul II ever set foot on Philippine soil. The 1995 World Youth Day went off as planned and was attended by millions. John Paul II spoke to the

Catholics of the Philippine church, telling them they had a pivotal role to play in the evangelization of Asia: "In the first millennium the Cross has been planted on the soil of Europe; in the second on that of America and Africa. We can pray that in the third Christian millennium in this vast and vital continent there will be a great harvest of faith to be harvested."

Catholics in the Philippines are known for their great devotion to Mary. Hundreds of towns and churches are named after the Blessed Mother. The patroness of the Philippines is the Blessed Virgin Mary of the Immaculate Conception. Some of the most famous pilgrimage destinations are Marian shrines: remember the walking pilgrimage taken by General Orellana and his men to St. Domingo in honor of Our Lady of La Naval after their 1646 battle with the Dutch? Another renowned shrine is the sanctuary of Our Lady of Peace and Good Voyage, named for the 17th century image of the same name enshrined in Antipolo Cathedral in the mountains east of Manila. Each year, many thousands of Filipinos perform the *Alay Lakad* or "Walk Offering", traveling through the night by foot to hear Mass at the shrine in the morning. Further south, the shrine of Our Lady of Peñafrancia in Bicol draws nine million pilgrims each year. To put that in perspective, Lourdes draws six million annually while Guadalupe draws ten million.

A more recent example of the devotion of Filipinos to Mary is the lofty statue of Mary, Mother of All Asia, which was completed in 2021 at Montemaria near Batangas City. The statue was designed by Filipino sculptor Eduardo de los Santos Castrillo to celebrate the 500th anniversary of the arrival of Catholicism in the Philippines. Topping out at an impressive 322 feet in height, it is presently the tallest statue of the Virgin Mary in the world. A line-art version of the statue with the Philippine sun behind it may be found at the opening of each chapter of this book.

Two of the more uniquely Philippine devotions are the devotion to the Black Nazarene and the Santo Niño de Cebú. The Black Nazarene is a life-size wooden image of a dark-skinned Jesus carrying His cross. It is enshrined in the Minor Basilica of the Black Nazarene in Manila's Quiapo district. The image is dark because of the dark Mexican wood it was carved from. It was made in Mexico and brought to the Philippines in 1606. The image has a long history of miraculous cures. It is brought out in procession every year on January 9. The faithful press handkerchiefs to the image in procession hoping to receive special graces thereby. In recent years, the Black Nazarene procession has drawn up to six million devotees.

As for the image of the child Jesus known as Santo Niño de Cebú, we have already learned of its origin in Chapter 9: it was presented to Rajah Humabon by Magellan in 1521 on the occasion of his conversion. It is the oldest Christian artifact in the Philippines and is housed in the Minor Basilica del Santo Niño de Cebú. The image has been replicated all over the Philippines and is one of the country's most recognizable cultural icons. The festival of the Santo Niño is a major occasion in the Philippines. Falling the Thursday after Epiphany, it is observed with dawn processions and novena Masses stretching nine days. On the final day of the novena, the Santo Niño image is brought together with the image of Mary known as Nuestra Señora de Guadalupe de Cebú and housed in the National Shrine of St. Joseph in Mandaue City, thus "reuniting" the Holy Family. The images are then returned to Cebu City where there is a reenactment of the first Mass in the Philippines and the baptism of Rajah Humabon. The following Saturday comes the great Sinulog Festival, a grand celebration of dancing that draws millions. Meanwhile the image of the Santo Niño undergoes the Hubo rite, in which the crown and regal vestments are stripped from the image and replaced with plain robes to the chants of *Christus Vincit; Christus Regnat; Christus Imperat*, that is, "Christ Conquers; Christ Reigns; Christ Commands." The Hubo ritual is supposed to signify the humility of Christ, who divested Himself of His divine splendor to live and die as a man for the sake of our salvation.

Filipino priests do not only minister within the Philippines. In modern times, Filipino priests have been sent all over the world, especially to the United States and other places with priest shortages. If you are a Catholic in the United States, chances are you've run into Filipino priests at some point!

Catholicism is at the heart of the question of Filipino identity. It is undeniable that the Catholic faith is at the center of traditional Filipino culture. Few countries have embraced Catholicism like the Philippines. Mass attendance is higher in the Philippines than in the West, with almost 30% of Filipino Catholics identifying themselves as "very religious" according to surveys. Yet, it is also undeniable that the Catholic faith was brought to the Philippines by Spain and is, in some sense, unable to be disentangled from Spain's colonial history. Many self-styled progressive Filipinos would like to reject the Catholic identity of their people as just another relic of colonialism. But how can one reject the Catholic Faith brought by Spain without repudiating an integral part of Philippine identity? If the 400-year-old Philippine Catholicism were rejected for something else, would whatever replaced it be any more authentically Filipino?

It is good to remember that the Catholic faith is not indigenous to any country. It came to the Philippines from Spain, but it came to Spain through missionaries from the Greek world during Roman times. And the Greeks learned it from the apostolic missions of St. Paul and the Apostles, who came from Judea. But the faith was not even indigenous to Judea. It was brought to earth by Christ, the God-Man, who revealed it from the Father. The Catholic faith has a supernatural origin. Of course it is not of the Philippines, for it is not of this earth at all. The issue of Catholicism being not indigenous is a moot point entirely.

While the desire of many Filipinos to connect with the non-European roots of their culture is understandable, the quest for a "pure" cultural expression can be elusive. By comparison, what would a "pure" expression of Mexican culture look like? Suppose we strip away everything Spain brought to Mexico. What are we left with? The Aztecs, who pre-dated the Spanish, were not indigenous to Mexico, either. The other tribes of Mexico considered them

Chapter 32: Catholicism in the Philippines

foreign conquerors. If we then erase everything contributed by the Aztecs, we are left with the culture of the Mixtec peoples, who in turn succeeded the Mayans and the Toltecs. These succeeded the Olmecs, but the Olmec culture was heavily borrowed from other native cultures which came out of central Guatemala and never lived in Mexico at all. As with Philippine culture, scraping off centuries of cultural additions to in hopes of arriving at an elusive "pure" Mexican culture ends up leaving us with nothing. There is always another page to turn, always another level to go down. Everything comes from somewhere else.

The solution, of course, is understanding that culture is merely the sum total of all the customs, arts, social institutions, and achievements of a particular people that have been passed down. Catholicism *is* Filipino culture just as surely as any pre-colonial customs and beliefs. One cannot surgically excise parts of their own culture any more than we can remove parts of our inherited genetic imprint.

Chapter 33

The Filipino Diaspora

In modern times, Filipinos have brought their unique culture all over the world in what could be called a Filipino *diaspora*. A diaspora is dispersion of people outside their homeland. As of 2020, there were 4 million Filipinos living in the United States, making the U.S.A. home to the largest number of Filipinos abroad. Saudi Arabia, Canada, the United Arab Emirates, Australia, and Japan are also popular destinations for Filipinos. Wherever Filipinos live and gather, little snippets of Filipino culture are lived out in their communities the world over. For example…

It was a perfect Pennsylvania summer Saturday. Nick and Linda Carlucci and their four children made their way to the large open-air pavilion set up behind the Quindo's suburban house for Jake and Isabella McEwan's wedding reception. They had come straight from the church but already the place was packed with guests.

"Aemelia told me this would be a small reception," said Mrs. Carlucci, "but there must be 200 people here already!"

"You're surprised, mom?" nineteen year-old Ray quipped. "It's like you've never been to one of the Quindo family parties before."

Before Mrs. Carlucci could respond, three of the Quindo family's younger children approached, huge smiles plastered on their merry faces. Little Julia, age four, had already managed to dribble grape juice down her chin and onto her shiny blue dress. "Come on, Aunty Linda and Uncle Nick! We will take you to your table," nine year-old Xavier announced.

The Carluccis were happy to comply and were soon led to their table under the pavilion. There, they were greeted by numerous people they knew in common with the Quindos. The kids were all drawn off by friends, leaving Mr. and Mrs. Carlucci a few minutes by themselves to chat.

"Bella looked so beautiful, didn't she? I'm so happy she found such a great guy like Jake," said Linda, a little tear forming in the corner of her eye as she remembered the recently concluded nuptial Mass at Holy Savior Catholic Church.

"I wonder if Jake knew what he was getting himself into," Nick replied, looking around. "I mean, his family fits into just three or four tables. The Quindos and their family must take up the other twenty! It's amazing how many aunts, uncles and cousins they have."

"Don't be a bonehead, Nick," scolded his wife. "You know quite well that not all these people are family members. When Filipinos love you, you become part of the family."

"They really are a great family," said Nick with a sincere smile.

"Where did you get that?" Mrs. Carlucci burst out, seeing her eleven year-old daughter Gina bound up holding a large icon of the Virgin Mary in an ornate metal frame.

"It was in the Quindo's family room. I told Aunty Aemilia's grandmother that it was pretty, so she said I could have it. Isn't it gorgeous?"

Before Mrs. Carlucci could utter a word of reproof, the bride and

Chapter 33: The Filipino Diaspora

groom approached, greeting them joyfully. "Thank you so much for coming, Aunty Linda and Uncle Nick!" said Isabella in between hugs. "I'm so glad the weather held up. Mommy was so worried it was going to rain."

"God gave you a perfect day," Mrs. Carlucci began as the tears built up again, "And you look so beautiful."

"Awww, thank you," said Isabella, hugging her again. "But don't cry or you'll make me cry and my makeup will run!"

Jake and Isabella were soon pulled off in another direction to greet other guests. Mr. and Mrs. Carlucci took the opportunity to get in line to sample some of the food that was already being served buffet-style. Each chaffing dish contained a different delicacy—from corned beef and cabbage to celebrate the groom's heritage, to a variety of delicious-looking Filipino delicacies.

"I love the pancit," Nick declared, helping himself to a healthy portion. "But the bitter melon…I just can't get into that."

"It's an acquired taste," added Linda as she piled a few chunks onto her plate.

Grace before meals was intoned by Father Klacik of Holy Savior, and the Carluccis began to eat, now surrounded at their table by a few of their kids and various members of Quindo extended family. By the time the plates were cleared, the music had already changed from old standards to more up-beat pop songs. The younger folks took to the patio to dance while Mr. and Mrs. Carlucci remained at the table and sampled some of the cake.

"I've been trying to get over here all day!" announced Aemilia Quindo, mother of the bride, settling herself into a chair next to Linda. She looked exhausted but extremely content. Her husband, Luis, stood behind her wearing the traditional Barong formal shirt. He greeted the Carluccis heartily and shook their hands.

"Was the food ok?" Aemilia asked.

"Delicious as always," Nick replied.

"The wedding was so beautiful," said Linda, "Jake and Bella make a lovely couple, don't they?"

"They do. He really is a good guy," Aemilia said. "Even Luis approved, and he's been a tough critic of boyfriends."

"It's true," Luis agreed, with a smile. "Better to scare 'em a little."

This pleasant story of Filipinos eating and greeting at a wedding reception took place in Pennsylvania, but it could have taken place in any of the many places that Filipinos have put down roots. As the world becomes more mobile and Filipinos continue to move abroad, hopefully interest in their history and traditions will continue to grow as well.

INDEX

9/11 terrorist attacks 251

abacá 153
Abdul Hamid II, Sultan 184
Acapulco, Mexico 132–136, 137, 139, 144
Ache, Young Prince (Rajah Matanda) 47–48, 60, 71–72, 76–77
Aglipay, Gregorio 197–198
Agricultural Land Reform Code 227
Aguinaldo, Emilio 162–163, 165, 167, 171–172, 174–175, 178–181, 184, 197, 199–200, 223, 260
Agurto, Bishop Pedro de 114
Alaska 212
Alay Lakad (Walk Offering) 270
Alcarazo, Juan de 123–126
Allison, John More 204
Americanos 127
Ampatuan, Andal 254
Anda y Salazar, Simón de 141, 144–146
Antipolo Cathedral 270
Aquino, Benigno (Ninoy) 236–237
Aquino, Benigno III 259, 262
Aquino, Corazon 237, 241–248, 253, 262
Arabia 50, 51, 53
Arellano, Alonso de 85
Argentina 62, 154
ARMM (Autonomous Region in Muslim Mindanao) 253, 259
Arroyo, Gloria Macapagal 251–255, 262
Arula, Jibin 231
Asian Financial Crisis 249, 255
Asiatic Squadron 167, 168, 171
Association of Veterans of the Revolution 181

Augustín, Basilio 163, 171
Augustinians (religious order) 114, 194, 266
Australia 205, 209, 212, 275
Aztecs 96, 272–273

Baclaran 236
Bagong Katipuneros (New Katipunan) 252
Bagong Lipunan 233, 234
Baguinda Ali, Prince 51
Baguio City 236
Baker, Newton 199
Baldwin, Frank 185
Banco Español-Filipino de Isabel II 153–154
Bangsamoro 259–260
Bankaw Revolt 126–127
BARMM (Bangsamoro Autonomous Region in Muslim Mindanao) 259
Basco y Vargas, José 152
Basilan 97
Basilica de Santo Niño de Cebu 65, 84, 114, 270–271
Bataan Death March 206, 209
Bataan Peninsula 205, 206, 208–209, 211
Batan 204
Batanes Islands 152
Batangas 20, 163, 180, 270
Batasang Pambansa 243
Battle of La Naval de Manila vi, 106–107
Battle of Trafalgar 150
Bautista, Francisco 268–269
Benavides, Bishop Miguel de 113
Benedictines, religious order 266
Benedict XVI, Pope 118
Bicol Peninsula 6, 270

Black Nazarene devotion 270–271
Blanco y Erena, Ramón 162
Bobadilla 108
Bohol 7, 73, 113, 123
Bojinka Plot 267, 269
Bonaparte, Joseph 150
Bonaparte, Napoleon 150
Bonifacio, Andrés 161–162
Bonin Islands 86
Borneo 7–8, 12, 35, 48, 51–52, 55–56, 71, 90–91, 94
Brazil 62, 175
Brunei iii, 48–49, 51–52, 55–59, 71, 72, 87, 89–91, 94–95
Buansa 51
Buddhism 34, 50, 56–57
Bud Dajo vii, 186–187
Buencamino, Felipe 175
Bulacan 141, 163
Buluan 254
Bureau of Insular Affairs 194, 196
Burgos, Fr. José 160
Burias 7
Bush, George H. W. 235
Butuan iii, 24–32, 39, 41, 43, 62–63, 104

Cagayan River 6
Calcutta 139
Calderón y Roca, Felipe 175
California 135
Calungsod, Saint Pedro 115–116, 118
Cambodia 26, 236
Camp Abubakar 250
Camp Vickers 185
Canada 275
captaincy general 87, 89–90
Carmelites (religious order) 266
Carter, Jimmy 236
Castilian War iii, 89, 91, 93–94
Castrillo, Eduardo de los Santos 270
Catholic Church vi, 8, 111, 118, 150, 160, 194, 196, 198, 237, 265–271, 272–273, 276
Cavite 160, 163, 171
Cebu iii, 7–8, 32–39, 41, 49–50, 53, 64–65, 73–75, 84, 87, 90–91, 95–96, 104, 112–114, 123, 126, 161, 218, 227, 236, 260, 266, 271

Cebu City 7–8, 95, 113, 271
cedulas 162
Cerón, Álvaro de Saavedra 85–86
Chamorro 115–117
Charles III, King of Spain 140, 147
Charles IV, King of Spain 150
Charles V, Holy Roman Emperor 4, 81
Chavacano 96
China 5, 11, 21, 23, 26–28, 31, 43–44, 46, 49–50, 52, 58, 104–105, 107, 109, 112, 121, 133, 152, 154, 203–204, 218, 227, 233
Chino (see also Sangley) 128
Chottry Court 144, 147
Christianization 110–111, 123, 127
Church of St. Potenciana 113
Clark Air Force Base 215, 245–247
Clavería y Zaldúa, Narciso 157–159
Colambu, Rajah of Butuan 62–65
Columbus, Christopher 62
Commission on Good Government 242
Commonwealth of the Philippines 200, 211
communism 201, 223, 226–227, 229, 233, 235–236, 243, 247–248
Concepción (ship) 62, 69
conquistadors vi, 258
Constitution of 1973 241
Corcuera, Sebastián Hurtado de 97–98, 101, 103–105, 110
Cordillera Central 6
Corregidor 205–206, 215, 231
Cortez vi, 73
Cotabato 232
Cruzat, Fausto 195
Cry of Pugad Lawin 162
Cuba 140, 165–167, 174

Dapitan 161
Dasmariñas, Luiz Pérez 121–122
Davao City 8, 236, 251–252, 260
Dewey, George 167–168, 171–174
De La Salle Christian Brothers (religious order) 266
Divine Word Missionaries (religious order) 266
Diwata-1 264
Diwata-2 264

Index

Doctrina Cristiana 122
Dominicans (religious order) 112, 114–115, 194, 266
Drake, Dawsonne 144–147
Draper, William 140, 147
Dula, Lakan 47–48, 60, 71–72
Duncan, J. W. 186
Dutch vi, 89, 103, 105–110, 119, 134, 155, 270
Dutch East Indies 204
Duterte, Rodrigo 247, 260–262

East India Company 139–140, 144
Elcano, Juan Sebastián 65–69, 71–72
El Shaddai movement 267
encomienda system 120
Estrada, Joseph 250–253
extrajudicial killing 262

Fajardo, Diego 105
Fariscal, Aida 268–269
Fernando VII, King of Spain 151
Filipino diaspora 275
Fortress of San Felipe 160
Fort Balanguigui 157
Fort Drum 215–218
Fort Pilar 97, 101, 108
France 114, 139–140, 149–150, 154, 160, 193, 218
Francis, Pope 266
Franciscans (religious order) 194, 266
Freedom Constitution 241
Freemasons 160–161, 198
French Indochina 203

galleons 105–106, 121, 132, 134–135, 137, 144, 152
Gamboa, Pedro Sarmiento de 86
Garcia, Carlos 227–228
George III, King of England 140
Global War on Terror 251
Goiti, Martin de 76
Gomez, Fr. Mariano 160
Great Britain 139–140, 144, 146, 150, 193
Gregory XIII, Pope 112

Guadalcanal 212
Guam 86, 115, 174, 179
Guzmán, Francisco de Tello de 94, 121

Hara Amihan (Juana), wife of Rajah Humabon 64, 84
Hare-Hawes-Cutting Bill 200
Hawaii 204, 237–238, 240
Hay, John 184
Hayam Wuruk, King of Borneo 56
Homma, Masaharu 206, 209
Homonhon 62, 257
Honasan, Gregorio 243, 247
Hong Kong 5, 128, 155, 162–163, 167, 171, 174
Hospicio de San José 190
Hsieh, Likan 28–31
Hubo ritual 271
Hukbalahap 223–224, 226, 229
Humabon (Carlos), Rajah of Cebu 64–65, 68, 74–75, 84, 113, 271

Iglesia ni Kristo 266
Illius Fulti Præsidio 112
Ilocos 145, 197, 263
Iloilo 178
ilustrado 154, 159, 184, 191
imperialism vii, 165
India 12, 26, 34, 41, 50, 52, 55–56, 85, 130, 133, 139–140, 144, 147
Indio 128
Indochina 154
Indonesia 11, 12, 25, 41, 72, 79, 204
Industrial Revolution 149, 151
Insulares 127
Intramuros 121, 133, 141, 163, 172, 174, 190
Ireland 111
Isabella II, Queen of Spain 151, 154, 159, 263
Islam iii, 35, 48–53, 55–56, 59–60, 90, 110
Isla de Convalecencia 190
Italy 193, 218

Jabidah Massacre 231–232
jade 17, 19–23, 25, 30, iii
Jamalul Kiram, Sultan 184

Japan 11, 39, 44, 64, 85, 115, 133, 136, 193, 203–204, 212–213, 219–220, 227, 236, 275
Jáudenes, Fermín 171–172
Java 55–56, 130
Jesuits (religious order) 96, 113–116, 266
Jesuit Colegio de Manila 113
John Paul II, Pope Saint vi, 114, 118, 236, 267, 269
Jolo 51, 101, 186–187
Jones, William 198
Jones Law (1916) 198–199
juramentado 100, 185

Kapampangan 49, 123–124
Karim Al Makhdum 51
Katipunan 161–162
Kiling, Rajah of Butuan 27–28
Kiram-Bates Treaty 184–185
Kota Batu 91, 93–94
Koxinga 106, 108–109
Krueger, Walter 215

Laguna de Bay 6
Lamitan 97
Lanao 98–99, 104, 185
Laos 236
Lapu Lapu, Rajah of Mactan 65–69, 72
Lara, Sabiniano Manrique de 108
Las Casas, Bartolomé de 112
Laurel, José 221–223, 245
Lawton, Henry Ware 179
La Liga Filipina 161
Legazpi, López de vi, 73–77, 86, 87, 113, 126
Leyte 7, 123, 126, 213, 219, 222
Liberal Party 227, 229
Lim, Danilo 252–253
Limasawa 62–64, 73
López de Villalobos, Ruy 4, 73, 79, 86
Louis XVI, King of France 149
Luzon 4–7, 17, 20, 22, 34, 39, 41–43, 48–50, 53, 59, 71, 76–77, 89–90, 94, 96, 104–105, 112, 127, 129, 134, 145–146, 153, 160, 162–163, 171, 173, 175, 178, 180, 185, 194, 204–206, 214, 218, 224, 236, 246, 260

Ma'i iii, 3, 5, 7, 9
macanjas 115, 117
Macapagal, Diosdado 227–229, 263
MacArthur, Douglas 204–205, 209–210, 212, 213–215, 222–223
MacArthur Jr., Arthur 179–180, 204
Mactan 65, 69, 75, 112
Madras 140
Magalos (see also, Moros) 35, 38, 53
Magellan, Ferdinand iii, 4, 8, 61–69, 71–72, 74–75, 82, 84–85, 110, 114, 257, 271
Magsaysay, Ramon 226–228
Maguindanao 254–255, 259, 263
Maguindanao Massacre 254, 263
Malacañang Palace 180, 243–245
Malaysia 12–13, 17, 41, 260
Malolos Constitution 174–175
Malvar, Miguel 180
Mamasapano 259
Mandaue City 271
Mangudadatu, Esmael 254–255
Manila Pact 226
Marcos, Ferdinand Jr. (Bongbong) 263
Marcos, Ferdinand 220, 227–243, 247–248, 251–252, 260, 263, 267
Marcos, Imee 263
Marcos, Imelda 232–234, 237
Marinduque 7
Marquesas Islands 86
martial law 179, 233
Mary, Mother of All Asia statue 270
Mata'pang 115–118
Matalam, Udtog 232
Matanda, Rajah (*see* Ache)
Manila (also, Maynila and Selurong) vi, 6, 42–43, 47, 53, 60, 72, 76–77, 87, 89–90, 93–97, 104–106–115, 120–122, 129, 131–135, 137, 139–141, 143–147, 152–155, 159, 162, 163, 167–169, 171–172, 174, 176, 178, 180, 187–188, 191, 194, 196, 205–206, 214–215, 218, 223, 226, 231, 233, 236–237, 243–245, 251–253, 255, 260, 266–268, 207, 279, 282
Mazatlán 136

INDEX

McKinley, William 166, 174, 198
Mecca 53
Meralco (Manila Electric Rail and Light Company) 188–189, 191
Mercantilism 131
Merry del Val, Rafael Cardinal 196
mestizos 96, 103, 127–128
Mestizo de Bombay 127
Mestizo de Español 127
Mestizo de Sangley 128
Mexico vi, 73, 80–83, 85–87, 90, 95–97, 103, 105, 111–112, 120–121, 131–133, 135–136, 144, 150–152, 154, 175, 271–273
Mexico City 73, 81–83, 86, 136, 150
MILF (Moro Islamic Liberation Front) 250–251, 254, 259
MIM (Muslim Independence Movement) 232
Mindanao 4, 8, 12, 26, 32, 34–35, 37, 49, 51–53, 73, 77, 85, 90, 94–98, 101, 104, 108, 110, 113, 118, 121, 127–128, 158, 173, 184–187, 191, 200, 205, 213, 218, 231–233, 236, 247, 250–251, 253, 255, 258–260, 263, 266
Mindoro 7, 76, 214
Ming Dynasty, China 43–44, 58, 104, 106, 108
Minor Basilica of the Black Nazarene 271
MNLF (Moro National Liberation Front) 232–233, 247, 250
Mohammed Shah, Sultan of Brunei (also, Awang Alak Betatar) 58–59
Moluccas (*see* Spice Islands)
Montojo, Patricio 167
Moros vii, 35–39, 76, 89–90, 94–101, 104–105, 108–110, 118–119, 121, 157–159, 183–187, 189, 191, 231–232, 259
Mount Apo 8
Mount Arayat 6
Mount Pinatubo 246
Mount Pulag 6
Murad, Abdul Hakim 269

Nacionalista Party 199, 227, 229
Nahuatl 96

Nanking 204
National Shrine of St. Joseph 271
Negritos 12, 17, 128–129
Negros 7
Neira, Álvaro de Medaña de 86
New Britain 212
New France 114
New Guinea 86, 212
New Hebrides 86
New Spain 73, 86–87, 95, 112, 120, 135, 137, 150
New Zealand 212
Niaosung people 21–23
Nimitz, Chester 213
NPA (New People's Army) 233, 236–237, 243
Nuestra Señora de Guadalupe de Cebú 271
Nueva Ecija 163

Oakwood Mutiny 252
Ocampo, Pablo 230
Onoda, Hiroo 219–220
Operation Classic Resolve 245
Orellana, Lorenzo Ugalde de 105, 106, 270
Osmeña, Sergio 214, 221–222
Otis, Elwell Stephen 176, 178–179
Our Lady of Peace and Good Voyage 270
Our Lady of Peñafrancia 270

Pacific Ocean 3, 5–6, 62, 85–86, 115, 134, 166–167, 203–204, 211–212, 218, 269
Pact of Biak-na-Bato 163, 165, 171
Paduka Mahasari Maulana (*also known as* Sharif Al-Hashim) 52–53, 99
paganism 118
Palau 86
Palawan 14, 52
Pampanga 6, 140, 145, 163
Panay 7, 76, 123, 203
Pangasinans 49
Papua New Guinea 212
Paramisuli, Princess 53
Pasig River 42, 47, 141, 151, 168, 178, 187, 189–190, 245
Paul VI, Pope 114, 267
peninsulares 127, 159, 194, 197

People Power Revolution 237, 241–242, 247, 251, 267
Pershing, John J. 187
Persia 52
PHILCAG (Philippine Civic Action Group-Vietnam) 231
Philippine-American War 173, 178, 180, 183–184, 188, 197
Philippine Assembly 180, 193, 198–199
Philippine Benevolent Missionaries Association 266
Philippine Commission 180, 188, 198
Philippine Independent Church 197
Philippine National Guard 193
Philippine Organic Act 180, 194, 198
Philippine Senate 198–200, 247
Philip II, King of Spain 4, 73–74, 81, 83, 86–87, 112, 126
Pilar, Pio del 178
pirates 35, 45–47, 76, 80, 96, 119, 121, 132, 134, 157, 158
Pius X, Pope Saint 195
Pizarro vi
Polavieja y del Castillo-Negrete, Camilo Garcia de 162
polos y servicios 122
Portugal 61–62, 73, 81, 82, 85, 87, 89, 96, 119
Proclamation 2045 236
Proclamation 889 232
Propaganda Movement 160–161
Public Lands Act 197
Puerto de Monterrey 135–136

Qing Dynasty, China 104, 106, 109
Qudarat, Sultan of Basilan 97–101, 103–104, 110
Queirós, Pedro Fernandes de 86
Quezon, Aurora 225–226
Quezon, Manuel 199–201, 206, 211, 221–223, 225, 228
Quezon City 223, 226, 236, 244, 260
Quirino, Elpidio 223–224, 226, 228, 260

Rabaul 212
Ramos, Fidel 247–248, 250

RAM (Reform of the Armed Forces Movement) 243–247
Real Audiencia de Manila 120–121, 141, 145
Recollects (religious order) 114, 194, 266
Redemptorists (religious order) 266
reducciónes (reductions) 114, 122
Reina Cristina (ship) 168, 170–171
Religious of the Virgin Mary (religious order) 266
Retez, Yñigo Ortiz de 86
Riccio, Br. Vittorio 108
Rivera, Fernando Primo de 163, 165
Rizal, José 160–162, 236, 259, 266
Rizalists 266
Rojo del Rio y Vieyra, Bishop Manuel 140–146
Rolex 12 235
Roosevelt, Franklin 204–205, 222
Roosevelt, Theodore 180, 198
Rosario 205
Roxas, Manuel 222–223, 228
Ruiz, Saint Lorenzo 115, 236
Russia 193

Sabah 231
Saiful, Sultan of Brunei 90–92, 94
sajonista 190
Salamanca, Juan Cerezo de 97
Salamat 98–100
Salamat, Hasim 250
Salazar, Bishop Domingo de 112–113, 141, 145–146
Salcedo, Juan de 76
Salesians (religious order) 266
Samar 7, 73, 214
Sande, Francisco de 90–94
Sandugo (holiday) 73
Sangley 128–129, 133, 145
Santiago (ship) 62, 65
Santo Niño de Cebú devotion 84, 270–271
San Antonio (ship) 62
San Juan Bridge 176, 178
San Pedro, Fr. Agustin de 104
San Vitores, Blessed Fr. Diego Luis de 116–118

Index

Saudi Arabia 275
Sa Huynh people 23–25
Second Vatican Council vi, 267
Selurong (earlier name for Manila) 59–60
Seri Lela, Pengiran 91–94
Seri Ratna, Pengiran 91–92
Seven Years War 140, 145
Shariff Aguak 254
Siaiu, Rajah of Limasawa 63–64
Sigala, Datu of Bohol 73
Sikatuna, Datu of Bohol 73
Silang, Diego 145
Silang, Gabriela 145
Sin, Jaime Cardinal 237, 266–267
Sociedad Económica de los Amigos del País 153
Solomon Islands 86, 212
Song Dynasty, China 27, 31
South China Sea 5–6, 23, 31, 218
Spain vi, vii, 4, 61–62, 64, 66, 72–75, 80–81, 83–87, 90–91, 95, 97, 105, 112, 120, 127–128, 131–132, 134–135, 137, 139–140, 145–146, 150–152, 154–155, 159, 161–162, 165–167, 169, 171–174, 183, 194, 197, 203, 258, 272
Spanish-American War 167, 174, 203
Spice Islands (*also* Moluccas) 71–73, 79–82, 86, 96–97, 110
Sri Bantug, Rajah 39
Sri Bata Shaja, Rajah 28, 30–31
Sri Lumay, Rajah 34–35, 37–39, 49, 53, 73
Subic Bay Naval Base 247
Suez Canal 154
Sulayman, Rajah 76
Sultanate of Lanao 52
Sultanate of Maguindanao 52
Sultanate of Sulu 51–53
Sulu Archipelago 8, 12, 51–52, 184, 218
Sulu Sea 7–8, 49, 97, 158
Sumatra 12, 26, 34, 41, 49, 51
Swift, Charles 188

Tablas 7
Taft, William 180, 190, 198

Tagalog 41–45, 47, 94, 96, 103, 129, 163, 177, 200, 258
Tagalog Revolt 163
Tagle, Luis Cardinal 266
Taiwan 12, 21, 25, 44, 50, 105–106, 108–109
Tamblot's Rebellion 123, 125–127
Taniguchi, Yoshimi 220
Tarlac 163, 206, 208
Taruc, Luis 223–224, 226
Tejeros Convention 174
Thailand 26, 249
Third Republic 221–229
Tisdale, John 168–171
Tokugawa Shogunate 115
Tondo iii, 39, 41–50, 53, 60, 71, 76
Tornatrás 127
Torre, Bernardo de la 85–86
Torre, Francisco de la 140, 146
Treaty of Paris (1763) 145
Treaty of Paris (1898) 174–175
Trinidad (ship 1521) 62, 71
Trinidad (ship 1762) 144
Tupas, Rajah of Cebu 73–76
Tydings-McDuffie Act 199–200, 213, 219, 222
typhoon 5

United Arab Emirates 275
United States vii, 128, 165–166, 171–176, 178, 180, 184–185, 187, 191, 193–194, 196–201, 203, 219, 222–223, 227, 230–231, 235, 237–238, 243, 245–247, 251, 259, 272, 275
University of Santo Tomas 113, 236, 267
Urdaneta, Andrés de 81, 83–86, 131, 132, 137
Urrao, Datu of Samar 73
USS Maine (ship) 166
USS McCulloch (ship) 171
USS Olympia (ship) 168–170

Valderrama, Fr. Pedro 64
Vanuatu 86
Vera, Santiago de 121
Veracruz 136

Victoria (ship) 62, 69, 71–72
Vidal, Ricardo Cardinal 266–267
Vietnam 23, 26, 111, 203, 229–231, 236
Visayas 4, 7, 17, 23, 32–34, 41, 49, 53, 62, 64, 69, 76–77, 90, 95–96, 108, 113–114, 127

war on drugs 261
Wilson, Woodrow 198–199
Wood, Leonard 186
World War I 191–193
World War II vi, 192, 203, 219, 223–224
World Youth Day 1995 vi, 267, 269

Yangtze River 203
Yellow Revolution (*See also* People Power Revolution) 241
Yousef, Ramzi 269
Yung-lo, Chinese Emperor 56

Zambales 129
Zamboanga 97, 104, 108, 110, 261
Zamora, Fr. Jacinto 160
Zheng Jing, son of Koxinga 109
Zhenzong, Emperor of China 27–31

If you enjoyed this book, you may also be interested in these other high-quality works from Arx Publishing...

Angels in Iron by Nicholas C. Prata
"I ended up spending the entire day reading *Angels in Iron*; the book was impossible to put down. As Prata vividly described the perilous progression of one of the most fascinating battles ever, my daily routine was shoved aside....A thrilling read, and especially recommended for boys age eleven and up."
—*The Kolbe Academy Little Home Journal*

Three Years Behind the Guns: The True Chronicles of a "Diddy Box" by John B. Tisdale
"Many of my friends and I have read [*Three Years Behind the Guns*] with the greatest interest. I can vouch for many of the facts; and the description of the Battle of Manila Bay is one of the best I have ever seen published.
—**Admiral George Dewey**

Belisarius: The First Shall Be Last by Paolo A. Belzoni
"An ambitious tale, filled with action, spectacle, and intrigues of all kinds....Not only is it driven by costumed action and Dune-like plots-within-plots, the novel exalts a youthful leader who is virtuous to a fault, is unfailingly loyal to God and country, who manages setbacks with aplomb, is handy with weapons and gets the pretty girl in the end."
—**John J. Desjarlais, CatholicFiction.net**

Centurion's Daughter by Justin Swanton
"This was not a book dashed off and rushed to publication but something that had been lovingly labored over....First of all, let me say, I loved it....I strongly recommend this book and would say it is appropriate for young ladies and gentleman 15 years and older and their parents of course. This would be a great Christmas gift, Confirmation gift for your Confirmandi or addition to a High School Curriculum."
—**Latin Mass Network**

Crown of the World: Knight of the Temple by Nathan Sadasivan
"*Knight of the Temple* is written in a style of historical fiction that was prevalent in American Catholic literature several decades ago and follows in the footsteps of such Catholic classics as *The Outlaws of Ravenhurst* and the novels of Louis de Wohl, but with greater intensity. *Knight of the Temple* is a really excellent work, fraught with tension."
—*Saint Austin Review*

For further information on these titles, or to order, visit:
www.arxpub.com

www.ingramcontent.com/pod-product-compliance
Lightning Source LLC
Chambersburg PA
CBHW030135170426
43199CB00008B/78